AMAZON
Highlights
Peru • Brazil • Colombia • Ecuador

Roger Harris

D0711697

Edition 1

Bradt Travel Guides Ltd, UK
The Globe Pequot Press Inc, USA

Bradt

About this book

Planning a trip to the Amazon? This book is for you. It helps you decide the where, what, when and how of exploring this vast region.

Prospective visitors to the Amazon can choose from among many guidebooks to individual Amazon countries, but few travel books cover the region as a whole. These other guides are often bloated with a surfeit of details; the long lists of budget hotels and complicated minutiae of public transport are targeted at backpackers and independent travellers. *Amazon Highlights* offers more selective information: it is written for the traveller who is looking for a tour operator to help them plan and organise their trip.

The book has two main aims. First, it helps those considering a tour to decide what they'd like to see and do. Using this book you can construct your ideal itinerary. When you liaise with tour operators you'll already have the necessary information to ask the right questions. Second, the book provides an insightful and informative guide to carry during your trip. With that in mind, the author provides overviews of towns, nature reserves and cities that are the region's highlights. He also includes a summary of practicalities and a short list of recommended accommodation.

This book provides more extensive wildlife and natural history information than any other guide. The author draws upon his academic background in biology as well as 20 years travelling in the region to provide practical accounts of the flora and fauna based on what you are most likely to encounter.

In addition to the author's recommendations we have called upon the expertise of leading tour operators – those who know best what the area has to offer – to recommend their favourite itineraries and activities. Bradt has carefully chosen the included tour operators based on their reputations for excellence, and they have generously contributed to the production costs of the book. These companies are featured in the 'In Conversation with...' spreads that can be found in the country sections of the guide. You can read a description of each of these tour operators on pages 134–5 and 137.

These pages are unique in bringing together the selections of a top writer and top operators, making this the ideal guide for planning your Amazon adventure.

Author

Afflicted with an incurable travel bug acquired during his childhood upbringing in Africa, Roger Harris now regularly travels throughout South America – camera in one hand, notebook in the other – on his quest for ever more arcane knowledge. Throughout this book, he draws  on his degrees in biology and his experience of leading dozens of natural history and photography tours to the Amazon and other parts of Latin America.

Author's story

Since my childhood in Africa, I've been fascinated with nature. So after I got my Biology degree from the University of York I headed to South America. My first view of the Amazon was flying over it at night. I'd heard about deforestation, but the reality only sank in when I saw thousands of pinpoints of light across the dark forest. Each speck of light was a fire: the rainforest was ablaze. A few years later I leapt at the chance to lead natural history and photography tours to the area around Iquitos and beyond. Teaching people about the rainforest while exploring its wonders is a privilege and a responsibility.

I wrote my first Amazon travel guide in 1997 to encourage travellers to visit. It's not just a jungle, I like to say. Some say that the Amazon is the lungs of the planet, but when I'm there, immersed in its endless complexity, I'm getting more than a literal breath of fresh air. For me, the forest is more than an external thing. It is a sensation, a feeling, an emotion. I merge with the tall inscrutable trees, leaves of infinite shades green, alien bird and insect sounds and musty fungal odours, as a pesky mosquito draws my blood. I am part of the Amazon. It is part of me.

Acknowledgements

I am indebted to numerous people who have given their time and expertise to help with this book. In particular, I thank Julie Schroer for proofreading the entire manuscript, and tireless support, encouragement and cups of coffee when they were most needed. I am very grateful to those people who offered their specialist knowledge of specific areas, helping make sure the book is fresh and up to date, and as accurate as we could make it. I cannot praise enough Scott Humfeld of GreenTracks and Analia Sarfati of Muyuna Lodge for comments on the Iquitos chapter, Mark Aitchison of Swallows and Amazons for his help with the chapter on Manaus and Kurt Beate of Nomadtrek Adventure Travel for reviewing the information on Ecuador's natural areas. Ed Hudson and Steve Alexander provided valuable insight and information for the chapter on Leticia. Special mention is due to Dr Stuart Pimm, Dr William Lamar, Dr Ted Kahn and Dr Bill Cooper who advised on the natural history sections and generously provided many of the spectacular photos gracing the pages of this book. I also owe a debt of gratitude to the editorial and administrative team at Bradt for their endless patience and understanding. Without the kindness and generosity of all these people, this book would not have been possible. Of course, any errors remaining are my own.

Forest at dawn, lower Urubamba River, Peru (PO/MP/FLPA)

Foreword
Ed Stafford

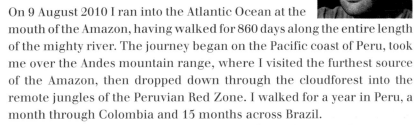

On 9 August 2010 I ran into the Atlantic Ocean at the mouth of the Amazon, having walked for 860 days along the entire length of the mighty river. The journey began on the Pacific coast of Peru, took me over the Andes mountain range, where I visited the furthest source of the Amazon, then dropped down through the cloudforest into the remote jungles of the Peruvian Red Zone. I walked for a year in Peru, a month through Colombia and 15 months across Brazil.

Having spent many years of my life in South America this journey was for me the ultimate immersion in a continent that I already loved. Travelling without any support team, the entire trip would not have been possible without a strong faith in how hospitable the people of the Amazon are. More often than not when emerging from the dense undergrowth from a direction with no paths in our ragged clothes we would be met by inquisitive yet smiling villagers whose first question was not 'Who are you?' but 'Are you hungry? Would you like some food?'

Nobody can sum up the Amazon as a particular type of rainforest – it is simply too large and too diverse. Can it be a paradise packed with animals and birds, where crystal-clear waters trickle over secret waterfalls? In places – yes. Can it be a 'green hell', a tangled mess of twisted vines and razor grass that tears your skin and is virtually impenetrable to cut through with a machete? Oh yes – it certainly can.

Where else on earth can you get the same sense of exploration than in the largest rainforest left on the planet? In an age where satellite mapping has exposed the entire world, the mystery below the tightly woven forest canopy is still hidden, cities are still lost, and people are still living in isolated pockets without interaction from outsiders.

From the region's ancient civilisations to its colonial settlers and scientific explorers, this book provides a wonderful historical background to an incredible place. A gem of a travel guide, it packs in natural history, geography, relevant journey planning tips, handy local maps and much more. Roger Harris's wealth of knowledge is evident in every entry, making this book a must for all travellers to the region.

Ed Stafford was the first man to walk the length of the Amazon River, an epic feat captured in the Discovery Channel documentary *Walking the Amazon*. ❂ www.edstafford.org.

Contents

List of maps

Feedback request

If you have any comments about this guide (good or bad), we would welcome your feedback. Please email us on ✉ info@bradtguides.com. Alternatively you can add a review of the book to www.bradtguides.com or Amazon. Periodically our authors post travel updates and reader feedback on the website. Check 🖱 www.bradtguides.com/guidebook-updates for any news. The author also appreciates any feedback or updates, which will be posted on the book's companion website, 🖱 www.amazontravelbook.com.

Introduction

The unsolved mysteries of the rainforest are formless and seductive. They draw us forward and stir strange apprehensions... In our hearts we hope we will never discover everything. We pray there will always be a world like this one... The rainforest in its richness is one of the last repositories of that timeless dream.

E O Wilson, *The Diversity of Life*, 1992

John Muir, founder of the national park system today used worldwide, once said, 'The clearest way to the universe is through a forest wilderness'. You walk between tall, gray columns of giant trees, dappled innumerable shades of green. You taste the oxygen-rich air, heavy with moisture. It imbues you with an inexplicable euphoria. You wander on as though in a dream. Strange fragrances waft among the compost odour

Looking over the rainforest from a canopy tower, Cristalino State Park, Brazil (GTW/IB/FLPA)

of decaying vegetation. All around, exuberantly lush vegetation bursts out, spills upon, over and under itself. Vines and lianas cavort, twist and tumble in every direction.

A spot of colour might be a flower... then it moves and turns out to be a butterfly. The tinny whine of cicadas pervades the forest, but the sound stops respectfully as you walk close.

An alien cooing spreads through the forest. Your naturalist-guide is an expert on the local wildlife, so he identifies the strange sound as a bird called the screaming piha.

You kneel down to peel off the top layer of damp leaves covering the hard clay soil. Countless scurrying motes of life incessantly move towards their inscrutable destinations. Between and within the papery leaves are masses of tiny white threads – tendrils of fungi seeking sustenance from the dead. Yet they are part of life, unlocking vital nutrients once held by the living plant, freeing them for re-use. Just a few inches away a seed sprouts. Its roots already push down through the leaf litter. Its small, soft leaves reach up towards the precious light.

Here in the Amazon, on the banks of the world's biggest river, you're surrounded by endless tracts of tropical rainforest: green in overwhelming abundance, one of the world's biodiversity hotspots and home to more types of plants and animals than anywhere else on earth. But what does the Amazon mean to you? Sensationalist nature shows? Lurid B-movies? Glossy nature magazines filled with photos of wildlife too colourful to seem real? A brooding wilderness full of weird animals, repulsive bugs and strange people? Until you've been there, impressions are mere illusions.

Over the past 20 years I've been lucky enough to visit the Amazon many times. I've sailed along the full length of the river twice, and led dozens of natural history and photography tours. Yet, even now, having been there so often and encountered so many bizarre creatures with my perspective as a biologist, the Amazon's mystery remains. Perhaps because it is ultimately indescribable, nature's truth cannot be conveyed, only sensed, and then only fleetingly. Seeing it on TV, even in the best nature documentaries, offers merely a glimpse of a greater whole.

So you walk on, along the muddy trail. You observe more closely, trying to take it all in, but it is endless – a surfeit of sensory input. The beauties and intricacies of the forest are infinite. How unjust, how cruel, that we humans should pillage this treasury of life. Yet it remains intact in many parts.

The giant Victoria water lily is the world's largest freshwater plant (SS)

Introducing the Amazon

1 History and People

El Dorado, disappearing explorers, lost cities, the Cat People, head hunters; much of the Amazon's mystery and interest lies in its history and people. Why do such things intrigue us so? As humans we are drawn to stories. Our intellect understands that the Amazon is important for its biodiversity, unique plants and animals, its immensity and wildness. But without the human context, these only weakly stir the imagination. To travel in our minds we want to put ourselves there - to imagine. We can imagine Lope de Aguirre in his rage and madness as his quest for El Dorado fails. We can wonder at people who live as part of nature, rather than beside it. Some part of us still wants to touch that primordial existence. It is through stories of the Amazon that we can relate to its reality. So it is with its history and people that we begin our exploration of the Amazon, its rainforest and river.

History

Ancient civilisations in the Amazon

The history of the Amazon is often treated from a Eurocentric perspective. We may want to pin down the 'discovery' of the Amazon, but the region's human story reaches much farther back. The rainforest's damp and heat conspire to obliterate the remains that might give us extensive evidence of human habitation. Archaeological excavations at Caverna da Pedra Pintada in Brazil have pushed back the time of verifiable human occupation to at least 11,000 years ago. One view is that these people migrated across a land bridge connecting North America with Asia during the last Ice Age. The migration progressed southwards and the people crossed the Isthmus of Panama, into northern South America and the Amazon region. Archaeologists recently proposed, however, that colonisation from Asia occurred primarily via coastal migration. The land bridge provided the coastline, but rather than trekking across land, it is thought that Palaeo-Indians may have used canoes to make their way into the Americas.

A more speculative idea is that 2,000 years ago the Chinese crossed the Pacific and influenced the native cultures, but this is hotly debated. Others propose that the pattern of migration went in the opposite direction, from South America. Thor Heyerdahl's *Kon-Tiki* expedition across the Pacific in 1947 proved that a long journey across the ocean was possible with a simple craft made from locally available balsa wood. Still others, notably R Buckminster Fuller, cite evidence of Phoenician voyages to the South American coast around 200BC. Yet opinion remains divided; scholars vehemently disagree over whether any such voyages took place.

We may never know if non-South American cultures impacted Amazonian peoples, but we can be certain that the peoples of the Andes exerted considerable influence on societies around them. These latter cultures, in particular the **Inca**, developed advanced architecture, mathematics, astronomy and agricultural systems. Their works include megalithic monuments – Machu Picchu being the supreme example – and gold, pottery, textile and stone artefacts. These rank among the greatest cultural and creative accomplishments of pre-industrial humanity. Inca presence in the Amazon lowlands was limited but significant, with Inca outposts trading in gold, pottery, agricultural produce and slaves. Despite Inca influence, forest-dwelling peoples remained hunter-gatherers, as they did until outsiders – the Europeans – appeared on the scene.

The arrival of the Europeans

The recorded history of the Amazon begins with explorers who discovered the river's mouth. Sea voyages led by Pinzón, Ojeda and Vespucci had travelled past the Amazon's mouth by 1500. Those captains noted the change in the ocean's colour and the offshore presence of fresh water. They had encountered the Amazon's immense outflow, which reaches beyond the sight of land hundreds of miles into the Atlantic.

On 26 April 1500, the Portuguese commander **Pedro Álvares Cabral** made the first landing on the eastern side of South America by a European. He is now remembered as the founder of Brazil; it was not until 40 years later that Spanish conquistadors entered the Amazon heartland.

Indeed, the river's history properly begins with the first voyage down its full length. In 1541, **Francisco Orellana** departed Quito, Ecuador, in search of gold, spices and unknown lands. The

Pedro Álvares Cabral, the first European to land in South America (WP)

legend of El Dorado haunted the imagination of Spanish adventurers. For them, the easy conquest of the Inca and their riches were recent memory. Every noble, soldier, footpad and pirate yearned to emulate Francisco Pizarro, who had ransomed the Inca king Atahualpa for a room filled with gold.

Gold and spices remained elusive, but Orellana did traverse the breadth of the continent. His expedition emerged at the mouth of the river in August 1542. Along the way, Orellana encountered a tribe of indigenous people dressed in grass skirts whose adept bowmen attacked his fleet. Not caring to investigate further, perhaps understandably, Orellana resumed his downriver journey. His chronicler Carvajal assumed the tribe he had encountered were the Amazons, women warriors of Greek legend: 'These women are very white and tall ... and they are robust and go about naked, but with their privy parts covered, with their bows and arrows in their hands, doing as much fighting as ten Indian men.' From this encounter, Orellana named the river after the Greek Amazons.

Although Orellana encountered hostile tribes, made endless detours among the maze of waterways, and experienced the loss of men, vessels and horses, and starvation and disease, he completed his journey more or less intact. The same cannot be said for the second attempt to navigate the river's full length.

Again inspired by the lure of El Dorado, a motley crew of 300 Spaniards and 2,000 indigenous departed Lima in 1559. The band of soldiers, brigands, pirates and criminals recruited for the expedition crossed the Andes to Moyobamba where they built craft for the downriver journey. Led by Pedro de Ursúa, the expedition soon deteriorated into a debacle. The young noble had made the mistake of bringing his wife, the Doña

Lope de Aguirre, leader of the second full-length journey down the Amazon (WP)

Inez, along for the ride. Records of the time report her as being the most beautiful woman in Peru. Perhaps distracted by the Doña, he botched the expedition's organisation. Progress bogged down, and it was not long before **Lope de Aguirre**, whom de Ursúa had selected as captain of the horse, took over, and the usurper promptly executed his benefactor. Aguirre's paranoia led to more executions. As the expedition progressed, murder added to lives lost through disease, encounters with hostile locals, starvation and drowning.

The chronicler apparently lost track of the geography. To this day there is doubt as to whether Aguirre left the Amazon River at its mouth, and some scholars speculate that he made his way northwards along the Negro. If so, he would be the first European to have used the Casiquiare Canal, which links the Amazon and Orinoco watersheds.

We do know that Aguirre turned up in Venezuela in 1561, with only a few dozen of his men remaining. Despite the attrition, he pledged to take Peru from the King of Spain. He penned a tirade protesting the king's right to New World riches; some consider his letter to be the first-ever declaration of independence from royal rule. But bravery was not enough and Aguirre's rebellion was short-lived. His few remaining supporters deserted following a promise of pardon from the governor of Venezuela.

As the royal soldiers gathered for the coup de grâce, Aguirre ran his sword through his daughter – who had faithfully accompanied her father throughout the voyage – declaring that no soldier would violate

Lost cities of the Amazon

Since it began in the mid 16th century, the story of the lost city of gold, El Dorado, is so compelling that history has never quite let go. So we can imagine the enthusiasm of Colonel Percy Fawcett, a British explorer who went in search of a rumoured lost city in the jungles of Brazil. Perhaps he hoped to emulate the discovery of Machu Picchu by Hiram Bingham in 1912. But Fawcett disappeared without trace. His expedition is recounted in a book, *The Lost City of Z*. A film of the book starring Brad Pitt was scheduled for release in 2011. However, in fitting irony, and like so many Amazon enterprises, the film became a failed dream after Pitt pulled out of the production.

The mystery of Fawcett's disappearance is unresolved to this day. In 1977, when German photojournalist Karl Brugger published *The Chronicle of Akakor*, many were ready to believe his tales of hidden cities in Amazonia. The story tells of the Ugha Mongulala, a tribe 'chosen by the Gods'. Arriving in golden airships 15,000 years ago, white-skinned strangers civilised the tribe and built great stone cities. But Brugger's story is less fact than fiction. His sole source, called Tantunca Nara, was later revealed to be a fellow German, Günther Hauck. Director Steven Spielberg incorporated some elements of the Akakor story in *Indiana Jones and the Kingdom of the Crystal Skull*.

But lost cities of the Amazon are not all fiction. In 2008 the discovery of a fortified citadel in a remote mountainous area of Peru was announced. According to archaeologists, the Cloud People of Peru, a tribe with uniquely white skin and blonde hair, inhabited the site. In another discovery in 2010, satellite imagery and aerial photos showed the remains of giant earthworks spanning 155 miles (250km). The account, published in the journal *Antiquity*, called the remains evidence of a 'sophisticated, pre-Colombian, monument-building society'. So it does seem that life imitates art. As long as there is a wilderness to be explored, and a fascination with the unknown, we shall continue to imagine and look for lost cities of the Amazon.

her. He was hanged, drawn and quartered, and named a traitor to the Spanish crown. Needless to say, chroniclers of the time did not leave us with a favourable impression of the man.

The struggle for the Amazon

Despite the Spaniards' efforts to explore the Amazon, most of the region today is Portuguese-speaking. To explain this apparent anomaly we turn to the exploits of Captain **Pedro de Teixeira**, who was the first to complete the upriver journey.

In 1494 the Treaty of Tordesillas allotted a portion of South America to the Portuguese. But they showed little interest until 1637, when two Franciscan missionaries floating downstream arrived in Fort Presépio, present-day Belém, at the mouth of the Amazon. Fearing Spanish domination, the Portuguese felt compelled to travel upstream to deter further incursions into their territory.

Captain Teixeira left Belém on 28 October 1637. Forty-seven canoes, powered by 1,200 South American indigenous and African slaves, transported 70 Portuguese soldiers upstream. One full year after his departure, he arrived in Quito. This accomplishment secured the Portuguese claim to the world's greatest rainforest.

In 1751 the Treaty of Madrid formalised Portugal's claim, dividing South America between the two countries, and marking out the international boundaries roughly as they are today.

The advent of scientific exploration

The century or so after the early expeditions marks a hiatus in European Amazon exploration. It was seen as a 'green hell'. If demise didn't come from wild beasts, hostile tribes or disease, it would come from simply getting lost in the vast unmapped wilderness. Europe's Age of Reason and a generation of scientist-explorers began to change that. These educated, articulate scholars realised the Amazon's riches were not in gold and spices, but in its biological wonders.

Among the first and most influential of the scientist-explorers was the Frenchman **Charles-Marie de La Condamine**, who departed Paris in 1735 for an expedition that was originally meant to take just two years. He returned a decade later. His endless curiosity filled his *Abridged Narrative of Travels through the Interior of South America*, published in 1745.

One of La Condamine's discoveries in particular had a dramatic impact on Europe's nascent industrial revolution. Along the Japurá River, he observed how the Omagua tribe used the sap of a certain tree to make galoshes, rings and even bulb syringes. Others had seen bouncing balls and waterproof items made from this same substance – the substance that today we call rubber. La Condamine was the first to take the material back to Europe. Industries there and in the United States soon found innumerable uses for the valuable commodity.

In the 1740s La Condamine's research had suggested the existence of a natural canal – the Casiquiare – connecting the Amazon and Orinoco river systems. Sixty years later, in February 1800, **Baron Alexander von Humboldt** began a four-year expedition into the Amazon's interior, with the primary goal of establishing whether the two rivers were indeed linked. In this, he succeeded; Humboldt entered the Casiquiare and measured the length of the natural canal to be 200 miles (322km). Considering the lack of modern navigational instruments, his survey was remarkably accurate; the canal is actually 220 miles (354km) long.

Before Humboldt's survey, most 18th-century geographers doubted the canal's existence. Proving it did exist was a big success for Humboldt, but it was not the only one. His contribution to the field of botany ranks as a major scientific achievement. He collected more than 12,000 plant specimens, most of them new to science.

Humboldt's scientific work was accurate, detailed and exhaustive. He wrote on botany, zoology, pharmacology and geology, creating what is still today considered a database of the region. Although Humboldt increased awareness of the rainforest, he never actually saw the Amazon River itself.

Following in Humboldt's footsteps, botanists, zoologists and geographers from all over Europe and North America

Alexander von Humboldt, one of the 19th century's great scientist explorers (WP)

descended on the Amazon Basin to discover its hidden riches, and unveiled a seemingly endless variety of plants and animals. Inspired Western naturalists from humbler backgrounds were to find new species and build their reputation on Amazon discoveries.

Naturalist Charles Darwin sailed past the river's mouth in 1834 on his famous round-the-world voyage in HMS *Beagle*. Alfred Wallace, Darwin's contemporary and co-discoverer of the principle of natural selection, spent four years in the Napo River area of present-day northeastern Peru, near Iquitos. Botanist Richard Spruce, a friend of Wallace, spent much longer in the area; over 15 years, he collected and documented thousands of Amazon plant species. He fended off hostile indigenous and recovered from tropical fevers. Spruce's place in history was secured when he smuggled quinine seeds to the outside world. In one of the early acts of bio-piracy, Spruce broke the South American monopoly on the anti-malarial drug and thereby helped European powers colonise tropical areas in Africa and Asia where the disease was rampant.

Henry Walter Bates collected more species of insects than anyone before him (WP)

Another of Wallace's companions arrived in Brazil in May 1848. **Henry Walter Bates**'s monumental collection involved the drawing and cataloguing of close to 15,000 insect specimens, more than half of them unknown to science. His research proved that some harmless insects mimic more dangerous species. Now called Batesian mimicry in his honour, this evolutionary strategy is recognised by biologists today as a process in generating biodiversity. In 1863, Bates published *The Naturalist on the River Amazons* (see page 272). The work is rightly regarded as the best contemporary account of Amazon natural history.

From source to mouth, one way or the other

Traversing South America by journeying down its greatest river dates back to 1540, when Spanish conquistador Francisco Orellana first completed the journey downstream. In 1638 Portuguese captain Pedro Teixeira completed the first upstream journey. Joe Kane kayaked down the Amazon from its source to the mouth in 1986. In 2007, Slovenian Martin Strel completed a swim of 3,497 miles (5,628km) down the Amazon, taking 66 days. In 2010, Ed Stafford, who wrote the foreword to this guide, became the first man to walk the length of the river; it took him 860 days.

People

The Amazon's cultural diversity is as precious as its biodiversity. The indigenous peoples and languages are perhaps even more at risk

The Amazon is thought to be home to around 200 tribes including the Surui tribe, who live in the Rondônia region of Brazil (SS)

of extinction than the plants and animals. What we see today are vestiges of the diversity that existed before European incursions into South America. Perhaps 2,000 distinct cultural groups, comprising a population of several million, once inhabited the Amazon. Following European settlement in the 16th century, most of these either died out or were assimilated into the dominant European cultures from Spain and Portugal.

Yet even today the Amazon harbours numerous unassimilated indigenous groups; it is thought that 200 tribes of 300,000 people or so remain. In 2007, the Brazilian government reported 67 uncontacted tribes in its territory. In mid-2011, an uncontacted tribe in Colombia made the headlines when it was photographed from the air. A few months later, the tribe was feared to have been eliminated by drug runners. Ecuador and Peru are also home to tribes who have not had significant contact with the outside world. But powerful pressures threaten them. Disease, competition with settlers, ranchers, oil exploration, mining and logging companies are reducing indigenous populations. As they disappear, so do their unique ways of life, languages, religions and cultural wisdom.

Today, we recognise the value of indigenous tribes and cultures, but a Western reader can't escape the guilt that accompanies the exploitation of the region's people. At the outset, knowledge of valuable products such

Head hunters

Head hunters are as much part of Amazon lore as piranhas and giant snakes. The practice has long been banned in Peru and Ecuador, where it was formerly carried out by the Achuar/Shuar tribal groups in the upper Marañón watershed. Uniquely among such cultures worldwide, the Amazon head hunters shrunk the heads of their enemies.

Our concept of headhunting is often coloured by sensationalist filmmakers who have taken the ritual out of context, with films and novels portraying frenzied savages immobilising victims with deadly blow darts, and viciously slicing off heads to shrink at weird cannibal rites. All of this is pure fiction. The reason for headhunting revolves around the spirit world. Indigenous people believe the soul resides within the head, which is beautiful and revered; the body is seen as merely a vessel for the head. To own an enemy's head is therefore to possess his soul and use its power... if you know how. First, blow darts are for hunting game and not to be used on humans, as the enemy must be nobly killed with hand weapons. The shrinking process is straightforward, requiring the removal of all fat and muscle from the head by boiling. What remains of the head is filled with hot sand which begins to contract and harden as water is removed from the tissues. The victor must conduct interminable magical rites to control the enemy's soul. The eyes and mouth are sewn shut to imprison the soul in the head, because it would otherwise haunt the possessor's dreams. Long periods of celibacy and isolation are also necessary. Three years of incantations, rituals and potion-making must pass before the head is fully empowered as a magic fetish.

The complexity of headhunting rituals deterred warriors from casually seeking victims, and taboos affect whose head could be chosen to make into a trophy. A head could only be taken as an act of revenge and the individual could not be personally known. A person whose relative dies by weapon or witchcraft was justified in seeking vengeance and only the murderer's head could be taken and shrunk. Far from the lurid atavistic version of this practice, headhunting was a ritual which served as a social control, apparently rare even before it was actively suppressed.

as rubber and quinine was exported with no benefit to the indigenous communities. Exploitation quickly moved to direct abuses of the rights of the local people, through land grabs and enslavement. Nineteenth-century industrialists apparently had no moral constraints. During the rubber boom, local people were indentured on plantations and farms. Their labour provided raw materials to fuel the growth of the West's industrial expansion. The cost was high: forced labour, disease and malnutrition exacted a heavy toll. These atrocities contributed further to the attrition of the indigenous population. The remaining indigenous tribes are mostly fractured and displaced, and most of those you meet have been acculturated, preferring to speak Spanish rather than their own language.

Today, nevertheless, the peoples of the Amazon represent a wide range of beliefs and customs compared with developed countries. Acculturated people are often Christian, but many tribal people are animists who believe that all living things possess a spirit. Shamans help govern the interaction between the real and imaginary worlds, and are said to be able to see the invisible magic darts that cause pain, curses and illness. This skill is enhanced by the use of plant-derived hallucinogens (properly called entheogens).

The indigenous people have a wide range of myths and legends to explain their place in the universe. The creation myths of different tribes usually reflect some part of the natural environment. Indeed, reliance

Face painting is common among many tribes present in the Amazon, such as the Karaja (SS)

on the 'natural order' provides indigenous people with the context for their day-to-day survival. Whether hunting, fishing or cultivating the land, the people depend on traditional beliefs to understand the rhythms of nature. Hence technologies imported by Western aid organisations rarely succeed; the mechanised, scientific 'one size fits all' approach is alien to the holistic agricultural tradition.

Before the Europeans arrived, communities living close to the Amazon's main stream raised fish and turtles in pens. Social interactions were dominated by seasonal flooding. Conflict was highest during annual floods when food stocks were low, and warring parties would often raid neighbouring villages for food. In times of plenty, flooded forest habitat was capable of supporting large populations. Today, with the decline of wildlife, hunting and fishing provide no more than half the dietary needs, and people rely on subsistence agriculture and trade to provide the remainder.

Common indigenous practices

Although tribes vary in the details of their lifestyles, the indigenous people of the Amazon invariably rely on the forest and rivers for sustenance. Tribes closer to settled regions have more contact with outsiders and have adopted many aspects of outside society. But many other tribes or individuals within tribes retain their traditional way of life. Most tribes practise some form of 'slash-and-burn' cultivation, and grow manioc, bananas and papaya. They use the forest to gather fruit and medicinal herbs. The men hunt animals and fish, while women are responsible for raising children, cooking and tending plots. They also make items for daily use, such as baskets and pots. You can still see evidence of their skills at basketry and pottery among the handicrafts for sale at most native villages and in souvenir stores in larger towns. Among unassimilated tribes, families live communally, in large shared dwellings. The practice of an individual family house, which you see in most places today, is imported from Western culture.

Significant Amazon peoples

Although much reduced in number, the Amazon tribal population includes several tribes who maintain a semblance of their former lives. These live mostly in remote areas of Brazil, Peru, Ecuador and Colombia. Near urban areas, indigenous people have assimilated into the general population of *mestizos*, those of mixed ancestry. In most cases, relatively unassimilated tribes are the most remote; their territories were too inhospitable for the colonisation that decimated other tribes in Amazonia during the 19th century.

A member of the Javari tribe making a dugout canoe: fishing is still an important way of life for many indigenous people (SS)

Significant Amazon tribes today include the Yanomami of Brazil and Venezuela, numbering about 20,000; the Achuar/Shuar of Peru and Ecuador, with a population of 30,000; the Tikuna, numbering about 25,000 in the area where the frontiers of Brazil, Peru and Colombia meet; and several others numbering more than 10,000 each.

Languages

Spanish is the dominant language of the Amazon Basin except in Brazil, where Portuguese is most widely spoken. In the Andes, Quechua was the lingua franca of the Inca Empire. Today, Quechua is the dominant language among many people living in western Amazonia.

At least 170 different ethnic groups in the Amazon speak their own language. Most dialects spoken by Brazilian tribes derive from one of four languages: Gê, Tupi, Carib and Arawak. While most indigenous languages in eastern Amazonia are based on one or a combination of these four languages, in some cases the language bears no relation to these core groups. For example, linguists do not know the origins of Gŭycan, the Yanomami language.

2 The Natural World

In recent years it seems that the emphasis of nature shows has changed since I was raised on the style of scientist-presenters such as David Attenborough. Today, such programmes like to entertain viewers with dramatic scenes of adventuresome, muscular daredevils wrestling with giant snakes or huge fish. To my mind, however, the real fascination is in the intricate, delicate details of the Amazon's natural history: a hummingbird pollinating a *Datura* flower; a knife fish using its electric field to navigate muddy waters; a morpho butterfly's iridescent random path across a light-dappled glade; a multihued tropical sunset's reflection in the waters of a black lake. Such beauty is difficult to convey on screen; the only way to truly appreciate it is to experience it for yourself.

The Amazon at a glance

Location Northern South America. The Amazon River flows west to east across South America, approximately along the equator. The Amazon watershed includes seven countries: Peru, Bolivia, Ecuador, Colombia, Venezuela, Guyana and Brazil.

River volume Almost a fifth of the world's water passes through the Amazon River delta. The Amazon watershed – the river basin – drains 2.7 million square miles (7 million km²), covering just under half South America's total area. That's almost the size of the 50 contiguous United States (see diagram below).

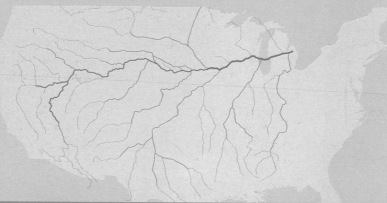

Size of the Amazon Basin compared with the contiguous United States of America

Source Nevado Mismi, at 17,000ft (5,200m) in the Peruvian Andes, 120 miles (190 km) from the Pacific Ocean

Mouth The mid-Atlantic coast of northeast Brazil

Total length 4,000 miles (6,440km)

Navigable length Ocean steamers (+3,000 tons) to Manaus (1,000 miles; 1,600km); small riverboats to Achual (2,786 miles; 4,480km). During flood season the total length of navigable waterway throughout the river basin can exceed 1.2 million miles (2 million km).

Maximum depth 300ft (100m)

Maximum width 1-6 miles (2-10km)

Width at mouth (of the delta) 300 miles (480 km)

Longest tributary Rio Purus, Peru to Brazil 2,100 miles (3,380km)

Biggest blackwater river Rio Negro

Biggest whitewater river Rio Solimões/Amazon River

Proportional areas of rainforest in each country Brazil = 62.4%, Peru = 16.3%, Bolivia = 12.0%, Colombia = 6.3%, Ecuador = 2.1%

(Data provided courtesy of JunglePhotos.com)

The origins of the Amazon

As you wander along a rainforest trail, it's easy to imagine that the trees and plants have been there forever. On our timescale, the rainforest ecosystem is ancient, but geologically speaking, the Amazon is relatively recent; its existence spans perhaps one fiftieth of earth's history.

About 100 million years ago, an undersea ridge bisecting the Atlantic Ocean began pushing the continents of Africa and South America apart. Some 15 million years ago, inexorable tectonic shifts pushed the South American Plate over the Pacific Plate. To the west, the Pacific Plate was forced downwards as the South American Plate moved over it. Along South America's western edge, the Andes mountain range began to rise, forming the continent's 'backbone'. The tremors and earthquakes common to western South America are the continuing legacy of the geological forces that continue to push the Andes ever higher. Today, the Andes is the world's second-highest mountain range, with numerous peaks over 20,000ft (6,000m).

Between 5.3 and 1.6 million years ago, the rising Andes obstructed westward flowing rivers. These blocked rivers created a huge inland lake, the biggest ever. Marine animals were trapped in a freshwater environment; some adapted and remain to this day. Hence, the rivers are home to freshwater dolphins and stingrays, along with other animals normally found only in marine environments.

To the north, another great geological event was unfolding. Around five million years ago, South America joined North America, forming

The source of the Amazon lies at over 16,000ft (5,000m) in the Peruvian Andes (TR/MP/FLPA)

the Panama Isthmus. Closure of the link between the equatorial Pacific and Atlantic oceans changed currents and climate patterns. Placental mammals from North America invaded southwards, leading to the extinction of many of the previously isolated primitive mammals of South America. Some 1.6 million years ago, tectonic movements tilted the entire South American Plate, and the Amazon flowed east, in its present direction, into the Atlantic. So the river we see in maps and satellite images is perhaps two million years old, a blip of geological time.

However, such time has been enough to shape the land we experience. As the Andes pushed upwards, weathering eroded the highlands on the edges of the Amazon Basin. Sand and mud were washed down, filling the vast, low-lying expanse to the east. Underlying rock sank under the weight and yet more silt piled on the deposits. Over millions of years, starting when the area was an inland lake and continuing today, rocks of the Andes have become the soils of the Amazon.

Immensely deep alluvial deposits fill the vast network of ancient valleys that comprise the present-day river system. As you stand on a riverbank along the Amazon, remember you're on a pile of mud more than 2½ miles (4km) deep – mashed and crushed rocks, sand and silt from the Andes.

What's in a name?

Along the eastern foothills of the Andes, waters gather and merge until they meet the westernmost major tributary, the Ucayali. About 60 miles (100km) south of Iquitos, Peru, this joins the main stream. Some consider this to be the start of the Amazon River – it's called Amazonas by Peruvians. But Brazilians call it the Solimões, not recognising the Amazon River proper until it flows past Manaus.

The Solimões meets the Napo at the Meeting of the Waters near Manaus, forming what Brazilians believe to be the Amazon River proper (WWL/GT)

From the air, and relative to the Andes, the Amazon is a vast, flat plain. But get closer and you see hills, knolls and bluffs, carved by meandering rivers. The Ice Ages, the most recent of which ended 10,000 years ago, created this topographical variety. The sea level was 100ft (30m) or more lower than today, so east-flowing rivers ran much faster. Huge torrents cut deep channels in the mud. Carved by primordial floods, the high banks your boat sails past are above today's highest flood levels. The result is a variety of terrain that contributes to the Amazon's topographical and hence biological diversity. Beyond the reach of seasonal flooding, the vegetation on high ground – forests called *terra firme* – are quite different from the *várzea* forest found in flooded areas.

This scenario, of dynamic geology combined with climatic variation, conspired to create a shifting mosaic of habitats, pulses of forest expansion and contraction. These grand forces provided the conditions for generating the biodiversity we see today.

Geography

Beginning at its source more than 16,400ft (5,000m) high in the Peruvian Andes, less than 125 miles (200km) from the Pacific Ocean, the Amazon River rushes, flows and meanders almost 4,050 miles (6,500km) to the Atlantic. It's the world's second-longest river; the Nile is longer, but only just.

The main stream of the Amazon tracks almost exactly along the equator, bisecting the South American continent. Along the way, it collects the waters from 1,100 major tributaries, 12 of which are over 1,000 miles (1,600km) long. Many of the Amazon's tributaries are among the world's largest rivers in their own right: the Negro and the Madeira rank as the fifth- and sixth-largest rivers. At 2,000 miles (3,200km) long, the Madeira–Mamoré–Grande is the world's longest tributary. At its mouth, the Amazon produces about 262,000 cubic yards (200,000m^3) of water per second. That's about 80 Olympic-sized swimming pools – a flow greater than the world's next eight-biggest rivers together, or ten times that of the Mississippi.

Unlike most rivers that we think of as flowing downhill, along nine-tenths of the Amazon's course there is practically no change in **elevation**; once it leaves the Andes the river flows down a gradient of 1 in 50,000! Snow and rain in the Andes govern much of the Amazon's hydrology. Sunlight warms lofty peaks, and thawed snow rushes downhill. Then for

A source of debate

Ever since it was first depicted in maps of South America, geographers have debated the location of the Amazon's source. Several competing claims contend for the title, but it really depends on how you define the 'true' source. The definition of the source of a river is open to debate, and various contenders have staked a claim. In 1996, an international team claimed the Amazon's source is an underground glacier near Arequipa, Peru, as the highest location of the waters that feed it. The glacier gives rise to an icy creek, known as **Apacheta Crevice**, at 16,955ft (5,168m) on Volcán Chachani. In 2000, a National Geographic expedition identified the source as a thin sheet of water flowing down a rock wall on **Nevado Mismi**, at 18,362ft (5,597m) in southern Peru. This is the most distant point in the drainage basin from which water runs all year round, and the furthest point from the river's mouth. Given its contribution to the main river, **Lake Lauricocha** at 15,873ft (4,838m) in Peru is cited in the *Encyclopedia Britannica* as the source of the Amazon.

In any case, Peru can proudly claim that, by whatever criterion, it is home to the source of the world's greatest river.

A pink river dolphin in flooded forest along a tributary of the Rio Negro, Brazil (KS/MP/FLPA)

most of its long journey to the sea, the river meanders lazily across flat floodplains. With the spring thaw and seasonal rains, lowland river levels begin to rise. About 2% of the Amazon watershed is submerged during these **seasonal floods**. This 'flooded forest' is a small portion of the Amazon Basin's total area, but it adds habitat variety and hence species diversity. The floods persist for six to seven months of the year, challenging the region's wildlife and people to adapt to the constantly changing landscape.

Water is the forest's lifeblood. Rivers annually deposit nutrient-laden silt to fertilise the flooded forest. Enriched soils support sustainable agriculture and enhance the growth of natural vegetation.

The kinds of vegetation vary depending on the geochemistry of the waters that flood the area. *Várzea* **forest** grows in the floodplains of whitewater rivers. These rivers are a pale, murky yellow-brown, similar to milky coffee. The water is close to neutral (pH 7.0) and contains a high concentration of microbes and inorganic particles. *Igapó* **forest** is typical along black water rivers. The black tea colour derives from dissolved plant compounds. These rivers are quite acidic, which limits microbial activity and growth of aquatic flora and fauna, so mosquitoes are less abundant along them. **Terra firme forest** grows above the floodplains. It doesn't receive the annual input of nutrients from seasonal floods.

Muddy banks are constantly eroded by the river, leading to loss of crops such as this field of rice along the Peruvian Amazon (RH)

With every season's flood, accumulated silt changes the river's flow. Where the flow is diverted, the river leaves behind oxbow lakes and newly formed land. New channels create **'edge' habitat** essential for wildlife. Strong currents during annual floods or heavy rains scour weed-clogged streams and lakes. The river is a natural corridor along which animals migrate. Fish follow new watercourses, and aquatic birds follow the fish. Even small mammals ride on floating rafts of dislodged vegetation.

Floods speed up **erosion and deposition**. Without rocky areas to inhibit erosion, a river's course is unstable. On the river's outside curve the current runs faster. Here, the riverbank erodes, losing up to 100ft (30m) of forest a year. As you travel along the river, you can see

Flooding across the Anavilhanas Archipelago, Brazil (KS/MP/FLPA)

where the riverbank has collapsed. Slabs of soil have slid into the water. Trees lie askew in the river, a tangle of trunks and vines, ready to be swept away by the current. On the inside bend, the current slows. It drops silt, floating vegetation and anything else carried by the water. The inner banks grow towards the middle of the river. They become exposed when waters recede, and new land is thus created.

The process of erosion and deposition continues, year on year; the meanders of the river make their way downstream and sediment is picked up from the outside of one bend and deposited on the inside of another, further on. The process overall is a complex 'shifting mosaic' of innumerable islands, oxbow lakes, rivers, streams and sand bars – a wide variety of habitats for plants and animals.

The disturbances from seasonal flooding create conditions that isolate species populations and prevent migration. Such conditions promote speciation processes that have created the Amazon's teeming biodiversity.

Outside the inner Amazon Basin, other regions contribute to the variety of habitats encompassed by the watershed. Measuring some 1,840 miles (2,960km) from north to south, the Amazon Basin's outer margins comprise **montane forest** to the west and dry **grasslands** to the north and south. Here you will find a greater range of habitat types than anywhere else on earth.

Deforestation

Like its biological diversity, the Amazon's tragedy is superlative. We hear of areas the size of Wales being lost every year, but we can't fully grasp the real losses. More than a fifth of the entire lowland rainforest has been

A sawmill in Iquitos (RH)

lost. Cattle ranching accounts for two-thirds of the losses; a quarter are due to small-scale agriculture. Other causes include agribusiness, logging, mining, urbanisation, road construction and dams.

Sustainably harvested fruits, latex and wood could generate more than US$ 5 trillion annually. It's an economic equation some Amazon countries understand. In 2010, the Ecuadorian government denied oil exploration concessions in Yasuní National Park, which has among the highest biological diversity in Amazonia.

The rainforest is critical to the global climate, as it absorbs a tenth of yearly worldwide carbon emissions. But Amazon deforestation also produces about 200 million tons of carbon per year. Reducing deforestation and increasing sustainable harvesting would significantly impact the global carbon balance, and hence climate change.

Climate and weather

Climate, as opposed to weather, concerns long-term, large-scale patterns. Warm, humid conditions dominate the Amazon's climate, while local weather varies from day to day. Scientists are concerned about the effects of global warming on the Amazon's climate. Recent years have seen unprecedented droughts, resulting in lower river levels and drying out of the forest. Undoubtedly, long-term climate changes will affect the weather.

In terms of weather, the Amazon region does not have distinct seasons. Days are usually sunny with scattered cloud, and although rain is possible every day of your trip, it's unlikely. The central Amazon Basin and the eastern slopes of the Andes have a tropical wet climate. Amazonia's periphery experiences wet and dry seasons that last longer the greater the distance from the equator.

Rainforests are characteristically warm, although not excessively hot, and the temperature varies little around Iquitos, for instance, just south of the equator. **Temperatures** range from 75°F (24°C) in the morning to 86°F (30°C) in the afternoon, falling to 70°F (21°C) at night, rarely lower. Humidity is 80% or higher, which exacerbates the warmth. But there's occasional relief. Every year around December, the cyclical weather system known as El Niño (see below) causes a cold southerly wind (*friagem* in Brazil, *surazo* in Bolivia, *garúa* in other countries) to blow from Patagonia. During these weather systems daytime temperatures drop as low as 59°F (15°C).

Wind conditions here are typically light, and at ground level **winds** are more or less non-existent, as the forest canopy absorbs most wind energy. Strong winds can occur in the middle of broad rivers and lakes, but windy conditions on a river boat are not usually dangerous.

Contrary to our preconceptions, **rainfall** in the rainforest is not constant but intermittent. Rain descends on average three or four times a week, often in the form of short, spectacular downpours: an inch of rain may fall in an hour. In the upper Amazon, rainfall averages 120 inches (305cm) per year. Rainfall is predictably unpredictable: around Iquitos, almost every month recorded as the wettest one year has been recorded as the driest in another. In general, July to November tends to be dry, while the wetter season is from February to April. To the north, most rain falls between the months of June and October.

Tropical warmth and moisture create perfect conditions for **thunderstorms**. Cumulonimbus clouds bubble above the rainforest,

El Niño: a weather anomaly

Periodic weather fluctuations hit the Amazon due to the El Niño weather system. Temperatures drop, affecting Amazon wildlife. Some species, especially reptiles, undergo behavioural changes. Reptiles such as caiman bask in the open to warm themselves in the sun, and anaconda emerge from the cooler waters. Winds increase, cooling the surface of lakes and rivers. As the surface cools, the upper layer of cold water descends. The rich organic ooze of decaying vegetation at the bottom of lakes and rivers is stirred up and releases methane and other poisonous gases, creating an oxygen deficit. Desperate fish crowd close to the surface to gasp uncontaminated oxygen, dissolved in a thin layer where water meets air. Vast numbers of fish and freshwater crustaceans suffocate and floodplains become feasting grounds for carrion feeders, such as vultures.

Enormous clouds gather above the Amazon due to the warmth and moisture, promising spectacular rainstorms (OL/MP/FLPA)

stretching high into the sky, fuelled by rising thermals. These formations may rise to 33,000ft (10,000m) in a classic 'anvil' shape. The clouds harbour enormous energy, released in spectacular lightning displays and ear-splitting thunder.

As the Amazon is equatorial, daylight is about 12 hours all year round. The amount of **sunshine** depends on cloud cover, but it averages nine to 11 hours per day. Because the sun is directly overhead, it is more intense than in temperate latitudes. Take precautions to prevent sunburn (see page 151).

Flora

The Amazon's forests are very different from the forests you might be familiar with. Take a stroll along a forest path in Europe or North America, and you might encounter a dozen species of trees. In the Amazon, you'll count a hundred or more. Plants are the forest's foundation and building blocks. The animals and people that tend to garner most attention are entirely dependent on the tremendous diversity and abundance of the Amazon's plant life.

Amazon plants help to regulate climate through the production of oxygen and absorption of carbon dioxide. They also help manage water flow by storing and retaining rain water, and releasing it back into the atmosphere. Plants form soil, recycle nutrients and provide food, medicines and materials.

Spectacular Amazon plants

Giant water lily The world's biggest lily (see page 46)
Kapok tree One of the great rainforest giants (see page 31)
Orchids Astonishing variety of shapes and colours (see page 40)
Tree-ferns Among the most ancient plant groups (see page 42)
Ayahuasca vine Sacred plant of shamans (see page 44)

(WWL/GT)

Strangler fig Kills its host plant but provides habitat for dozens of animals (see page 32)
Floating meadows Rafts of grasses supporting abundant wildlife (see page 45)
Epiphytes Live on other plants, creating miniature forests within forests (see page 39)

Rainforest plants absorb and release so much water that they determine the amount of rainfall – one reason to suspect that deforestation influences weather patterns. When forests are cut down or burned, the released carbon dioxide adds to global atmospheric carbon. According to the UN's Food and Agriculture Organization, deforestation is responsible for a quarter of manmade greenhouse gas emissions.

We're cutting down forests, but life depends on plants. Plants harvest the energy in sunlight to power photosynthesis. Inside leaf cells, molecular factories transform light, air, water and earth into living matter. Animals in turn depend on plants for energy from food and life-giving oxygen. Warmth, strong light and lots of water speed up photosynthesis in rainforests, which are among the world's most productive ecosystems – second only to coral reef in terms of biomass produced in a given area. Tropical forests contribute almost a third of the world's photosynthetic production. They hold more than half the world's biomass, despite covering less than 5% of its area.

Non-tropical forest
Remaining tropical forest
Deforestation

Trees

Trees are the rainforest as we experience it. They also support countless other species. Trunks, stems, branches, leaves, fruits and roots are habitats for animals and smaller plants. Rainforest trees need specific environmental conditions: year-round high temperatures and heavy rainfall. The species composition of the forest depends on the terrain and the geochemistry of rivers. Areas above annual flood levels, terra firme, have the most species. Biodiversity of terra firme is highest in northwestern Amazonia, the most species-rich region in the world.

Structure and function, diversity and design

At least 50,000 woody plant species have been recorded in the Amazon – about a fifth of all plant species. Rainforest around Cuyabeno, Ecuador, harbours the world's greatest variety of trees, with over 100 species per acre. That's ten times the level of variety found in an equal area of temperate forest.

Most rainforest trees are broadleaved evergreens that shed leaves continually, a few at a time. Palms and acacias, not found in temperate forests, add to the variety. Yet the strikingly similar appearance of rainforest trees hides their true diversity.

When you walk along forest trails away from rivers, you pass through floodplain forest to upland forest. But, because of the trees' similarity, the change can be imperceptible. Typically, trees have straight trunks and smooth, grey-to-brown bark splotched with moss and lichen. Leaf structure is also remarkably invariable – dark and narrow, with pointed 'drip-tips' and a waxy surface to help heavy rain run off easily, inhibiting colonisation by fungi and epiphytes.

Surveying the forest, you see broad crowns of trees. These so-called 'emergents' rise above

The flooded forest of the Cuyabeno Wildlife Reserve, Ecuador, promotes the diversity of plant life (PO/MP/FLPA)

The trees that defy time

Because plants grow so fast in the tropics, it was commonly believed that Amazon trees were younger than trees of similar size from temperate regions. Most tropical trees lack tree-rings. These provide the easiest way to date trees, so in their absence it's difficult to verify a tree's age. Recent scientific studies show that trees of the Amazon are much older than previously believed. Some have been growing for at least 1,400 years. Using carbon-dating techniques, a team from the University of California in Santa Barbara found that most of the trees felled in an area near Manaus were 500 to 600 years old, with a couple exceeding 1,000 years. This discovery could benefit forest management, if loggers were to leave the older, slower-growing species behind to maintain the canopy, harvesting only the faster-growing ones.

the canopy. To support themselves, forest giants have flared bases and buttress roots to stabilise them in the thin soil, too shallow for a taproot. Impressive root systems branch out to cover an area the size of a tennis court, while also increasing the area available for absorption of nutrients from the leaf litter on the rainforest floor.

Plenty amid starvation

Look under the mat of rainforest litter and you will find bare clay. Termites, fungi, algae, insects and worms rapidly decompose the thin layer of rotting leaves; dead vegetation decomposes 60 times faster than in temperate coniferous forests. Minerals and nutrients are so quickly incorporated into plants that most organic matter is locked up in living organisms. This is how infertile tropical soils support lush growth. The forest absorbs nutrients so effectively that plants use 98% of the phosphate dissolved in rain before the water reaches the forest floor. Innovative ways of maximising nutrient use have evolved.

Brown-throated three-toed sloth, Peru (IA/MP/FLPA)

Certain kinds of symbiotic fungi (mycorrhizae) surround and penetrate epiphyte and tree roots to greatly increase the root absorption area. Nitrogen-fixing bacteria enable acacias to thrive in soils that are deficient in nitrogen.

Habitats and vegetation

Trees form the forest's vertical structure, and while the tangle of growth may appear chaotic, it is actually organised in three or five overlapping vertical layers.

In the **emergent (or overstorey) layer**, forest giants tower above the canopy. Trees such as fig, teak, mahogany, kapok or silk-cotton and many others reach 130ft (40m) or more. Epiphytes cloak lower branches, and greatly add to floral diversity.

The **canopy layer** is made up of uniform-looking trees which form the main canopy,

The different layers of the rainforest can often be glimpsed from the riverbank (MM/MP/FLPA)

growing 40–100ft (12–30m) tall. This is the site of highest biodiversity, where over nine-tenths of the forest's photosynthesis takes place. Canopy trees have tall, narrow crowns, to efficiently occupy space among each other. Crowns of the same tree species at the same height never overlap or cover each other, an arrangement called 'crown shyness'. Numerous palm and acacia crowns comprise this level. Around 900 palm species are described from the lowland rainforest. The common stilt palm has stilt roots to help support it in the thin soil. The moriche palm has among the largest leaves of any plant, and has so many uses that Alexander von Humboldt called it the 'tree of life'. The plant's fruits are edible, consumed fresh or as a juice, while the leaf stem is used to make mats and candles. Other palms important for income or subsistence include thatch palm, fibre palm and heart palm.

In the **understorey (or shrub) layer**, widely spaced treelets and shrubs reach upward from 3–20ft (1–6m). In forest undamaged by axe or saw, understorey plant growth is sparse. Small palms include the commercially valuable ivory palm and others with edible fruits. Tree-ferns and cycads are also found in this layer. Often mistaken for palms or ferns, cycads are a poorly known group, with more species likely to be discovered.

In mature forest, dense, closed canopy cuts off most light – up to 98% of it – so only shade-tolerant herbs, ferns, tree seedlings and fungi grow at **ground level**. Many herbs have long, narrow, often variegated leaves. Look for the beautifully variegated calathea and caladium, members of the arum family. A number of these species have been domesticated as popular houseplants. Some terrestrial arums provide edible corms, notably arrowroot, used in cooking as a natural thickener. The corm of the huge, pale-green elephant's ear is made into a taro-like flour. *Piper* is a genus of low-growing shrubs with pointed, oval, shiny leaves with four parallel veins and swollen nodes (where the leaf meets the stem). It's among the most diverse plant genera, with over 1,000 species described, many from the Amazon. Mushrooms (locally called *hongo*) come in all shapes and sizes. You might see agarics similar to the ones you buy in stores, or jelly-like forms, of which tree-ear is common. Selaginella and club-moss are abundant, ground-dwelling mosses.

Multiple roles for animals

Animals inhabit ecological niches corresponding to the layered forest structure. Life in emergent tree crowns consists mainly of birds and insects. Swifts and swallows race through the air in pursuit of insects that stray above the canopy. Small primates are often most active at night, because raptors prey on them by day.

Death by strangulation

Plants in the Amazon employ endless strategies to clamber above the canopy and reach life-giving light. Among the most elaborate techniques is that of the strangler fig, which is closely related to the common houseplant, the weeping fig, but with a more sinister ecology. Frugivorous birds ingest the figs and excrete the seeds, which germinate on a branch. From the seedling, shoots grow out and envelope the main trunk of a host tree. Ever tightening, the fig's tendrils encircle the trunk, cutting into the bark and blocking vital cellular water channels. Doomed, the victim tree is eventually enshrouded beneath tightly woven roots and stems. After several years, the host tree dies and decays, leaving behind the shell of the living fig tree. This strategy allows the fig to grow to canopy level much quicker than if it had to wait for the light and warmth created by a forest gap. But the strangler fig is not all bad: once grown, its maze of tangled roots and trunk crevices offers shelter for a wide variety of lizards and insects.

The canopy, the site of highest biodiversity, harbours birds, mammals and reptiles. Tiny poison frogs inhabit tree-holes and bromeliads. Plants provide food and shelter for animals that in turn help the plants to reproduce. Rodents, bats, hummingbirds and insects pollinate flowers. A unique characteristic of tropical trees is the production of tough blossoms directly from the trunk – caulifory. This aids pollination and seed dispersal because climbing mammals find it easier to reach the flowers and fruit.

In the canopy's shade, small arboreal carnivores such as the ocelot and margay prowl thick branches, preying on sloths, monkeys and rodents. This habitat is ideal for tree-dwelling snakes hunting camouflaged tree frogs.

Below the canopy, lianas, bark, branches, leaves of shrubs and tiny twigs are colonised by opportunistic, shade-tolerant miniature ferns, along with mosses, lichens, algae and other simple plants. Within this mini-forest live detritus-feeding micro-animals: isopods, springtails, silverfish, millipedes and earth-dwelling oribatid mites. They break down dead plant matter and in turn are hunted by micro-predators: centipedes, hunting spiders, pseudoscorpions and predatory mites. Non-arthropod fauna are there too: tiny worms, nematodes and minute molluscs.

Giant leaf frog (WWL/GT)

Classification

Biologists use strict rules to identify organisms precisely. The rules underlie the science of classification or taxonomy, which is the basis for measuring biodiversity. Biodiversity in turn is needed to quantify the biological value of a habitat, which determines conservation and land management decisions.

The scientific name of a species is in Latin, the universal language of biologists. It comprises the genus (plural: genera) and species. This is written in italics. The genus name begins with a capital letter. The species name is lower case, such as Choloepus didactylus (two-toed sloth).

This book uses Latin/scientific names for plants and animals only where there is a need to avoid confusion, or if there is no common name. For a list of all species mentioned, along with their scientific names, please visit the book's companion website (⌘ www.amazontravelbook.com). You can use the printable checklists for keeping track of the plants and animals you see during your trip.

Pumas prey on smaller mammals on the forest floor
(CM/MP/FLPA)

Ground-dwelling forest mammals have compact bodies to help them move through tangled undergrowth. Jaguar, puma and smaller cats hunt rodents, shrews, tapir, deer and peccary on the forest floor. Anteaters feast on the abundant ants and termites. In the soil and leaf litter, a host of invertebrates help fungi and microbes quickly decompose organic matter to provide vital nutrients to fast-growing vegetation.

Forest edges and gaps

The different layers of the forest contribute to much of its biodiversity, but, where light is abundant, the layered growth typical of mature forest breaks down. Instead, 'edge habitat' dominates, home to specialised plants and animals. Edge habitats are spectacular for sheer exuberance of growth. Early explorers only saw the edges of the forest along rivers and trails, so edge habitats thereby defined our idea of 'jungle'. As much of your travel will be along rivers, lakesides and trails, the plants here will be your 'take-home' impression of rainforest.

Related to beans and peas, acacias and mimosas are trees 15–100ft (4.5–30m) tall, and are dominant along rivers and lake edges. **Acacias** often have elaborate, red-orange flowers, and many have large, attractive seed pods, like giant beans. The scarlet-flowered coral tree has hard, red-and-black, poisonous seeds used in native handicrafts, such as necklaces, bracelets and earrings. Retama is a yellow-flowered legume with large oval leaflets, common along slow-moving whitewater rivers. The ice cream bean tree produces a long, thin fruit that grows to 5ft (1.5m) or more. Break open the pod to find a delicious, almost fluffy white flesh. It is used to flavour ice cream. Hundreds of different kinds of **mimosas** are endemic to the Amazon. Some species are small and shrubby, while others grow to 32ft (10m) high. The globular yellow or creamy-white flower sprays produced by mimosas inspired the eponymous (champagne and orange juice) cocktail's name, and are one way to tell a mimosa from closely related acacias. Another distinction is that mimosas usually have delicate, feathery leaves. Their pods are generally small and fragile.

Legumes tend to have low levels of toxic compounds, so they have evolved ingenious ways of defending themselves against the depredations of hungry plant eaters. One defence mechanism exhibited

Much of what you see alongside rivers and lakes are the edges of the forest, a habitat that contributes to species diversity (PO/MP/FLPA)

by the 'sensitive plant', a small shrub, is leaves that close when touched. Many other legumes are defended with large, sharp thorns, and are often home to a second line of defence – hordes of stinging ants.

One common strategy for fending off unwanted herbivores is **plant–insect symbiosis**. Reaching 65ft (20m) in height, the *Cecropia* is one of the commonest trees of river edges. It has large, five-lobed leaves, a greyish stem and a noticeable absence of epiphytes. But look closely and you'll see tiny holes in the stem. From these, aggressive stinging ants sally forth when the plant is disturbed. Be sure to recognise these trees and avoid touching them.

The waxy red flowers of heliconias, such as this *Heliconia rostrata*, or crab claws, are pollinated by hummingbirds (RH)

Heliconia plants are common along well-lit riverbanks. Related to the banana, they can be identified by their similarly large, pale-green leaves. The shape of their waxy red and yellow flowers has given rise to their popular name: crab-claws. Hummingbirds pollinate the flowers, tent-making bats use the leaves for shelter and antbirds forage among the undergrowth.

Cloudforest

Far above the sultry lowlands of the Amazon's tropical rainforest is a different world – the cloudforests of the Andes. The Andes are South America's backbone, running north to south along the length of continent's western side. This is the world's longest and second-highest mountain range. For a third of the Andes' length, rivers on the eastern flank drain into the Amazon Basin. From the Amazon lowlands, as you travel west into the Andes, meandering rivers give way to smaller streams. Trees are smaller, their branches festooned with epiphytes. Palms are less abundant and tree-ferns dominate the undergrowth. The forest floor is covered with mosses, ferns and fungi.

The cloudforest (*selva de neblina* or *bosque nuboso*) feels quite different from the lowland forest. It's quiet and more subdued. Sounds are muffled by thick vegetation. You can't see as far ahead, cloaked by the ever-present mist. The shorter trees, with their thick, gnarled trunks, imbue a sense of ancient landscape, a place where mythical creatures roam. Mystery lies around every turn of the trail.

In Amazonia, altitudes with persistent, frequent or seasonal low-level cloud cover provide the most favourable conditions for cloudforests; this zone varies from about 1,500 to 10,000ft (500–3,000m). Rainfall is frequent, while much of the water cycle is completed within the ecosystem. Water condenses on the vegetation and drips to the ground. Temperatures are cooler than in lowland forest, varying from 46 to 68°F (8–20°C). Cloudforests typically develop in valleys and on mountainsides, where clouds can settle.

Cloudforests are the most endangered tropical habitats. Colombia has lost more than 80% of its original cloudforest. Causes include clearing for crops, conversion to tea or coffee plantations, and logging. Climate change will disrupt the delicate balance of temperature and moisture that favours cloud formation. Drying out of the forests stresses epiphytes, moisture-loving frogs and invertebrates. Such changes are unfolding faster than plants or animals can adapt. The good news is that governments now recognise the value of such habitats. About one-third of cloudforests worldwide are protected.

Cloudforest landscapes are often shrouded in mist (TF/MP/FLPA)

Cloudforests have lower species diversity than lowland rainforest, but **biodiversity** is still high. Higher altitude areas include *páramo* (treeless alpine plateau) and scattered patches of *Polylepis* woodland; elfin forest and montane cloudforest occur at lower elevations. These forests also feature high levels of endemism, species often have small ranges and are unlikely to be seen elsewhere, and hummingbirds and orchids reach their highest species richness here. Rare mammals such as the spectacled bear are found nowhere else.

Given the terrain and range of habitats, cloudforests offer endless opportunities for travellers. River rafting and caving are for the adventurous, and if you're relatively fit, a trekking holiday is the best option. Specialist tours are available for birdwatchers and nature lovers. The Andes is studded with active volcanoes, so the area offers numerous opportunities to explore geology close up.

Visiting Amazonian cloudforests

Peru and Ecuador offer the best opportunities to experience Amazonian cloudforest. Much of Colombia's cloudforest is already degraded, although well-preserved areas remain around the Magdalena Valley. Significant areas of Ecuador and Peru remain intact. The area around Baños in Ecuador is relatively accessible, while the Cosanga Valley and Yanacocha are virtually pristine. The Antisana Ecological Reserve offers some of the richest montane habitats in the country. In Peru, the best place to explore cloudforest is in Manú National Park, given its infrastructure for tourists. Other notable locations include the area around Machu Picchu, Machiguenga-Megantoni Reserve and Alto Rio Piedras in the Madre de Dios region. See pages 191–256 for information on the Peruvian and Ecuadorian cloudforests.

Morpho butterfly caterpillars on a tree trunk in Manú National Park, Peru (TM/MP/FLPA)

Epiphytes

Among the treetops there is enough light to allow smaller plants to grow – ideal habitat for epiphytes (wrongly called 'air plants'). Incessantly reaching for light above gloomy lower layers, epiphytes perch on tree limbs, but are not parasitic. Rooted in soil accumulated on branches or in crevices, they take all their nutrients from rainwater, leaf litter, and dead microbes and insects. Epiphytes depend on their host tree to raise themselves to canopy height but do not 'feed' off the host, although they sometimes festoon boughs so heavily that their weight comprises up

Bromeliads and numerous other species growing as epiphytes in subtropical forest, Colombia (MC/MP/FLPA)

to one-third of the tree's. A burden of epiphytes can sometimes snap branches off the host tree. Although the 'high life' has its advantages, things are not that easy. Epiphytes must withstand the rigours of life in the treetops – the danger of desiccation from winds and hot sun, and fierce competition for space among the branches.

A tenth of all higher plants are epiphytes. The biggest epiphytes are bromeliads and arum lilies; other important groups include orchids, philodendrons, peperomias, forest cacti and ferns.

Smaller, more primitive 'lower' plants cram the remaining space. Many lower plants can tolerate complete drying out so they can colonise parts of trees that are hostile for more delicate plants. You might think moss only grows on the ground, but in the canopy, velvet-green moss carpets every twig and branch. Crinkly lichens and slimy algae encrust branches and treetrunks. Some of these tiny epiphytes, called epiphylls, live only on the leaves of bigger plants.

Bromeliads: aerial aquariums

High in the branches of trees you will notice the most conspicuous epiphytes: various species of bromeliad, also called 'vase plants'.

The central rosette of the bromeliad's leaves is ideal for catching water (WWL/GT)

Often large and abundant enough to obscure the host tree's branches, bromeliads produce spear-like blossoms. They are easily identified by their bright-green, waxy, strap-like leaves, arranged in a rosette and often lined with small, curved thorns along the edges. About half of all bromeliads are epiphytic; the best known of the bromeliad family is the pineapple, but it's not an epiphyte.

The bromeliad's vase-like leaf-rosette holds water – as much as 1¾ gallons (8 litres) in the biggest specimens. It's an aerial mini-aquarium supporting water ferns, algae and microscopic plants. Larvae of aquatic insects graze the aquatic plants, and are in turn food for the arboreal frogs who depend on bromeliads for a place to hide, mate and raise tadpoles. Sometimes you will find a brightly coloured poison frog within a bromeliad.

As epiphytes, bromeliads do not directly harm the host tree, but their weight can sometimes cause damage. After heavy rain, water accumulates in the vases of dozens of bromeliads, and the extra strain can cause branches to break and even trees to fall.

Orchids: evolution's sculptures

The exquisite forms and colours of orchids were mysterious to early botanists, but we now know that their beauty results from intricate relationships with pollinating insects. Most orchids are perennial epiphytes which are pollinated by small euglossine bees, but wasps, beetles, butterflies, flies or even birds may also act as pollinators. To prevent access by the wrong insect, orchid flowers often have complex traps and passages. Each flower has its own unique method to attract the insect and to ensure pollen is placed on the insect's body. The insect must negotiate the obstacle course before it fertilises the flower. Some orchids provide nectar or extra pollen to bribe their pollinators to make the effort. Other species trick the insect instead, with flowers that mimic the female bee in size, shape and colour patterns in order to deceive the male. Even their perfume smells like her pheromone. Enamoured by the deception, the male bee buzzes from flower to flower in futile attempts to mate. Over time, tight bonds have evolved between orchids and insects, which explains much of the elaborate complexity of orchid flower shapes and colours.

Mostly found high in the canopy, orchids are exposed to hot sun and drying winds, and are in constant danger of drying out. They have swollen leaf bases called pseudobulbs to help them conserve water. Orchids also have thick, waxy leaves to minimise evaporative water loss. Pale, light-resistant roots affix the plant to branches and absorb nutrients from dripping rain. On a cellular and molecular level, orchids are rather like cacti. Like those of their prickly cousins, the leaf pores of orchids close during the day to reduce evaporation.

Visitors to rainforests often expect trees to be adorned with bouquets of brightly coloured orchids. In reality, the flowers are not easy to see from the ground. Most rainforest orchids grow on branches high up, hidden by dense vegetation. Only a few

The bright colours of orchids trigger the mating instinct of male insects, obliging them to visit and pollinate the flower (WWL/GT)

flower at any one time, so we see mostly leaves. Orchids are less diverse in lowland rainforests than in cloudforests in the Andean highlands. Around 125 kinds have been found around Iquitos, whereas a 2004 study found 110 species in just a small patch of undisturbed cloudforest.

Orchids are among the most threatened plants. Many species are very rare, restricted to just one or two remote locations. Attracted by their beauty, collectors have pushed many orchid species to extinction. Over-zealous collecting is less of a problem now, since the trade in wild botanicals is controlled. However, widespread habitat loss continues to threaten orchids.

Other epiphytes

You can recognise philodendrons and monsteras by their heart-shaped, leathery leaves, climbing stems and long, stringy roots dangling down to the forest floor. You might recognise some species from your local gardening store. In the Amazon you'll see them in their native habitat, growing up the trunks of trees – hence they're commonly called creepers. **Monsteras**, also known as Swiss cheese plants because of the holes in their deeply divided leaves, have a dual nature. When sprouting on the forest floor, they grow towards shadowed places, such as between the flat buttresses of tall rainforest giants. These tree trunks provide support as the plant climbs upwards. As the plants begin to grow up the trunk, they change preference and instead grow upwards towards the light.

Arum lilies are not climbers, but they grow to huge sizes. Their shiny, dark-green, arrowhead-shaped leaves can grow up to 6ft (2m) long. The flowers are white or yellow, and are unmistakable with a single petal or 'spathe' curved around the fleshy, finger-like head of pollen-bearing flowers. Many arum lilies are epiphytic, but other species grow on the forest floor, where they are quite common. Look out for them as you walk along jungle trails.

Ferns

Some ferns grow as epiphytes, while others are soil-bound at ground level, and certain species are adaptable enough to thrive in a variety of habitats. Because their reproductive cells need free water during the crucial fertilisation phase, ferns are more abundant and widespread in moist tropical rainforests than in drier habitats.

The terrestrial **maidenhair fern** is familiar to indoor gardeners. Notable for its thin, deltoid leaves and wiry, black stems, you'll see it growing along forest trails. Natives use it for mosquito repellent and a variety of other purposes. **Bird's nest fern** is an ornamental, native to Japan, but cultivated in the Amazon. It has the form of a bromeliad, but without the vase to hold water.

Tree-ferns don't grow as epiphytes but are puny compared with real trees. However, they are the giants of the fern world. They boast a long lineage as 'living fossils', relics from the age of the dinosaurs. Their crown of typically fern-like leaves is supported by a tall, black stem about 10ft (3m) high, thick as a man's arm and covered in coarse black hairs.

Ferns are an important and diverse group of rainforest plants (WWL/GT)

Lianas and vines

In contrast to epiphytes, which live entirely on other plants, vines and lianas get their nutrients from the thin forest soil. Rather than try for a spot high in the canopy by chance distribution of seeds in the manner of epiphytes, lianas and vines cheat in the competition for light. To avoid expending energy on growing a huge trunk, their seeds germinate next to taller plants, then grow up them. These plants add much to the forest's botanical diversity. They physically connect trees, develop intricate networks across the rainforest canopy, and provide skyways for ants, caterpillars and arboreal mammals. You occasionally see a troop of leaf-cutter ants disappearing up a liana high into the canopy. On the other hand, dense vines at forest edges impede larger animals on the ground, including humans!

Vines and lianas provide aerial walkways for arboreal rainforest creatures (ss)

Lianas

Like ropes entangling the masts of some fantastic sailing ship, knotted stems straggle up thick trees and vanish high into the canopy. These are liana stems. In brightly lit gaps, lianas hitch a ride upwards on young, fast-growing trees, while in mature forest they work their way up the trunks of existing trees. Large trees thus give lianas access to brighter levels of the canopy. Some lianas might live for over a hundred years.

Woody lianas can extend half a mile (900m) from where they're rooted, trailing over acres of trees. A liana can literally be the downfall of a tree. The weight of a liana, with its matrix of interconnections with

Red and green macaws congregate on a vine in Manú National Park, Peru (MPF/MP/FLPA)

other trees, spreads the stresses and strains of swaying action across several trees. When one tree falls, connections between lianas may pull down others.

In deep terra firme forest, some lianas grow as big as trees and are strong enough to support a person's weight. If your tour includes a forest walk you might even have the chance to swing on a liana; a true vine would simply snap, so Tarzan swings on lianas, not vines.

There are over 15,000 species in the Amazon, many of which are distinguished only by flowers or leaves hidden from sight in the canopy. Some, including the water vines (which are not true vines), contain water within their hollow stem. Your tour guide might point one out and cut its stem for a drink of fresh, pure water. But drink with caution – a similar species is used in *curare*, a paste used for poison on the darts of blowpipes.

Among the best-known lianas is **ayahuasca**, also called spirit vine or vine of the soul, which is widely used in religious ceremonies because of its powerful hallucinogenic properties.

Liana growth forms vary from slender stems to massive trunks. They may be in the shape of a simple cylinder or with helical twists, or two or three plaited together. Monkey ladder, which grows in *várzea* forests, has a flattened, wavy stem. A few lianas have protective thorns or spines, while others have hooks and suction cups on the end of long, thin exploratory shoots to get a firm hold on nearby trunks and branches. Inevitably, some trees have evolved a defence, since lianas can be a burden. The smooth bark and frequent shedding of bark by such trees as capirona, *palo santo* (holy stick), and *Terminalia* inhibit liana growth as well as epiphyte colonisation.

Vines

Some 90% percent of vine species are tropical. These fast-growing plants are generally restricted to well-lit areas around forest edges. They have thin, spindly, often thorny stems and most are short-lived. They

Red petals and prominent stamens are diagnostic features of the passion flower family
(WWL/GT)

drape trees and shrubs with a mass of green, enveloping riverbanks and forest glades. Missionaries believed the blooms of the passion vine symbolised Christ's Passion, confirming the Lord's blessing on their New World endeavours. The passion fruit vine, also called *granadilla*, has edible fruits locally called *maracuya* and used to make a soft drink.

Cissus, with three-lobed leaves and sprawling tendrils, is a true vine (grape family), but relatively poor in species. Vines in the morning glory or bindweed family grow fast. You can recognise these plants from their papery, heart-shaped leaves. Delicate, trumpet-shaped flowers open early in the day. Bees swarm in a frenzy of nectar-feeding and pollination, but the flowers wither by the afternoon. It's all over in one glorious morning.

One of the many commercially important vines is the *camote* or sweet potato. Another of interest to pharmaceutical companies is *uña de gato*, or cat's claw, which has long been used for its medicinal properties, including anti-cancer activity. Along with several other vines, it is becoming rare around towns and cities due to over-collecting. A further important family of vines is the cucumber. Amazon cucumbers aren't much like the familiar varieties we see in our supermarkets, and wild cucumbers are small, bitter, and in some cases poisonous.

Floating meadows and water plants

Water plants congregate in such abundance in shallow lakes and along slow-moving tributaries that they form mats, often spanning entire water bodies. These 'floating meadows' provide food for fish, arthropods and the world's only herbivorous aquatic mammal, the manatee. Underwater roots shelter small fish, amphibians, crustaceans and molluscs. Above-water vegetation supports arthropods and other invertebrates, in turn sustenance for vertebrate predators.

Water plants quickly colonise oxbow lakes and slow-flowing rivers, and the process is even faster if manatee are absent. Flood-tolerant carricillo cane first takes over, accompanied by forage grasses. If floods do not dislodge floating vegetation, it remains, and eventually claims, the waterway for the forest.

A young caiman hiding among water lettuce, Peru (D/DT)

Where conditions permit, aquatic plant species can be especially abundant. The commonest are water hyacinth and water lettuce. The mosquito fern can also be seen; it has pairs of simple leaves, only a twenty-fifth of an inch (1mm) wide, the smallest leaves of any plant.

In the main stream's lower reaches, water chestnut is common along sluggish *igapó* rivers. This arum, with typically arrowhead-shaped leaves, grows on a tall, stout stalk with a huge, edible, pineapple-like spadix (spike).

Giant water lily

The Amazon or Victoria water lily (*Victoria amazonica*, previously named *V. regia*) is the mother of all water lilies. In permanent *várzea* swamp, the pads grow up to 6ft (2m) across. Due to lower nutrient levels, in blackwater lakes the lilies are only half the size. Both the pad's underside and the stalk bristle with large spines to deter manatees and herbivorous fish. Its network of supporting ribs is said to have inspired the design of the Crystal Palace for London's Great Exhibition in 1851.

The flower of the giant water lily turns purple after it is pollinated by scarab beetles (WWL/GT)

The sordid sex life of lilies

The lily's sex life involves bribery and kidnapping. Perhaps these are justified as 'crimes of passion' as they ensure cross-fertilisation. White, melon-sized flowers open in the evening, exuding a strong perfume. Nectar bribes scarab beetles to enter the flower. Once the beetles are inside, the flower closes, and the beetle is imprisoned overnight. Sticky with nectar, it becomes covered in pollen. Next morning, the flower opens again and the freed scarab flies to new flowers, completing the cross-pollination. Once pollinated, the flower turns purple and loses its scent. The beetle is no longer needed and future visits are unnecessary. Both organisms benefit: the beetle has a meal and secure home for the night and the lily gets pollinated. If your trip is during the flowering season (which varies by location), look out for the purple and white flowers.

3 Wildlife Highlights

Why are you planning a trip to the Amazon? If you are expecting huge flocks of birds, monkeys swinging from every tree, or to get close to exotic animals, then you need to realign your expectations. This is not Africa or the Galápagos Islands. The Amazon's beauty is a holistic experience. Even if you are a keen birder (and you won't be disappointed if you are), there is so much more than just birds. Rather than straining to see a distant sloth or elusive monkey, sometimes it's better just to take in what is around you. It is the wildness of the Amazon and its pristine, primordial atmosphere that makes the wildlife here so special.

Note: this chapter paints the Amazon's wildlife in broad brushstrokes, and is intended to give an impression rather than an exhaustive account. See page 272 for a list of books you can consult for scientific names and complete taxonomic listings.

Biodiversity in the Amazon

Physical characteristics aside, the Amazon breaks numerous records on account of its unfathomable variety of plants and animals – its biodiversity. The Amazon rainforest is home to more types of plants and animals than anywhere else on earth. The variety of reptiles, birds, mammals and insects and other groups is unparalleled.

Birdwatchers visiting the rainforest think they're in heaven. A sixth of the world's bird species (see page 66) are found in the Amazon – about 1,300 different kinds. Mammals too are well represented (see page 51). Scientists have found 427 mammal species, almost a tenth of the world's total. More than half of the Amazon's mammals are bats. In its explosion of diversity, nature takes the opportunity to exploit every conceivable niche. Most other mammal species are small and furtive, but the Amazon does, of course, boast charismatic larger species such as the jaguar.

The Amazon's other animal groups can also be described in superlatives. The 378 reptile species (see page 84) include the anaconda, the world's largest snake, crocodilians, turtles and a plethora of lizards and geckos. Scientists have also found about 430 different kinds of frogs, toads and other amphibian species in the Amazon (see page 91). These include the tiny but gorgeously coloured poison frogs, which are among the most toxic animals on earth. Just as weird and wonderful are transparent frogs, and species disguised as fallen leaves, a snake's head or even bird droppings on a leaf (see page 96).

Poison-dart frogs are vibrantly coloured to warn predators of their bad-tasting skin (WWL/GT)

Most people can name at least one species of Amazon fish, the much-feared and much-maligned piranha (see page 116). The electric eel is another fearsome species. But the Amazon is a popular destination for angling, and it's not piranhas or electric eels fishermen want on their hooks. The peacock bass is one of the most sought-after freshwater fish. A few hours fishing in the Amazon might yield dozens of species; the diversity of Amazon fishes far outranks that of any comparable area in temperate climates. Scientists have named more than 2,000 fish species from the Amazon.

Yet all these numbers are dwarfed by the diversity of invertebrates (see page 97). Scientists estimate the Amazon is home to at least 2.5 million insect species, most of which have not yet even been named. Groups such as arachnids, isopods and worms are even less known. Even if you're not a fan of bugs and creepy-crawlies, such astonishing variety cannot fail to impress.

The silky short-tailed bat is an important disperser of seeds from the fruit upon which it feeds (CM/MP/FLPA)

Mammals

(See *Aquatic Life*, page 111, for descriptions of aquatic mammals.)

As you walk along a dark forest trail all you see are plants, more plants, and maybe a few bugs. It's easy to wonder where the hundreds of different kinds of mammals you read about are. The simple fact is that you're unlikely to see many wild mammals in Amazonia. Bear that in mind, and you won't be disappointed. You can spend a week in the Amazon without seeing a single wild mammal. However, if your trip takes you away from urban areas, the chances are that you will spot several sloths and two or three species of monkeys. You're likely to see bats flitting around at night and, if you're lucky, you might see one or two of the other mammal species mentioned here. But consider those a bonus. People have lived years in the Amazon without seeing a jaguar or giant anteater.

Most likely mammal sightings in one week

Here are a few mammals that you can realistically expect to see on a typical week-long tour or river trip in lowland Amazonia.

Sloth The most abundant large mammal in the rainforest (see below)

Pink dolphin Common, incautious and easy to spot from a river boat (see page 111)

Monkeys Three or four monkey species are commonly spotted (see page 54)

Woolly monkey (WWL/GT)

Amazon mammal ecology is worth a book in its own right. All species are part of the complex food web linking predator with prey, of symbiotic and parasitic relationships that contribute to vertebrate biodiversity. Much of this diversity is out of sight, high in the forest canopy.

Canopy mammals

Many Amazon mammals spend their lives in the forest canopy. These species interact with other animals and the surrounding flora. Such interactions often revolve around the reproductive cycles of trees. Many arboreal mammals pollinate flowers. Trees attract pollinators with large, strongly perfumed blooms coloured white for bats or rodents. You can recognise such flowers because they often grow directly from the tree trunk, a condition called cauliflory. Tasty fruits tempt monkeys who inadvertently disperse the seeds. Dispersed seeds often end up far from the parents; like the teenager leaving home, they may have a better chance in new surroundings.

Sloths

Consider yourself unlucky if you don't see at least one sloth on your trip. These animals, the most abundant large mammals in the rainforest, perch at the tops of trees during the day and don't move. How easy could it get to see them? Unfortunately, they're well-camouflaged and those treetops are a long way off. But with a sharp-eyed guide to help, you're practically guaranteed to see a wild sloth.

As the world's slowest land animal, the sloth moves about 6½ft (2m) a minute. When under pressure it can race (in relative terms) along branches at 15ft (4.5m) a minute. The sloth is nature's couch potato – the world's laziest creature. Its priority is to save energy, and it spends up to four-fifths of its life asleep or dozing. Like a reptile, the sloth's body temperature varies with the environment. Minimal movement and a slow metabolism enable the sloth to survive on a low-energy diet of leaves. This strategy is successful – sloths comprise two-thirds of all canopy mammal biomass.

Sloths eat large quantities of leaves to meet their nutritional needs, but their peg-like teeth are poorly suited to the job. Undigested leaves make up to a third of their body weight. Their digestive system can neutralise only a few toxic chemicals at a time, so they feed on just a few kinds of trees. This may also explain why the non-poisonous *Cecropia* is a favourite tree despite being defended by stinging ants.

The sloth's grooved fur encourages algae growth, creating a mottled, greenish coat. It grows up its back (which is down in their typical repose), opposite to that of other mammals. The direction of growth helps heavy rain run off the upside-down sloth. The sloth's fur also allows it to harbour its own ecosystem; several moths, spiders and types of mites live in the microcosm of its fur.

The sloth's camouflage is its first (and only) line of defence against predators. Sloths high in the canopy may suffer aerial assaults from eagles, while rainforest cats look out for sloths on the forest floor. They are especially vulnerable when moving to new feeding trees or while making their weekly trip to ground level to defecate. (Yes, that is once a week.) Good swimmers, they paddle fearlessly across rivers and ponds.

Sloths spend most of their languid lives in the trees, rarely coming down to the forest floor, but they are good swimmers when the need arises (SS)

In western Amazonia you'll most likely see the brown-throated three-toed sloth. In eastern Amazonia, the pale-throated three-toed sloth replaces it. Hoffman's two-toed sloth has the smallest range, west of Iquitos to the Andes and the Napo.

Sloths belong to the Xenarthra (also called edentates), a group of primitive mammals that includes anteaters and armadillos. Typified by primitive or absent teeth, these animals survived the Pliocene invasion of placental mammals into South America some five million years ago.

The collared tamandua, or southern anteater, feeds mainly on ants and termites (IB/FLPA)

Tamanduas

The collared or southern tamandua is a small arboreal anteater – a specialist predator on ant and wasp nests. Related to the giant anteater (see page 60), it shares adaptations: powerful claws, long snouts and jaw-bones fused into a tube for the long, sticky tongue. Thick fur and small eyes and ears protect against aggressive stinging insects. The tamandua grasps branches with its coiling, prehensile tail. Like the giant anteater, its range encompasses all of Amazonia.

Pygmy anteaters

The smallest anteater is the silky or pygmy anteater. Less than a foot (30cm) long and weighing less than a can of soft drink, it scores high on the cuteness quotient, with lustrous, silky, grey-gold fur. Pygmy anteaters are widely distributed across Amazonia in secondary forest, but you're unlikely to see one; they live solitary, mainly nocturnal lives out of sight in the lower canopy.

Monkeys

During your first walk in the rainforest your expectations of monkeys swinging from the branches of every tree soon plummet. Monkeys are common but rarely within sight or sound of humans. In areas where monkeys have been heavily hunted, they disappear into the forest before you realise they were there. Your best chance of seeing them is when they are foraging near remote lodges or along a river or lake edge.

Sometimes, monkeys are as curious of you as you are of them. If your guide knows the correct call he may, with a bit of luck, attract a troop closer to your binoculars.

The conservation outlook for Amazon primates is not promising; three varieties are officially endangered and the rest are threatened. The dominant primate family is the neotropical Cebidae. Characteristic of the cebid monkeys is a prehensile tail acting as a fifth limb. Marmosets and tamarins comprise the other important group. Some 35 lowland forest monkeys are known, with new ones still being discovered. A new species of titi monkey was discovered in the Colombian Amazon as recently as 2010, although taxonomists debate its classification status.

During your trip, the primate you are most likely to see is the **common squirrel monkey**. Squirrel-sized and slender, it has a greenish gold coat and yellow-orange forelimbs. Though classified as a cebid, it lacks a prehensile tail. During the day, they roam in troops on the lookout for fruiting trees. Squirrel monkeys are often kept as pets, but they're usually unhealthy and have fleas and mites, so don't feed or hold them.

The six species of **saki monkey** are all relatively rare except for the monk saki monkey. As its name suggests, the monk saki's hairy crest above its naked face conveys the appearance of a monk's tonsure. It may be spotted in the wild because the long, fluffy, non-prehensile tail dangles down when it sits on a branch. You could see one of several species, depending on where you visit. The equatorial saki monkey has the narrowest range, along the western upper Napo River.

The large **black spider monkeys** have long, thin limbs and coarse fur. A punk hair-do emphasises their curiously human expression. A patch of skin on the tail's underside adds grip as it swings among branches. The black spider monkey is common where not hunted, and depending on where you visit, you might see one of two or three species.

The common squirrel monkey is among the most widespread and abundant New World monkeys (IB/FLPA)

The **woolly monkey** is superficially similar to the spider monkey. It has a prehensile tail and skinny body, but has thick, dense, dark-brown fur. The common woolly monkey feeds in groups at middle to higher canopy levels. The tastiest of monkeys (so we are told), this is the most intensively hunted primate; hence it is rare or extinct in much of its former range west of the Rio Negro.

Howler monkeys often appear in nature films about the rainforest, and with good reason: their impressive calls resound for great distances through the dense forest. They are world's noisiest land creatures, audible up to ten miles (16km) away. The calls signal status and territory, allowing the howlers to communicate through dense vegetation where visual gestures wouldn't be seen. The red howler is found only in northern and western Amazonia. East of the Purus River in Brazil is the red-handed howler, and the black howler replaces it further south. Intensively hunted for meat, they are rarely sighted.

Attractive-looking, smallish, and grey-brown with a pale face and a prehensile tail, the **capuchin monkey** is the so-called organ-grinder's monkey. Its hair resembles the cowl, or *capuche*, worn by monks.

The red uakari monkey's corpulent appearance and pink face have led it to be dubbed the 'English monkey'
(WWL/GT)

Brown capuchins are found throughout the Amazon Basin, with the wedge-capped 'weeping' capuchin being found in northern Brazil. The white-fronted capuchin ranges through central Brazil to the Andes. Capuchins are intelligent, noisy monkeys, foraging in the mid to lower canopy for small animals as well as fruits and nuts.

Both the black uakari and red or white uakari are on their way to extinction in the wild. Quite large, with stumpy tails, **uakaris** are habitat specialists restricted to flooded forest, making them easy prey when hunted from boats. Among primates, they are at greatest risk in South

America, considered highly endangered. The red uakari's pink, naked face and corpulent body inspired its nickname *mono Ingles* ('English monkey'). This species lives along the Javari River, north up to the main stream.

The **night or owl monkeys** – the world's only truly nocturnal monkey – include nine recognised species at present. Grey-brown in colour with three black stripes down its face, the *douroucouli*, as it is known locally, is sometimes kept as a pet. Night monkeys have enormous eyes to enhance night vision, and lack prehensile tails. They feed mostly on fruit, insects and nectar. Night monkeys range throughout Amazonia, except for northwestern Brazil.

Marmosets and tamarins

The 14 Amazon marmoset and tamarin species are placed in a different family from true monkeys. They are small with non-prehensile tails. Unlike monkeys, they have claws instead of fingernails.

The **pygmy marmoset** is small enough to sit in your hand. It's about half a foot (15cm) long, and weighs little more than an iPod. Its tawny-yellow to reddish colour, and mane around the face, give rise to the local name *leoncito*, meaning 'little lion'. Often kept as a pet, it is quite common and found throughout western Amazonia, prefers lowland flooded-forest areas and is potentially at risk as a result of deforestation.

If your trip is in western Amazonia, the **saddle-back tamarin** is the primate you are most likely to see in the wild after the squirrel monkey. So called because of the 'saddle' of dark red-brown fur on its shoulders, it has a black head and forelegs and a white muzzle. Troops often forage along river edges, where you can easily spot them from a skiff. Like the squirrel monkey, it is found only west of Manaus in areas north and south of the Amazon main stream.

The pygmy marmoset is the world's smallest monkey and among the smallest primates (TW/FLPA)

Porcupines

Five types of these spiky rodents inhabit the rainforest canopy. Porcupines typically feature thick, sharp spines, long-clawed feet, tiny ears and a prehensile tail. The commonest species is the Brazilian porcupine; its range extends across the entire Amazon region. Porcupines are not often spotted in the wild because they are quiet, slow moving and nocturnal, preferring to spend the day curled up in a tree hole or an empty termite nest.

Squirrels

Six of the Amazon's squirrel species are similar in appearance and difficult to tell apart. They resemble northern temperate squirrels, red to brown in colour with bushy tails, and feed primarily on nuts and seeds. Squirrels perform useful ecosystem functions: the southern Amazon red squirrel gnaws and buries large, hard nuts and thereby perpetuates the reproductive cycle of nut-bearing trees, especially palms. Some tree species rely on the squirrel to break the seed coat. Another squirrel species, the Amazon dwarf squirrel, is monkey-like in its behaviour – it actively forages for insects and feeds on exuded resin it scrapes from the tree bark, rather in the manner of the pygmy marmoset.

Racoon family

Classified as a racoon, the **kinkajou** is the clear winner of the cutest rainforest animal contest. Thick golden fur, wide brown eyes and a docile manner endear it to all. Its diet consists of fruit and occasionally

The kinkajou is one of the most photogenic of Amazon mammals (PO/MP/FLPA)

insects. Uniquely for racoons, the kinkajou has a prehensile tail. Being strictly arboreal, the tail helps it move among high canopy branches. About the size of a large house cat, it is found throughout Amazonia in a wide range of forested habitats, even close to human settlements.

With a similar niche and sometimes mistaken for a kinkajou, the **olingo** is about three-quarters its size, and is brown with a faintly banded non-prehensile tail. It is uncommon and restricted to western Amazonia; scientists believe the several species presently recognised may be only one.

More terrestrial than the olingo, the **coati** accordingly demonstrates several more racoon-like characteristics. It has a ringed, tapered tail and long, low body. It takes a wide variety of food, from insects and small vertebrates to fruits, nuts and flowers. It is equally at home probing for food with its long snout under leaf litter or among canopy branches. Found across the Amazon region, coatis are easily tamed and often kept as pets.

Bats

The bat, locally called *murciélago*, gets a hard time from many quarters, but these little winged mammals perform numerous ecological services. Bats are renowned as specialist predators of nocturnal flying insects. With such an abundance of prey, tropical bat species diversity is high. Depending on the exact boundaries and details of classification, scientists recognise about 200 from Amazonia, which has the most diverse bat fauna in the world, about a fifth of the world's total bats, and comprising more than a third of the region's total mammal species.

Greater sac-winged bats roosting on a tree, Ecuador (MC/MP/FLPA)

The majority of bats are insectivorous. The vespertilionid bats, found across the Americas, and the spear-nosed bats have convoluted 'nose-leaves' to emit sound, and large ears to detect it.

In this hotbed of evolution all these kinds of bats have exploited a variety of niches, avoiding competition for a single food source. Not all bats are insectivores; there are frog-eating bats, bird-eating bats, fish-eating bats and even bat-eating bats. Many species are fruit- and nectar-feeders.

The best known of all bats – and Hollywood's favourite, of course, – is the **vampire bat**, found throughout Amazonia. Of course, their diet of fresh blood is not especially wholesome. But vampire bats rarely attack humans. Their usual victims are cattle or wild mammals, and they also feed off birds. Contrary to horror movies, vampire bats do not suck blood. A vampire's sharp incisor (not canine) teeth cut a small flap of skin, gently so as not to startle the prey. The bat then laps blood as it seeps from the wound, while its anti-coagulant saliva prevents clotting.

The **false vampire**, or spectral, bat is the New World's largest bat, with a wingspan of 2½ft (80cm) or more. This species is an omnivore. Besides fruit and insects it feeds on amphibians, reptiles, small birds and mammals – even other species of bats!

In contrast, another large Amazon bat, the greater bulldog or fishing bat, is a specialist. It plucks fish from the water using a technique similar to that of an osprey.

Neotropical fruit bats evolved from insectivorous bats, rather than a separate ancestor as is believed to be the case with Old World fruit bats. Frugivores disperse seeds and nectarivores pollinate many trees. Bat-pollinated flowers are often cauliflorous, large, white and heavily perfumed. Many bats leave their hiding place just before or after dusk to forage overnight, having spent the day roosting in well-hidden spots, including tree-holes, leaf-tents or caves.

Forest floor mammals

Many of Amazonia's mammals are semi-arboreal. Species such as porcupine, coati, tamanduas and others cross easily from tree to forest floor. These medium-sized animals are equally at home among lower branches or in shady undergrowth. Larger animals tend to stay on the ground, but not always. If scared, a tapir charges headlong into water, whereas a jaguar or puma bolts into a tree.

The **giant anteater** is the largest edentate and one of the largest rainforest animals. It is strictly terrestrial, searching the forest

A giant anteater foraging for insects, Peru
(IA/MP/FLPA)

floor where ants and termites are most plentiful. Most likely the giant anteater's terrestrial habit evolved to avoid competition with its arboreal cousins, the tamanduas. Insects are no match for it. Its powerful claws rip open nests in seconds. Tough, hairy skin protects it against stings and bites. The anteater probes for its abundant food with its long snout and sticky tongue. You often see holes near forest trails where an anteater has dug through an ant's nest. Its strong front legs also come in handy to defend itself and it can easily kill a dog. Rare in rainforest and locally extinct in many places, the giant anteater is a threatened species. They are easiest to see in grassland savannah habitats.

In the same order as sloths and anteaters, **armadillos** are well known to US southerners familiar with the nine-banded armadillo. The largest Amazon species is the giant armadillo. Due to over-hunting it is extinct over much of its former range. Armadillos are rarely seen, on account of their quiet, nocturnal and solitary habits. If you do see one, it will more than likely be curled up in a tight ball to protect the vulnerable parts of its body. Broadly omnivorous, it feeds on ants and other insects, various small animals, carrion, fungi and fruit.

Brazilian tapir calling in rainforest
(IA/MP/FLPA)

The biggest South American land mammal is the Brazilian tapir. **Tapirs** are related to horses, but have three toes instead of a single hoof. They have an elongated, highly mobile snout, useful when searching out fruits, berries, tubers, fungi and herbs. Heavily hunted, tapir are rarely seen, except at mammal clay licks such as those in Manú and other protected areas.

Peccaries are the Amazon's wild forest pig. Commonest is the widespread collared peccary, or *sajino*, which is omnivorous and consumes any edible plant, small animals or carrion. Roaming in groups of ten or more, their presence is betrayed by a pungent, cheesy smell long before sight or sound. Aggressive animals, they can inflict serious wounds with their sharp tusks. Intensively hunted for meat, peccaries are listed as threatened.

The nocturnal **red brocket deer** venture into forest clearings or even to the edge of gardens and plantations. Although common and widespread, they are shy and retiring.

The Amazon's 'big five'

For most people, mammals are the most exciting and attractive wildlife. And usually, the bigger, the better. But the Amazon does not boast the glamorous wildlife of the African savanna. To appreciate Amazon mammals, keep your expectations in proportion. Most Amazon mammals are small and nocturnal, and the big ones are elusive. In Africa you might have a chance of seeing the so-called Big Five on a week-long safari, but not so in the Amazon.

What makes Amazon mammals special is the variety and intricacy of ecological relationships. The Amazon region is home to more bat species than anywhere else on earth, and more primates too. It also has more and bigger rodents than anywhere else. You can read about these in the main text, but in case you must at least know the trophy animals (photographic trophies only please), here is our pick for the Amazon's big five:

Jaguar The biggest cat in South America (page 63)

Tapir The biggest South American land mammal (page 61)

Pink dolphin One of a handful of freshwater dolphin species in the world and the only one of the big five you have a good chance of seeing in the wild (page 111)

Manatee The Amazon's biggest aquatic animal (page 112)

Capybara Other Amazon mammals are bigger, but this is the world's biggest rodent (page 65)

Honourable mention: the giant anteater – the largest in its taxonomic group and one of the Amazon's largest land mammals (page 60)

The capybara is the world's largest rodent, and can weigh up to 145lb (65kg) (WWL/GT)

Carnivores

Carnivores are well represented in Amazonia, although rare and elusive. The main terrestrial groups are cats and weasels. The dog family, with two rare and obscure species, is relatively thin on the ground.

Cats

Although they reign at the top of the food chain, wild cats are uncommon everywhere: over-hunting diminishes their conservation prospects and all South American felids are officially endangered. Four are spotted cats: golden-yellow with black spots or stripes. Two others are uniform in colour. For many, seeing a cat would be the ultimate highlight of a trip to the Amazon, but cats are highly unlikely to be seen in the wild on an average-length visit; they are rare, wary of humans and usually nocturnal. Observe carefully, however, and you can pick up evidence of activity. Look for tracks by muddy rivers or claw marks on a tree. If you are very lucky, you might see a cat on a trail at night or around water margins in remote areas. Each of the cat species is widespread across the neotropics, including most of Amazonia, away from developed areas. Local zoos sometimes display captured jaguars and smaller cats. Such zoos are usually inadequate in many respects, lacking facilities and expertise that characterise zoos in developed countries, so we don't recommend visiting them. Such a visit may, however. be your only chance to see live cats.

The **jaguar** is South America's biggest and best-known feline, and its only 'big cat'. Extinct over much of its former range, it is thinly distributed. It is the only predator big enough to tackle full-grown tapir, pouncing to break the spinal cord behind the neck. The name jaguar comes from the indigenous word *yaguar*, meaning 'he who kills with one leap'. Natives tell tales of titanic struggles between jaguars and anacondas, stories seemingly from the pages of an Edgar Rice Burroughs novel.

A rare sight: a jaguar peeking out through foliage, Brazil (CM/MP/FLPA)

The second largest rainforest cat, the **puma**, also known as the cougar or mountain lion, is the most widespread New World feline, with scattered populations throughout the Americas.

The **ocelot** looks like a miniature jaguar, about the size of a large domestic cat. It ranges through the Neotropics up into the southern US.

The ocelot is the most common of several spotted cat species in Amazonia (FL/FLPA)

The **margay** looks similar to the ocelot, but is smaller and somewhat rarer. Both the ocelot and margay are nocturnal, so spotting them is unusual.

The **jaguarundi**, about the same size as a margay but without spots, is diurnal in nature. Populations display a wide range of colour morphs: grey, red, tawny yellow, brown or even black. These cats prey on rodents, small reptiles, birds and the occasional snake.

The elusive **oncilla** or little spotted cat is about the size and build of a domestic cat with markings similar to an ocelot: dark spots arranged in lines on a tawny coat. It prefers more mountainous habitat to the other cats, but its range is poorly known.

Dogs

The two wild rainforest canids are the bush dog and the short-eared dog. Both are small and racoon-like, but little is known of their natural history. The bush dog hunts during the day in small packs of 10–12 individuals. This gregarious behaviour enables it to bring down larger prey. At night, it shelters in hollow logs or empty armadillo burrows. Uniquely among dogs, it has webbed feet. Although these species are widely distributed across Amazonia, they are exceedingly unlikely to be seen in the wild.

Weasels

Weasels perform a vital role in the rainforest food chain, with each species occupying a different ecological niche. The **grison** or

The bush dog is among the Amazon's rarest and most elusive mammals (WWL/GT)

hurón looks more like a skunk or a honey badger than a weasel. It eats small animals and sometimes fruit. The **tayra** resembles the grison, but is larger and darker, with longer legs and tail. A more generalist feeder on small vertebrates, insects and fruit, it occasionally climbs trees. Both species are widespread throughout Amazonia.

Large rodents

On trails or canoe rides you might see a creature resembling an over-sized guinea pig with long legs. It is one of several kinds of large rodent. Species in this group are dark coloured, with a low stance, long legs and either a small or no tail. All the species mentioned below are widely distributed across Amazonia.

The **capybara** is the world's largest rodent, weighing up to 145lb (65kg). Tan to yellow-brown, it feeds on grass and leaves and has a squarish muzzle. The capybara is easily tamed as a pet, a fact which along with its small ecological footprint, has led to small-scale ranching for meat and hides.

Agoutis, paca and **acouchys** are coloured orange-red to grey to black. Of these, only the paca has markings: rows of white spots. The black agouti is limited to western Amazonia, with the red-rumped agouti prevalent only in Brazil and the Guyanas. Feeding on a variety of seeds and forage foods, agoutis use their sharp incisors to open the tough, coconut-sized outer shell of the Brazil nut.

Opossums

Found only in the New World, opossums are the only marsupials (pouch-breeding mammals) outside Oceania. They are living survivors of the time before South America became an island continent. Most South

One of several species of mouse opossums (WWL/GT)

American marsupials became extinct when placental mammals invaded from North America. Only the opossums survived and they have diversified into a wide range of niches. Scientists have classified about 40 species of opossum in Amazonia, ranging from mouse-sized to as large as a racoon. Most opossum species are nocturnal, sleeping by day and foraging at night. Some species such as the American opossum range across Amazonia, but several species have highly restricted ranges.

Birds

The long bill of the straight-billed hermit allows this hummingbird to reach deep into flowers (CM/MP/FLPA)

One of the biggest mistakes you can make travelling to the Amazon is to forget your binoculars. If you do, you will miss much of the best wildlife of your trip and some of the best 'birding' in the world. In a day, just casually looking around, you might see 15 or 20 species of birds. Over a week, it's not difficult to see 100 or more species. Stay long enough, and 500-plus species in one place is typical. That's as many as nest in all of Europe.

Impressive as this is, though, it's still a fraction of what's there. In lowland Amazonia, there are nearly 2,000 types of birds, and Amazonia is home to at least a third of the world's bird species.

The birds that live in the Amazon year-round are supplemented seasonally by migrants from Patagonia or North America. The Amazon forest provides important winter habitat for temperate-region species. Alarming declines in US songbirds, notably the summer tanager and the yellow-billed cuckoo, are attributed partly to the destruction of Latin American rainforests where they spend the winter months.

The child in us wants to see macaws and parrots. Like most Amazon birds they are hidden until they fly out across a river or forest gap. If you are on a river cruise, you will probably see flocks flying over, calling noisily, especially in the early morning or evening.

Like no other group, parrots illustrate how the extraordinary diversity of Amazon birds makes life difficult for the birder who wants to name them! There are several species of macaw, and there are dozens of smaller species of parrots. So you have to look carefully at a flock as it flies overhead, screeching raucously.

Toucans are also obvious as they fly over the river, but again there are several species. You might see a brilliantly coloured hummingbird, but without a bird book it can be difficult to identify the type.

A few birds are easier to spot. Look for hawks, kingfishers, orioles, flycatchers and anis perching in the open, especially at watersides. Binoculars will help you enjoy the colourful plumage as well as nail the identification. That said, small birds can be hard to tell apart, even for experts.

Differences in song are sometimes the only clues to identity, so listen as well as look! In the forest itself you will hear many more species than you will see. The tinamous – partridge-sized birds that run along the forest floor – have loud plaintive whistles, but one rarely sees them.

Raptors

Amazon raptors include eagles, hawks, kites, falcons, vultures and owls. Commonest are the yellow-headed caracara, the black-collared hawk and the roadside hawk. In undisturbed swampy areas, the snail kite perches high in a tree when not searching for freshwater snails.

The black vulture is abundant around settlements, especially, and not surprisingly, at rubbish tips. Hence, this is one species you are guaranteed to see. The biggest lowland scavenger, with a wingspan up to 6½ft (2m), is the king vulture or *condor de la selva*, the royal title confirmed by an appropriately grotesque crown of orange, yellow and purple wattles.

Away from towns the most common vultures are the turkey vulture and the greater yellow-headed vulture.

Harpy eagle

Birders are particularly keen on spotting the harpy eagle, one of the largest raptors and the most powerful bird of prey in the world, but it is found only in remote areas of undisturbed forest. Adults stand 3ft (1m)

Birds you're most likely to spot

Raptors The yellow-headed caracara, black-collared hawk and roadside hawk are the most common sights (see page 67)

Orioles Golden-brown riverside birds with a loud, burbling call (see page 68)

Flycatchers Commonly seen near water, these include the greater and lesser kiskadees and the tropical kingbird (see page 80)

Finches and sparrows The red-capped cardinal is commonly seen along shrubby lakes and stream banks (see page 80)

The yellow-headed caracara is commonly seen perched on trees along riversides and lake edges (SP)

high, with a wingspan of 6ft (1.8m), and have huge yellow talons. They are major predators of monkeys and sloths, but luckily for our furry friends, this majestic bird is rare. It is sometimes seen perched high in undisturbed, old-growth canopy. If you see a soaring bird, it probably won't be a harpy but another large eagle; harpy eagles never soar.

Oropendolas weave complex hanging nests (TR/MP/FLPA)

Icterids

Oropendolas are the most-often seen members of the Icteridae family, which includes orioles and blackbirds. These riverside birds, coloured brownish with gold (*oro* in Spanish) on the tail feathers, have an unmistakable, loud burbling call. Their woven nests hang up to 6ft (2m), like large, pendulous fruits, from the branches of trees. The species you are most likely to see is the russet-backed oropendola, which is common along *várzea* borders. In terra firme forest the olive oropendola is common.

Caciques, with dark plumage and gold tail feathers, resemble the oropendola, but are smaller. Their boisterous behaviour and loud calls that often imitate other birds make them hard not to notice. Caciques nest communally in riverside shrubs and trees, often around villages and jungle lodges, producing woven nests with a compact, spherical shape.

Cowbirds such as the shiny cowbird are common on ranches, and cultivated and pasture areas. In the manner of cuckoos, these are brood parasites: they lay eggs of a size, shape and colour that mimic the unfortunate host's product.

Parrots and macaws

Endeared to us because of their renowned ability to mimic human speech, parrots are the quintessential tropical bird. Amazon parrots are diverse, with several dozen species. They use their powerful curved bill to break open hard nuts and seeds, notably those of the mucuja and tucumá palms.

The several rainforest macaw species are widely distributed and quite common. These birds are the largest types of parrots, distinguished by long tail-feathers, and seen nearly always in pairs. You can easily identify the scarlet macaw (*guacamayo rojo* in Spanish), blue-and-yellow macaw and green-winged macaw from their size and colouration.

A red and green macaw flock at a clay lick, Tambopata-Candamo National Reserve (KW/MP/FLPA)

The Amazon's most colourful birds

Hummingbirds, toucans and parrots are all species to which we're drawn on account of their bright colours, but the diversity of Amazon birds treats us to many more equally vibrant, although less-celebrated species. Take a moment to leaf through a copy of a bird field guidebook; your lodge or river boat should have a copy of one of the classic guides (see *Selected reading*, page 272). You'll be astonished by the variety of sizes, shapes and hues represented by these beautiful creatures.

Trogons are easily identified, with multicoloured plumage and straight tails, barred black and white on the inside. The most famous of these beautiful birds are the quetzals. Lowland Amazonia is home to the pavonine quetzal and the collared, black-tailed and blue-crowned trogons. These birds are fruit- and insect-eaters, and take both foods on the wing, having weak feet. They nest in disused insect nests or woodpecker holes.

Motmots are small chunky birds. Their unusual tails end in two racquet-shaped tufts. A scarlet breast and dark-green wings characterise the broad-billed, rufous and blue-crowned motmots.

The female of the blue-crowned trogon lacks the blue head feathers of the male, Manú National Park (SS)

Other parrots are smaller than macaws, have short tail-feathers, and prefer to fly in flocks. Common species include the festive parrot and mealy parrot. Along rivers in the evening you frequently see flocks of canary-winged parakeets flying to their evening roost. White-eyed parakeets and tui parakeets feed on coraltree blossoms and are often found close to moriche palms. These smaller parrots are difficult to identify in the field. They usually fly overhead so you will see only their silhouettes and little colour. Most are greenish and similar in appearance; differences are mostly in head-feather colours.

A great place to see parrots and macaws is at the famous clay-lick on the Tambopata River, Peru, where hundreds of parrots gather on clay walls along the riverbank. The birds are present mostly from late July to late September. This seasonality is believed to be based on availability of food plants and the birds' need to supplement minerals or perhaps detoxify the 'pre-season' unripe fruit. There are many less well-known clay-licks in Peru, as well as on the upper Napo in Ecuador.

Parrots and macaws are often kept as pets in hotels, lodges or jungle villages. You'll notice that the pet birds often have clipped wings to prevent them flying away.

Toucans

Their huge colourful bills have made toucans familiar rainforest icons, and they are often used to promote conservation or sell rainforest products (or Guinness beer!). Toucans have the biggest bills, relative to body size, of any bird, in some cases as long as the body itself. The bill is partially hollow, reinforced by an internal honeycomb structure, making it very

Araçaris, such as this chestnut-eared araçari in Brazil, are small relatives of the toucans (PR/FLPA)

light for its size. Fruits are the toucans' main food and their long bill is ideal for reaching figs and berries at the ends of thin branches. Distantly related to woodpeckers, toucans roost and nest in ready-made tree-holes. In addition to a diet of fruit, they prey on small animals and even the eggs and nestlings of other birds. This latter habit may be the primary reason for the long bill.

One of the biggest species is the **white-throated toucan**, which is black with a white chest, yellow rump and blue ring of bare skin around the eye. As long as the body, the bill is black with a yellow ridge on top. This species' frog-like croak is the only way to avoid confusion with the nearly identical **yellow-ridged toucan**, which has a polysyllabic yelp. A local guide should be able to point out the difference. Smaller toucans include the chestnut-eared araçari and the golden-collared toucanet.

Hummingbirds

Pre-Colombian cultures thought hummingbirds were messengers to the gods, perhaps because hummingbirds are rarely seen for long; they are small and flit among vegetation, almost too fast for the eye to follow. You will probably hear one before you see it. The humming is caused by the fastest wing-beat of any bird, at up to 80 beats per second.

Hummingbirds are ecologically essential to many trees, shrubs and epiphytes, of which they are the primary pollinators. They are attracted to red, orange and yellow flowers such as crab's-claw and aphelandra.

Hoatzin

The hoatzin (*shansho* in Peru, *pava hedionda* in Colombia) is unmistakable. It's a robust, portly bird about the size of a pheasant. Its head bears a prominent scruffy 'mohican' crest. Large, blue eye-rings of bare skin add to its comic appearance. It is a poor flyer, because its pectoral muscles are too small for sustained flight, limiting the seemingly clumsy bird to short, gliding flights. This reduced musculature makes room for the bird's oversized crop, which stores its diet of 60% leaves. Gut bacteria ferment the material for up to four times longer than most birds, and the

During the breeding season, hoatzins form small flocks in areas where habitat is ideal (KW/MP/FLPA)

by-products of this process are believed to be responsible for the hoatzin's unpleasant smell, and hence its rather unkind nickname, the 'stinkbird'.

Raptors and arboreal predators make an easy meal of the weakly flapping hoatzin, which therefore is quite wary and often flies off as soon as it is disturbed. But when the prospect of mating comes along, hormones throw caution to the wind and shyness is reduced. Up to a dozen birds squawk clumsily among trees, especially along borders of permanent *várzea* swamp. The flock co-operates in nesting with the mating pair, assisting them as 'helpers'.

The nest is built over water and, when threatened by a predator, the chick flings itself into the water below. It swims back to the nest tree where it uses its bill, feet and special wing claws to clamber back up. Scientists believe that the unique and apparently primitive wing claws evolved independently. They are not evidence for the widespread belief that the hoatzin is a 'living fossil' related to the fossil bird Archaeopteryx, one of the first birds to have evolved 120 million years ago. Egg protein analysis suggests it may be recently evolved from cuckoos. However, the bird is still weird enough to be classified in a family of its own.

Where there's ideal habitat, hoatzins may be very common. In such cases, they form flocks of 25 or 30 and ignore benign human presence unless they are breeding.

Hummingbirds employ two feeding strategies: hermit hummingbirds sneak around looking for isolated flowers, while other species exploit dense clusters, sometimes on flowering trees.

Stake out a flowering tree, and hopefully a curious hummingbird will soon whirr by. Many are small enough to fit in the palm of your hand, and they lead a precarious existence. In order to remain alive, they need a meal every two hours. Only pure nectar has enough energy to maintain their fast metabolism. With the fastest heartbeat of any bird, hummingbirds need so much energy that they consume several times their body weight in nectar each day. At night, they remain torpid until the morning. Their legs are virtually useless for walking, so they fly even the shortest distances. Woven from down, plant fibres, lichen, moss and even spider's silk, their nests are tiny, an inch across, and sometimes hung from the underside of a banana or heliconia leaf. Snug inside, the eggs are the size of peas.

Several species of hummingbird feeding on a ginger flower in an Ecuadorian cloudforest
(RN/IB/FLPA)

Hummingbird diversity is highest in the cloud and montane forest of the eastern Andes where, in Ecuador alone, over 100 hummingbird species are recorded. Colombia claims more species than any other country. Contrary to what most people expect, lowland rainforest is relatively poor in terms of numbers of hummingbirds, but there are still lots of species. You may get lucky and hear one flit by or, better still, have one hover in front of you for a few precious seconds.

Hummingbirds' charming names often refer to their exquisite plumage; the glittering-throated emerald, golden-tailed sapphire and black-eared fairy occur around Iquitos (see page 172).

Night birds

Several **owls** are endemic to the Amazon. The tropical screech owl has a gentle, cooing whistle often heard just after nightfall or before dawn. The ferruginous pygmy owl measures only 6in (16cm) high. Active day or night, it is sometimes seen perching on branches around tourist lodges.

Nightjars roost by riversides at night, and are easily picked out by their eye shine in torchlight. The pauraque is the most widespread, and the sand-coloured nighthawk is often seen at dusk near villages, towns and airports. Similar to nighthawks, but in a family of their own, **potoos** hide during the day by mimicking a dead branch. Their grey, splotchy plumage and stiff, upright stance enhance the deception.

The **oilbird** looks a lot like a nighthawk, to which it is related. However, the oilbird can use echo-location to navigate and it nests solely in caves. Moreover, it is the world's only nocturnal frugivorous bird and is placed in its own unique family.

Ground birds

Back down to earth, there are a dozen or so species of **tinamou**. These birds have rounded bodies, small heads and short tails. Being poor flyers they rely on dull, brown-black plumage to avoid predators. Shy, furtive and hard to see, their loud whistles are often heard, but the birds are rarely seen. In a gender-reversal role, tinamou males incubate eggs and raise the young, while females lay in several nests.

The **trumpeters**, lo and behold, have loud calls, enabling these sociable birds to communicate through thick undergrowth. Trumpeters prefer dense woodland where they forage on the ground for a variety of fruits and invertebrates. They are often kept as pets, making useful alarm animals.

The common potoo camouflages itself with its remarkable likeness to a dead branch (WWL/GT)

Cracids typically look like a cross between a turkey and a chicken. Chacalacas and guans are several species of similar-looking cracids that resemble streamlined chickens and likewise readily become semi-domesticated, although in the wild they spend most of their time in trees. **Curassows** are pheasant-sized, dark-coloured, semi-arboreal forest birds, widely hunted for meat. The wattled curassow (*paujíl* in Peru), has large, spherical, yellow wattles. Curassows are intolerant of disturbed habitat, and their conservation status is causing concern.

Other forest and woodland birds

Barbets are most diverse in Africa and tropical Asia, but a few are neotropical residents. They are robust birds about the size of a starling, brightly coloured, usually with bars or spots on the chest and wings. Typical is the black-spotted barbet, replaced in *várzea* forest by the scarlet-crowned barbet.

The diverse **cotinga** family of tree-dwelling birds has a broad range of habitats. Most are fruit eaters, but are highly variable in appearance and behaviour, notable for marked sexual dimorphism, as seen in the umbrella bird. Diverse in humid montane forests of Peru, Colombia and Ecuador, lowland species are numerous. Two attractive examples are the purple-throated fruitcrow, the female of which lacks the male's magenta throat fan, and the plum-throated cotinga, the male of which is shiny turquoise while his mate is dull brown and grey. Both these species occur around fruiting trees.

Another common cotinga is the screaming piha. This bird's call is a quintessential sound of the Amazon – a very loud, three-syllable 'weet-wee-ooo', with the last note trailing away. If the sound seems familiar, it's used in movies whenever the hero goes into a forest somewhere – even if that forest is in Africa, and even though this species lives only in the Amazon. The black-tailed tityra is the commonest cotinga in lowland forest, and is found especially around villages or tourist lodges, often with orioles.

Honeycreepers are related to tanagers and woodwarblers. Some authors ally them to wood warblers. The most widespread species is bananaquit, which

The female honeycreeper is dull brown compared with the brightly coloured male (DF)

feeds on flowers, being mostly nectivorous, but will take fruit and some invertebrates. Many honeycreepers pierce the flower's petals near the base with their bill to suck out nectar. This cheats the plant, which does not get pollinated as a reward for its nectar. Strictly arboreal, honeycreepers have a deeply cleft tongue that is fringed or brush-tipped to help lap up nectar. Plumage varies from blue, purple, yellow and green, with considerable sexual dimorphism. The male green honeycreeper and short-billed honeycreeper are both a dazzling purple with black wing coverts and throat.

Jacamars, found only in the New World, have small, compact bodies, lance-like bills and glossy green plumage. The paradise jacamar often perches high in forest, then flies out to catch insects on the wing. Other species live along river banks.

Manakins are a diverse group of small, highly mobile canopy birds rarely seen from the ground. They feed on fruits, berries and the occasional insect. Their breeding behaviour includes 'lekking'. Males form a dispersed group and each displays vigorously from branches, darting out and back almost too fast to see. They flick their wings as they do so, making whip-cracking noises. Manakin males are colourful but females of most species are dull green. The white-bearded manakin is found throughout lowland western Amazonia.

Pigeons and **doves** seem too boring to get much attention from casual birdwatchers, but in the wild they're fruit-eating specialists playing critical roles in the ecology of many rainforest trees. About a dozen columbid species occur in lowland rainforest. Pigeons and doves

Swifts

Swifts are supreme aerial insectivores, spending almost their entire life on the wing. Agile and rapid fliers, they are perfectly adapted to life in the air. Unable to perch, swifts cling to vertical surfaces or hop around on small weak legs. Indeed, males of some species never return to earth, even mating on the wing. Only to raise young do females return to ground. Swifts rarely rest – it is believed that some species even sleep on the wing. Swifts differ from swallows in two main respects easily picked out in the field: swifts have a blunt, squarish tail and have more curved, scythe-shaped wings. They are often overlooked because of difficulty in field identification. Look for the white-collared swift, a large species, with a notched tail. The fork-tailed palm swift associates closely with moriche palms within which it roosts and nests. It is seen alone or in small groups, common over clearings and towns in forested areas.

typically fly fast and direct, manoeuvring with fan-shaped tails. They are robust in appearance except for their weak bills and small heads. Generally dull-coloured, grey or brown, pigeons and doves feed among trees or forage on the ground for fruits and the occasional insect. Many rainforest species are shy and rarely perch in the open. The plumbeous pigeon is occasionally seen, but it's more common in humid forest and on forest borders with advanced secondary growth. It is virtually identical to the ruddy pigeon and impossible to distinguish in the field. Terrestrial columbids include ground-doves and quail-doves, the latter being more terrestrial. The ruddy ground-dove is associated with open areas and scrubland and is spreading in Amazonia, apparently because of deforestation.

Puffbirds have a tuft of bristles (the 'puff') around the bill. This presumably helps to catch aerial insects. They are small-to-medium, robust birds with thick, slightly hooked bills. Most are plain and drab in colour or have camouflaged or cryptic plumage. The swallow-winged puffbird is often seen in open *várzea* woodland. The black-fronted nunbird is often seen and unmistakable, being the only all-black bird with a scarlet bill.

Swallows and **martins** are characterised by a streamlined shape, small head and beak, but large, gaping mouth. In flight you can recognise them by their deeply forked tails and swept-back, pointed wings. They resemble swifts in some respects, but are not as adapted to aerial life. Swallows like to perch on branches, telephone wires and roofs. Most are gregarious and gather in groups or large flocks. Amazon species nest in cavities or holes and, unlike northerly species, tend to avoid using manmade structures. Two notable species are white-banded and white-winged swallows. These are seasonally common, appearing in large numbers at certain times of year. At other times, they will be completely absent. The brown-chested martin is quite common in areas with some vegetation, usually around water.

Tanagers are a diverse family of small birds akin to finches. Most of the 125 lowland species feed on fruit, making them important agents for seed dispersal. Perhaps the most beautiful is the paradise tanager, with turquoise underparts, a scarlet rump and

The blue-grey tanager eats mostly fruit and thrives around human habitations (DF)

77

apple-green cheeks and crown. Among palm trees near clearings and villages look for palm tanagers, often found with blue-grey tanagers or *azulejos*, the commonest type. The magpie tanager looks just like its European namesake. Other family members include the more strictly frugivorous euphonias, a genus of some 15 species.

Familiar garden birds of almost cosmopolitan distribution, only a handful of **thrushes** occur in the Amazon lowland rainforests. These birds are renowned for their fine songs. A thrush diet consists of fruits, seeds and insects, occasionally taken on the ground. Open cup nests in trees or bushes are typical. Shy, inconspicuous birds, most thrushes remain out of sight, except for the blackbilled thrush.

As the name implies, **woodcreepers** forage up and down trees. They use their specialised bills to prise out insects hidden in crevices. The shape of the bill therefore varies somewhat, ranging from short and wedge-shaped to long and sickle-shaped. Strong legs with angled toes similar to a woodpecker's help the woodcreeper to grip tree-trunks. Like woodpeckers, these birds have a stiffened tail with projecting spines that aid climbing. These poorly known arboreal insectivores and bark foragers are hard to spot, being cryptically coloured. About 20 species are known from Amazonia. The straight-billed woodcreeper is common in disturbed areas. Its song is a series of descending whistles. It may appear in pairs or in mixed flocks, and is often seen climbing smaller branches in lower and mid-elevations of the canopy.

As might be expected from the world's biggest tropical forest, **woodpeckers** are highly diverse. They have long, sticky

Birds such as this narrow-billed woodcreeper use their bills to probe under the bark of trees for small arthropods and other invertebrates (JCS/FLPA)

Avian oddities

Among Amazonia's strangest birds is the **umbrellabird**, named on account of its large, parasol-like crest. This, along with a pair of dangling throat wattles, is used for courtship. The male's dating paraphernalia are considerably larger than the female's – an example of sexual dimorphism. These help to amplify its singularly deep, loud and long-sustained, flute-like note. The umbrellabird lurks secretively around its nest in riverside trees so, although fairly common, it is not often seen.

The neotropical family of **antbirds** reaches its greatest diversity in Amazonia. These small, dull-plumaged birds follow army ants. As the army ants go on the attack, their camp followers forage for prey flushed out by the ants. A column of ants on the march followed by its associated suite of

The nest of the rufous hornero resembles a pizza oven (JCS/FLPA)

antbirds is one of nature's great spectacles. Many antbirds resemble other birds, leading to the appropriately named antshrikes, antwrens and antpittas. A typical lowland species is the ash-breasted antbird, which may be seen foraging under heliconia plants in open areas along the Amazon's main stream. The white-flanked antwren, one of the commonest such species in the upper Amazon, survives by gleaning insects in the middle and lower canopy.

The group that includes foliage-gleaners, horneros and spinetails are collectively called **ovenbirds**. Of about 70 species, 25 or so occur in lowland forest, many restricted in range. Despite the uniform appearance of these birds, their nest architecture is remarkably diverse. Horneros create dome-shaped mud nests that look like a traditional, wood-fired pizza oven. The nest of the pale-legged hornero is smooth and oven-like with a side entrance that spirals inward. This structure is often seen at the cleft of a branch in a cecropia tree and may be mistaken at first for a small termite nest. Spinetails and thornbirds make big, tangled stick nests.

The **horned screamer** is another curiosity, in its own family (*Anhimidae*). It is a large, goose-sized bird, greenish-black with a white belly, neck and shoulders, and with a prominent quill or 'horn' projecting from the forehead. Its very loud call sounds a bit like 'Yoo-hoo!'. Having trouble getting airborne, this mostly vegetarian bird makes a memorable sight as it flaps clumsily through trees and shrubs among vegetation-lined swamps, lagoons and lake margins. When alarmed, it will try to move quickly to higher branches before flying away.

tongues to snare insects in crevices. Some occasionally turn to fruit or specialise on tree-borne ant or termite colonies. With heavy, chisel-like bills, these birds are specialist excavators of old wood and their brains are thickly cushioned to prevent damage from the continuous pounding. Invariably, loud drumming first reveals their presence, but they prefer thick forest cover and are hard to glimpse, let alone identify. A keen-eyed bird watcher may spot the chestnut and lineated woodpeckers. Also included in the family are the piculets, a group of hard-to-identify, cryptically coloured birds.

Marsh and lake birds

Anis are among the commonest birds along vegetation-lined waterways. There are two species, the smooth-billed and greater anis, of which the latter is commoner. It's about the size and build of a small crow and pure black. Unlike most cuckoos, the family to which these birds belong, anis are non-parasitic; quite the opposite – they are social and gregarious, feed together and breed communally.

Flycatchers are commonly seen along rivers or the edges of large, open lakes. Many are attractive, yellow-breasted birds with a prominent black eye-stripe. The greater and lesser kiskadees and tropical kingbird are common along waterways. Most of the Amazon's flycatchers are small, greenish birds that are famously hard to identify.

Perhaps the most species-rich Amazon bird family, there are at least 200 flycatchers of diverse colour, occurring in every New World habitat from tropical lowlands up to the snowline. Many share the same technique for catching aerial insects: perching until one flies by, then sallying forth to catch it before returning to enjoy the meal. Others glean

Tropical kingbirds are commonly spotted along waterways
(PO/MP/FLPA)

foliage or take fruit. The fork-tailed flycatcher is a common seasonal migrant that forms large flocks among stands of tall riverside grasses.

Finches and **sparrows** have thick, robust bills specialised to crack open hard seeds, especially grains. You are most likely to see the red-capped cardinal. Its entire head and throat are scarlet, while the rest of the body is glossy blue-black above with white underparts. It's common along shrubby lakes and stream banks, in marshy areas with partially submerged branches on which to perch.

Small to tiny birds, **wrens** are remarkable for their melodious calls, trills, whistles and warbles. The most accomplished songster is the appropriately named musician wren. Members of both sexes often sing duets. These chunky birds have small bills and cocked tails. Eight species are known from the upper Amazon but most are not often seen, though they may be heard. Most likely to be spotted is the black-capped donacobius or mocking-thrush, which is one of the biggest species in the family (although experts have recently disputed its classification). It is common in marshy areas, around pools with vegetation, often seen low down or on the ground.

Aquatic birds

A world of rivers, streams, lakes and swamps, the Amazon is a haven for some 250 or so species of aquatic and shore birds. Many of these are easy to identify and readily visible, making them a lot of fun for novice bird watchers.

Herons or *garzas* are the most diverse group of Amazon water birds. Most common are the great and snowy egrets and the little blue heron. Also abundant in pastures is the **cattle egret**, found worldwide from the tropics to temperate zones. Morning boat rides along quiet rivers and streams disturb the elegant white-necked heron. It flies fruitlessly ahead of the boat, then tires and flops on to a branch. The compact, well-camouflaged striated heron, among the smallest Amazon herons, opts to stay perfectly still. You'll need sharp eyes to see this one. Also striped is the rufescent tiger heron (*pumagarza* in Peru), sometimes flushed out by a passing boat.

At night, look out for black-crowned night heron and the boat-billed heron, which does indeed have a huge, prow-shaped bill, ideal for

The rufescent tiger heron's stripes allow it to blend in with foliage at the sides of rivers and streams (SS)

foraging through water for shrimp, fish, insects and other small prey. The beautiful zig-zag heron is a relatively small species and a rarity birders will want to tick off their list.

Of **storks**, the only common species is the jabiru (*tuyuyo* in Peru), a tall, primitive-looking white bird with a huge black bill, with black skin covering the head and a swollen neck. It prefers drier areas and is often seen flying in flocks above ranchland.

Birdwatching in the Amazon: the major sights

Everyone can enjoy the variety of Amazon birds, but for the serious birdwatcher there are some sights not to be missed.

Flowering trees attract a wide variety of birds (PO/MP/FLPA)

The rainforest canopy at dawn An increasing number of tourist lodges have towers or walkways one can climb to look over the forest. Dawn is the best time to do this. In the hour or so from when it gets light to when it gets too hot, there can be a lot of activity, with parrots and toucans flying around and nectar-feeding birds having their first meal of the day.

A manakin lek You may find a manakin lek on your own by listening for the wing-clicking sounds, but they tend to be found in regular places, and your local guide may take you to one. The energetic displays by the colourful males alone are worth the price of your trip.

A clay lick Clay licks are the fast-food joints of the parrot world. Here you can see dozens, if not hundreds, of parrots or macaws cavorting along a river bank to take advantage of the nutrients provided by exposed river clay. (See *Parrots and macaws*, page 69.)

A flowering tree Tropical trees may flower profusely, and when they do they attract a wide variety of species. Some lodges put out hummingbird feeders, to entice various species.

A fruiting tree Individual trees, especially figs, may be loaded with fruit and attract parrots, toucans, guans, tanagers and mammals, including monkeys. Your lodge may put out fresh fruit to draw fruit-eating species.

An army ant swarm As the ants move through the forest, they disturb lots of insects and attract birds that specialise on the food provided. Experts find the swarms from the birds' calls.

The **sunbittern** (*tanrilla* in Peru), the only member of its family, is a graceful waterbird that is sometimes spotted along the margins of shady streams and quiet lakes. Another species in its own family is the **sungrebe**. Its short legs and lobed toes suggest its ancestor was an evolutionary step towards web-footed ducks and geese. Along muddy banks, sandpipers, snipes and plovers and other shorebirds forage for titbits left behind as the flood waters recede.

Ibises and the diverse **rail** family (Rallidae) including crakes, rails and gallinules, are also common and diverse in the Amazon.

Around lakes, several birds hunt for fish, including the osprey, the *anhinga* or snake-bird and the olivaceous cormorant.

The quintessential riverside bird, **kingfishers** are among the commonest birds of waterways and lake margins. They are stout, with short necks and long, pointed bills. Kingfishers perch on a branch waiting for a fish to swim by before plunging into the water after it. The six species are widespread and quite easy to spot. Most common are the ringed kingfisher and the slightly smaller Amazon kingfisher.

Of Amazonia's four kingfisher species, the Amazon kingfisher is the one you are most likely to see along large rivers (SP)

These species hunt along the edges of wide, deep rivers and open lakes. You might spot the pygmy kingfisher, just 5½in (14cm) long. The green and green-and-rufous kingfishers are less often seen as they prefer small, shady streams with overhanging vegetation. Kingfishers nest in riverbank holes. When waters recede after the flood season, holes excavated by burrowing catfish are exposed and make ideal burrows.

The lily-trotter or **wattled jacana** is a chestnut-brown, crow-size bird, common in undisturbed wetlands and backwaters. With long, skinny legs, it looks like a moorhen on stilts. The jacana is adapted to open, swampy habitat. The long, thin toes spread its weight to stop it sinking through floating vegetation. Because of its unusual physical and behavioural traits, taxonomists place the jacana in its own family, Jacanidae. It has a polyandrous mating system; females mate with many males and maternal duties become the male jacana's responsibility. Males incubate eggs and tend to the young. The jacana's eggs float so they are easier to recover should an accident occur. That's the male's job. When danger looms, the male runs away, skinny legs propelling him rapidly with the chicks tucked under his wings.

Reptiles

(See *Aquatic life*, page 115, for aquatic reptiles.)

Reptiles are successful due to their relative independence from open water. Waterproof skin and eggs enable them to colonise even the driest areas. Many get all the water they need from their food. Their slow metabolism lessens water and food requirements. Because reptiles are 'cold-blooded' they are restricted to relatively warm climates. But reptile blood is not cold: the animals' behaviour regulates their body temperature. To warm up, they bask in the sun; to cool down they seek shade. Such behaviour offers clues about when and where to look for them. As with other types of animals, the diversity of Amazon reptiles is paralleled nowhere else on earth. Land reptiles include snakes, lizards and tortoises – all represented in the Amazon.

To see reptiles, keep your eyes open and your mouth shut. Most species lie very still, hidden by their cryptic camouflage, and reptiles are highly sensitive to noise; make a sound and they will disappear before you know they were there. However, your chances of seeing at least one reptile are excellent, especially as most tours include at least one night of caiman spotting.

Snakes

According to psychologists, we're hardwired to be fearful of snakes. Luckily, however, we're not entirely bound by our evolutionary shackles, for otherwise we would not be able to appreciate the diversity

The Amazon's major reptiles

Spotting an anaconda tends to be top of everyone's list: it's the world's biggest snake, after all. However, it does tend to overshadow the other astonishing Amazon reptiles. Here's our pick for the Amazon's top five:

Anaconda The world's largest and arguably most famous snake (see page 86)

Black caiman One of Amazonia's four crocodilian species, and the biggest (see page 114)

Giant river turtle One of the world's largest species of freshwater turtle (see page 115)

Bushmaster The Amazon's largest venomous snake (see page 87)

Green iguana The largest Amazon lizard, often seen in the wild at river edges (see page 89)

The green iguana is one of the most commonly glimpsed Amazon reptiles (WWL/GT)

and beauty of this important group of reptiles. Of course, beauty is in the eye of the beholder, but it's hard not to at least admire the colours and forms of these creatures, so beautifully adapted to their environment. Tree-snakes for example, mimic vines, lying in wait for small mammals or frogs, while the rainbow boa, true to its name, shimmers before the eyes, reflecting iridescent colours of every hue. And of course we're fascinated by the biggest things, and who has not heard of the anaconda, the world's biggest snake?

Constrictors

The **anaconda** is almost synonymous with the Amazon. The 1997 film *Anaconda* represented the species with excessive artistic licence, but the reality is remarkable enough. The world's largest snake, this non-venomous constrictor reaches more than 26ft (8m) long and tips the scales around 500lb (225kg). Although not poisonous, its bite can inflict a serious wound. Anacondas kill their prey by constricting it within powerful coils. Constriction is thought to work by raising blood pressure so high that the heart stops. The process is swift and the victim is consumed whole; sharp, backward pointing teeth ratchet the body down the snake's gullet.

The **rainbow boa** (or *boa arco iris*) is about 6½ft (2m) long, and is orange-brown with black-purple circles along its back, but its iridescent skin shimmers and reflects all colours of the spectrum. The **emerald tree boa** is blue-green or red-orange, turning green and white in fully

The rainbow boa appears red, but its iridescent skin glistens in a whole spectrum of colours (WWL/GT)

Anacondas: people-eaters?

Your guide might tell you that anacondas do not eat people. Indeed, there is no reliable record of a person being eaten by an anaconda, although attacks are known. 'Huh?' you wonder when you're in an Amazon town gazing at a postcard that contradicts your guide's reassurance. The poorly composed photograph depicts a dead anaconda in the back of a truck, with a pronounced bulge halfway down the serpent's body. According to the back of the postcard, an Indian who had been missing for three days was found inside the snake. The photo made it onto the internet, where experts promptly debunked it as a fake. The same picture has accompanied tales of missing fishermen, dentists and others ad nauseam.

mature specimens. This species is nocturnal, hunting small mammals, birds and lizards near water. It does not lay its eggs, but carries them internally until they hatch, so the female gives birth to live young. Heat-sensing pits on its upper jaw help it detect body heat emitted by prey. Several types of snakes possess these thermoreceptor pits.

The **boa constrictor** is a large snake, reaching about 13ft (4m). It hunts large rodents, primates and birds, day or night. Subtle shades of dark tans and browns blend together to create a diamond pattern across the upper parts of the snake's body. Females have been known to give birth to up to 80 live young, but 20 is average.

The **garden tree boa** has a prehensile tail to curl tightly around branches. Individuals come in a variety of colours, from orange to grey. It is noted for its irritability.

Venomous snakes

Venomous snakes are mostly harmless to humans. In Amazonia, 23 snakes are considered poisonous, of which only a handful are dangerous to humans.

Pit vipers have thermoreceptor pits in their snouts, hence the name. The **fer-de-lance** (*jergón* in Peru) is responsible for most injuries to humans. Although its bite is painful, few incidents are fatal. These snakes, light brown with dark diamond patterning, are most active around twilight and just after dark. Fer-de-lances are commonly seen along trails, around riverbanks, cultivated areas and near human dwellings.

More imposing but rarer than the fer-de-lance is the **bushmaster**, the world's largest pit viper. It's Amazonia's biggest venomous snake

Speckled forest pitviper (WWL/GT)

and can be aggressive. Jungle lore says that if a bushmaster comes for you, you should rip off your shirt and throw it towards the snake. It will attack the nearest moving object (hopefully your shirt), giving you the chance to get away. However, such stories are overblown and should be regarded with caution. The bushmaster, along with most snakes, prefers to avoid encounters with people.

Two-striped forest pitviper (WWL/GT)

Other vipers include the nocturnal **speckled forest pitviper**, with bold, black-and-gold markings. This snake is nocturnal. Another nocturnal species is **the two-striped forest pit viper,** marked by two bright lines along its side.

Colubridae is the most diverse snake family, with about 50 genera in South America, most of which are harmless. Canopy-dwellers include the extremely slender vine snakes. The slow-moving but beautifully patterned dipsas is just fast enough to outrun its main food staple of snails. Green tree-snakes are swift-moving. When threatened, the non-venomous false fer-de-lance displays alarmingly and strikes vigorously with loud hisses. Spindle snakes are well adapted to burrow in the forest floor.

The **true coral snakes** number over 70 species. These are South America's representatives of the Elapidae family, which in the Old World includes cobras, kraits and mambas. Growing up to 4ft (1.2m) long, coral snakes have powerful venom. They may be active day or night and are found under logs and rocks. Owing to their secretive habits, coral snakes are rarely encountered. Although uncommon, bites can be serious and have caused death. Colouration is highly variable between species. The most familiar coral snake is red, yellow/white, and black, but they can be uniformly black or red, or red and yellow, bi-coloured black and white, or red and white. Some are not even ringed, but, rather, blotched ventrally. Langsdorff's coral snake occurs in the Iquitos region in three distinct colour morphs: red yellow-white, tan-white-pink and maroon-white.

The **false coral snake** mimics the venomous coral snake. Their subtly different patterns make it impossible to tell them apart unless examined in the hand: the only clear difference is the fangs in the back of their mouth.

In outward appearance, the false coral snake is virtually indistinguishable from its venomous counterpart (WWL/GT)

Iguanas and other lizards

The prehistoric-looking **green iguana** often basks on a tree branch overhanging a river, its long toes and nails grasping branches to help it stay aloft, but it will dive in at any hint of danger. Individuals grow to more than 6ft (1.8m) long, of which half is the tail.

Favoured for its meat, green iguana is known as the 'chicken of the forest'. The meat yields exceed those from cattle raised on an equivalent parcel of land. The hope is that iguana replaces beef to eliminate one cause of deforestation. We do not recommend seeking out iguana for a taste, but if you are presented with the opportunity try to establish whether or not it is farmed or wild-caught.

The **tegu** is a large lizard inhabiting most types of forest. It has shiny, grey-green scales and forages noisily among leaf litter for a variety of invertebrate prey, fruits, caiman eggs or anything else it can eat. The largest lizard, however, is the **northern caiman lizard**, which looks like a small caiman. This aquatic species is common but shy and hence rarely seen.

The northern caiman lizard is the largest of the Amazon lizards (WWL/GT)

Most lizards are small and furtive. **Geckos**, generally nocturnal, are often seen prowling around lights on walls and ceilings of hotels and lodges. You can recognise them by their splayed, spoon-shaped toes, which afford purchase on smooth walls while waiting for an insect that comes too close. Most will fit in the palm of your hand. Smaller lizards include **ameivas**, beautifully mottled in a wide range of colours. **Anoles** are slender, fast-moving insect-eaters. Uniform pale green or brown, they can change colour slightly and are often incorrectly called chameleons as a result. Males contend for territory or females with jerky push-ups while thrusting out their colourful dewlap.

Tortoises

The yellow-footed tortoise is found in rainforest throughout northern Amazonia, whilst isolated populations of the red-footed tortoise are found in Peru and Brazil. Breeding males fight in ponderous competitions for females. The tortoise's carapace is sometimes seen discarded by a dwelling, the animal being a popular delicacy.

Amphibians

To many, amphibians are sluggish, slimy and poisonous, but others admire them, knowing that most are active, beautiful and, on the whole, harmless. Indeed, they eat bothersome insects such as flies and mosquitoes. Amphibians have been around a long time; their ancestors were the first vertebrates to emerge on to land. As such, they share about half of our DNA.

All amphibians need water to reproduce. To overcome this limitation, they have evolved ingenious strategies to fill myriad ecological niches. Amphibians are at peak biodiversity in the Amazon Basin; representatives of all amphibian orders can be seen here: frogs and toads, salamanders and caecilians.

Frogs and toads

The special thing about Amazon amphibians is their tremendous diversity. We love the multicoloured poison frogs, but most frogs are cryptically coloured, because they have evolved to avoid detection. Some frogs have practically undetectable camouflage; certain species look like bird droppings, while others blend perfectly with leaf litter. Many species undoubtedly remain to be discovered.

Given their colouring, most Amazon frogs will simply escape your notice. You might glimpse a mere few on your trip, but you'll hear countless frog and toad voices. At dusk, croaks, whistles, trills, chirps and grunts betray the abundance of frogs of all sizes. As they prepare for amorous encounters of the night, the frogs' expandable throat skin

The Suriname horned frog has a very wide mouth, in keeping with its exceptionally voracious appetite (WWL/GT)

forms a vocal pouch that amplifies the calls. The male call attracts both females and other males. While males wrestle for position, the female chooses the dominant suitor. Different call types ensure species remain separate, and a skilled listener can tell frogs apart by call alone. If you have the chance to take a walk in the forest at night (highly recommended) you'll probably see many more species than you would during the day.

Usually insectivorous, adult frogs and toads are voracious. They eat practically any moving thing they can swallow – even each other. Some species mimic other frogs' calls, so when a curious female arrives she is promptly eaten!

Poison frogs

Poison-dart frogs, properly called poison frogs, are exquisitely coloured to warn predators of their bad-tasting skin. The **dyeing poison frog** of eastern Amazonia is shiny black, mottled with yellow stripes. Its name derives from a legend about its use as a dye by tribes in its range. One morph, the **blue poison frog** from northern Brazil, is iridescent turquoise, splotched with irregular black spots. The **Peruvian red-headed poison frog** is orange-gold decorated with black filigree, while among the commonest species inhabiting the forest floor is the **red-backed poison frog**, with scarlet head and torso, but mottled black hind legs.

These are among the most poisonous terrestrial vertebrates. Just handling the golden-yellow Colombian **golden poison frog** can be lethal. However, not all species are poisonous: of the 174 described species, only six are considered unwise to touch; the others are considered simply noxious or harmless.

Poison frogs sequester alkaloids from arthropods such as ants, millipedes and mites, and use the acquired skin toxins as a defence. But toxicity is diet-dependent – captive animals lose their poison if they are kept on a non-natural diet.

All poison frogs are small, and some are tiny, from just half an inch (1.5cm) long, ranking them among the smallest terrestrial vertebrates. So you'll be lucky to see a wild poison frog given their small size, although a good local guide may know where to find them. They are diurnal and active during the day, so look very carefully around stands of crab-claw plants, around and inside bromeliads, near fallen logs and around the buttresses of standing trees. Sometimes they can be heard along stream banks. Several species are arboreal and live out most of their life cycle in the canopy. Here they live as tadpoles in pools of water in bromeliads or tree-holes before completing metamorphosis. Most species live close to the ground where they live, feed and breed among leaf litter. Listen out for a low buzz or high-pitched trill, which may lead you to them.

All poison frogs take care of their eggs. Clutches comprise from two to 20 eggs, depending on species. Some species care for their tadpoles

Precious poisons

Like many poison frogs, Silverstone's poison frog has a narrow range, being restricted to the Cordillera Azul near Tingo Maria, Peru (WWL/GT)

Poison frogs are perfect examples of why we must preserve biodiversity. Only recently have scientists recognised that frog-skin toxins yield biochemicals potentially useful in medicine and industry. Chemical agents in amphibians' damp skins inhibit fungal colonies and are under close scrutiny as sources of new fungicides and antibacterials. Furthermore, frogs and toads yield neurotoxins produced as a defence against predators. The Ecuadorian phantasmal poison frog exudes epibatidine, an analgesic alkaloid 200 times more powerful than morphine. Drug manufacturers have yet to synthesise a homologous compound. Chemicals found in amphibian skin secretions are often unknown to science and undoubtedly many are yet to be discovered. About 800 known chemicals are under the medical microscope at present.

These secretions serve as drug models for the development of analgesics, anaesthetics, anticonvulsants, antiarrhythmics and many other drugs that could help ease human suffering.

The economic value of such products as pharmaceuticals could run to billions of dollars, but time is running out. Recent years have seen attrition of many species' populations, and several confirmed extinctions due to a variety of factors. Global climate change, destruction of forests, pollution, loss of habitat and a virulent skin fungus have all been implicated. Currently one third are threatened with extinction. Specialised frog and toad species tend to have very limited ranges, so they're vulnerable to local habitat changes.

Frogs and their brethren contribute to biological diversity, and are key players in maintaining the balance of life. Scientists are battling for our ecosystems to remain intact, so that the secrets of these creatures are not lost forever.

rather than abandon them to chance it in a pool of water, as do most amphibians. In some species, the fertilised eggs are attached to the male's back. These so-called 'nurse frogs' carry the hatchling tadpoles on their backs and deposit them in a tree-hole, low depression in the ground or in a plant axil. Here the tadpole develops alone without further care. In other species both parents provide parental care. Among one genus, *Oophaga* (meaning 'egg-eater'), females lay an infertile egg in the water to sustain the tadpoles while they adjust to their new home.

Contrary to common belief, Amazonian Amerindians have never used frog poison on tips of arrows. The poison has been used on blowgun darts only in Colombia. Only three frog species are used this way. Curare preparation relies primarily on plant derivatives.

Tree frogs and relatives

Chemical 'warfare' with poison is not the only way to escape predators. Tree frogs use other strategies. Many blend in superbly with vegetation,

Many species of Amazon frogs, such as *Dendrosophus triangulum* pictured here, show a wide range of colour variation (WWL/GT)

or mimic dead leaves and tree bark. Hylids have wide, rough and sticky toe pads for acrobatic climbing. All hylid frogs are entirely insectivorous. To avoid competition, different frogs are fussy about their preferred habitat. A niche might be ephemeral pools on the forest floor, high in the canopy or among reeds of waterside vegetation.

The 85 **neotropical glass frogs** lack pigment in the skin of their bellies. You can see both their heart beat and their blood circulate while looking at their internal anatomy. Their dorsal colours are brilliant green or sometimes bright blue, often with tiny yellow spots. These tiny frogs are very protective of their eggs, which they lay on leaves in the canopy overhanging streams. The hatchlings simply drop to the water below and develop as free-swimming tadpoles.

Other frogs

Many frogs do not have toxic skin secretions so, like tree frogs, they rely on camouflage to hide from predators. Many are also nocturnal,

A glass frog parent with developing eggs on a leaf, Ecuador (PO/MP/FLPA)

so you will have to go out at night to find them on floating vegetation, on a riverbank or oxbow lake. Here in the darkness the forest takes on a different tone, and a different community of creatures emerges. You might discover the Amazon horned frog, buried up to its eyes, patiently waiting for a meal to wander too close.

Toads

Large and small toads are common among the forest floor leaf litter, hidden by their cryptic colours. They're easiest to spot on nocturnal walks. As with most amphibians, toads are harmless (unless eaten; they have powerful skin toxins) and easy to observe. Toads are among the loudest of amphibians and when in chorus, called a 'congress', the hundreds of individuals calling can be deafening. Native to Latin America, the **cane toad**, which grows up to 12 inches (30cm) long, is now established in the US and especially northern Australia. It is regarded as a pest, preying on birds, reptiles and even small mammals, and having a serious effect on native species populations in these places.

The **Surinam toad** has a unique method of reproduction. During mating, the male presses eggs into the female's back. A layer of skin on her back grows over the eggs, and they incubate there until they are ready to hatch as little toadlets.

Other large toads include **narrow-mouth toads** and **true toads**. Several species of leaf toads inhabit the forest floor, where their cryptic camouflage blends in perfectly with dried leaves.

Caecilians

Their name might sound as though they're from Sicily, but caecilians are found only in tropical South America. These worm-like, nearly blind, legless amphibians live in moist, damp, shady forest soils. They are often seen after heavy rains and emerge from their underworld haunts only at night. Occasionally they can be seen burrowing through leaf litter at dusk. They expel copious amounts of slime and are nearly impossible to hold. This is a defensive mechanism, much like an eel's. They are predators and eat whatever they can catch and swallow. They search for standard amphibian fare: insects, spiders and other small creatures. Some species are aquatic, but most Amazonian species are terrestrial. Caecilians vary in length from about 4 to 60 inches (10 to 150cm) long, and are coloured bluish-grey to pinkish tan, while some are ringed with light blue or white. The mother typically guards the eggs and young for a short while after they have hatched, and filmed behaviour has shown the young eating their mother's shed skin in a feeding frenzy shortly after birth.

Salamanders

Many of the world's 597 salamander species are from New World rainforests. Most are in one genus, *Bolitoglossa*, with 262 species. They're quite common in the Andes, but scarce in lowland Amazonia. Their feet are entirely webbed, like a duck's, and they move along in a slow-motion waddle. They are usually brownish in colour, and some mimic bird droppings for camouflage. Look in damp leaf litter or in decaying logs, and on living plant leaves at night.

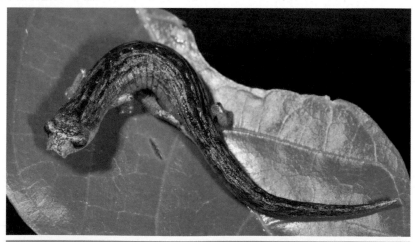

As salamanders are rather secretive, they are not often seen. This one was photographed in Yasuní National Park, Ecuador (PO/MP/FLPA)

Insects and other invertebrates

Do you dislike creepy-crawlies? Do you find insects and spiders repulsive, scary, or simply uninteresting? Your visit to the rainforest could change that. The beauty of invertebrates – creatures without a backbone – comes in many guises. It's easy to appreciate the lush colours of butterflies or the delicate weave of a hanging spider web, but their fascination lies in the crucial role of these organisms in the complex ecosystems that make up the Amazon region.

The metallic blue morpho is among the Amazon's most easily recognised and distinctive butterflies (SS)

Beetles

Beetles are the most diverse group of terrestrial animals. On a single tropical tree, one entomologist found 1,500 beetle species, with at least a tenth specialised on that tree alone. Such discoveries go some way to supporting seemingly extravagant claims that rainforests hold 95% of the world's species.

Despite the wide range of shapes and sizes among beetle species, they all have a single pair of membranous wings covered by a pair of hard chitinous plates called elytra. Hence the order's name, Coleoptera, meaning sheath-wing.

The **golden tortoise beetle** looks like a living Egyptian scarab, carved in gold, under a transparent, tortoise-shaped carapace. It's a chrysomelid, or leaf beetle, which are among the most diverse beetle families. Many feed on live plant material. Some are regarded as pests, though others control weeds or pollinate flowers.

Among the most beautiful insects are the **wood-boring beetles** (*Buprestidae*). Serious damagers of wooden buildings, in nature their feeding habits help speed up decomposition of dead wood. Popular with collectors, buprestids are also called jewel beetles because of their dazzling iridescence. Natives use the metallic green elytra from the giant ceiba borer beetle for necklaces and other adornments.

Fireflies, also called lightning bugs, are neither flies nor bugs, but beetles. Their spectacular displays twinkle in trees and at river edges during certain times of year, the light being generated by an enzyme reaction that doesn't produce heat. Each species has its own identification code of short and long flashes (like a visual Morse code), used to attract mates. Iridescent click beetles are also bioluminescent.

The **long-horned beetles** are among the longest insects. These giants of the beetle world include the titan beetle, which grows up to 8 inches (20cm) in length.

Scarabs are among the largest Amazon beetles. The rhinoceros beetles are large, robust beetles that grow 5 inches (12cm) long. Unfortunately, you may see the males' impressive antler used in handicrafts. A related giant is the Hercules beetle. The male uses an appendage modified from the head and thorax in contests over females.

Weevils (*Curculionidae*) are notable eaters of stored grains, though their lifestyles vary widely. They number 60,000 described species – more than any other beetle family, and about a fifth of all beetles. They look like miniature tanks, armed with a large, nozzle-like proboscis

The Amazon's major invertebrate sights

Army ants on the march Antbirds, small reptiles and insectivorous mammals follow army ants, preying upon individuals trying to escape the horde (see page 101)

Giant beetles The Hercules beetle and titan beetle test your idea of how large an insect can be (see page 98)

Morpho butterflies Splashes of iridescent blue fluttering through the green forest (see page 103)

Tarantulas Giant spiders beloved of Hollywood B-movies (see page 110)

Communal spider webs Huge stretches of nature's finest cloth, tattered here and there, hang down and around trees at forest edges

Mind-boggling variety An endless parade of different shapes, sizes and colours

Poo fighters: scarab beetles

True scarab beetles are usually quite plain, and large scarabs tend to be black or dark brown. They all share the dungball-rolling ability and powerful limbs to push the precious cargo around. This is buried in a suitable spot where the female scarab lays her eggs, from one or two to a couple of dozen, depending on the species. At night, dung beetles' eyes reflect gold-yellow. In their book Tropical Nature, Adrian Forsyth and Ken Miyata suggest taking a poo in the forest and watching for a while to see what happens. Sure enough, scarab beetles soon turn up.

with a set of jaws attached to its end, and a rounded carapace lined with small, longitudinal pits. They use their snout to bore into plant leaves, stems, seeds and roots for feeding. The palm weevil lays her eggs in fallen palms. Indigenous people harvest the thumb-size grubs for a nutritious snack, called suri. You might see them for sale in local markets (see page 164).

You can recognise a **rove beetle** by its foreshortened elytra, which leaves the posterior abdomen exposed. This group is very diverse: some are black and dull, while others may be iridescent green or blue. Aggressive predators of other insects, rove beetles are creatures of dark, damp crevices and corners, living among leaf litter, under rocks and logs and along muddy waterways.

Another important beetle family is the coccinellids or **ladybirds**; adults and larvae are important predators of aphids.

The **ground beetles** (*Carabidae*) are a cosmopolitan group of small to medium-sized, shiny black, fast-moving predators of other insects and small invertebrates. Despite the name, many ground beetles are found in trees.

Wasps

Wasps can spoil a summer's day, but most will leave you alone if you return the favour. They belong to group of insects, including ants and bees, or Hymenoptera, the second-most diverse insect order (about 100,000 described species).

Wasps vary greatly in size from the tiny to the worryingly large. Among the biggest wasps is the **tarantula hawk**. Up to 4 inches (10cm) long, it's the largest of the spider wasps. It uses its sting to paralyse tarantula spiders, laying its eggs in the victim. Despite its fearsome appearance, it is harmless to humans and not aggressive.

Wasps chew wood to a pulp, and glue pieces together to make paper-like nests (MC/MP/FLPA)

Some wasp species build large, intricate nests, while others build simple ones and many build none at all. A few wasp species are solitary, such as potter wasps, but most are communal, living in hives from five to ten individuals to many tens of thousands. Hive wasps operate a caste system incorporating a queen and workers, but each species has its own unique life history. Some live by scavenging, others live by robbing ants or larvae of other insects.

Minute parasitic wasps, able to fit in this printed 'o', lay their eggs in a caterpillar which then produces dozens more tiny wasps instead of a moth or a butterfly. Before they emerge from the caterpillar, the tiny maggots are in turn parasitised by an even smaller wasp – a hyperparasite.

Gall wasps lay their eggs in tree branches, and by some unknown chemical means, they force the tree to produce a spongy, amorphous tissue called a gall. These are mysterious, tumour-like lumps you might see on a branch or leaf. Safely within, the wasp maggot will develop into an adult to continue the cycle. That is, if it escapes predators or parasites, at least one of which may well be another wasp.

Some wasps have co-evolved complex relationships with plants. Fig trees depend on their symbiotic relationship with fig wasps, each fig tree relying on just one species of wasp to pollinate it. Around 900 kinds of neotropical fig tree are known, so there must be at least 900 fig wasps to go with each tree species.

Ants

Well adapted to darkness and high humidity, ants exploit forest production so successfully that they are numerically the most abundant rainforest insect: they comprise up to a tenth of all animal biomass. Ants are ubiquitous in the rainforest and crucial to its ecology.

Ant species are diverse in tropical rainforest. In the lowland rainforest of Peru, scientists counted 30 to 40 species per hectare; in

Leaf cutter ants can carry portions of leaf several times their body size (SS)

the Tambopata-Candamo National Reserve, a single leguminous tree yielded 43 ant species; and the entire Amazon fauna could number as many as 3,000 species. Ants are the dominant insects, second to none.

The glossy **black bullet ant** has an excruciating sting, presumably the origin of its name. It's also called the 24-hour ant, from the time taken for the pain (given numerous unprintable names by people who get stung!) to subside. The bullet ant's sting is more painful than that of the **giant hunting ant**, the world's largest ant – up to 2 inches (5cm) long. There are dozens of related species. They are solitary by day, scouting out their territory for prey opportunities, and at night they gather in small bands and sortie out to collect the booty.

Ant armies

Victorian naturalist H W Bates describes the nest-raiding activities of army ants. He tells of 'eager freebooters' who plunder other ant nests for eggs and larvae. Huge colonies of up to a million individuals form bivouacs in tree-holes and hollow trunks. Tens of thousands of worker ants hook limbs together to form the living walls of a nest. Within, the queen and her progeny are dutifully tended. At daybreak, the horde decamps and workers and soldiers sally forth in dawn raids, fanning out from the tree trunks and consuming all edible prey in their path. One entomologist describes army ant raids as 'an attack of 50,000 miniature wolves'. The flurry of activity caused by insects trying to escape the raiders draws to the scene insectivorous birds, like the antbirds, and parasitoid flies.

Insect architects

Ants, bees, wasps and termites are renowned for their architectural skills. All social insects have a caste system to delegate work to queens, workers, soldiers or drones. Each individual is efficiently communicated its task from chemical signals that emanate from the queen.

Wasps build combs similar to those of bees, but of chewed wood-pulp paper. You often see 6ft (2m) long finger-shaped nests of *Chartergus* dangling from the branch of a riverside tree. The potter wasp uses clay to build compact globular nests. The swarm-founding wasp moulds a clay nest about the size of your fist. This, being covered in a cement of clay and sand, is virtually impenetrable, except via a small entrance or flight hole. Another related species of the upper Amazon has rectangular clay nests a foot (30 cm) more on a side. It's distinctive on account of the long, slit-like flight hole.

The solitary species *Pelopaeus fistularis* builds a pouch-shaped nest, containing a single large grub. These wasps paralyse other insects, then leave them in the nest as fresh baby food for the larvae. Other kinds of wasps, including the sand wasp and the tarantula hawk, anaesthetise prey for their young, placing it in a tunnel dug in soft, dry ground wherein its offspring – usually only one per nest – is ensconced. Stingless bees build combs in nooks and crannies of trees such as the strangler fig. Others use silk from their own larvae to weave nests from folded leaves.

In some species the individual insects are part of the architectural design. Certain tree-dwelling **ants** have a caste of 'doorkeeper' ants. These stalwarts block the entrance hole with square-shaped heads employed for no other task. Some ants live on the outside of trees. Often seen on canoe rides, triangular mud nests are shaped around the underside of branches so rain does not enter and they point down to help the water flow off.

Termites are master builders, more closely related to cockroaches than the ants for which they're often mistaken. In flooded forest, termites build their globular nest up a tree trunk. To build lower down risks the nest being washed away by floods. These nests employ delicate, free-form architecture to maximise available space, minimise weight and maintain structural strength. Other termites build at ground level, with mushroom-shaped caps to prevent rain from washing away the nest.

Termites lack tannin in their chitinous shell, so they are easily damaged by light. To avoid sunburn, they remain in the nest. To move afield, they construct long mud tunnels, sometimes tens of metres up a tree trunk. Another way termites avoid sunlight is to move at night. *Nasutitermes* swarm on the ground, and provide an opportunistic snack for locals in Peru, who call them *paquira*.

Butterflies and moths

We do not know the exact number of scientifically described butterfly and moth species from the lowland Amazon. Accurate counts may never be possible. New species are continually being discovered, and with ongoing deforestation many are undoubtedly being lost.

Nymphalid butterflies such as this malachite (*Siproeta stelenes*) hold their forelegs so that they appear to have only two pairs of legs (BC)

Morpho butterflies are synonymous with the rainforest. Photographers, designers and collectors love their wings of iridescent blue, which may be 6 inches (15cm) across. When resting, the morpho's wings come together and show only their dull-coloured underside. These magnificent insects seem barely able to fly under their own impressive size and weight; their looping flight path appears both laborious and strained. They are highly diverse with over 80 species in the subfamily Morphinae. A related subfamily (Brassolinae) includes *Caligo*, a large butterfly with eyespots that are perfect replicas of owl eyes. The rest of the wings and body complete the deception, mimicking the owl's ear tufts and beak.

Most species of **pierid butterflies** appear to have only four legs, compared with the normal six of every insect. Their two hidden forelegs are held close to the body and only the two pairs of rear legs are used for standing.

The **longwings** group of nymphalid butterflies have a convoluted evolutionary interaction with their host plant. Cyanide compounds produced by passiflora vines put off most insect herbivores, but not the longwings. The longwing female seeks a passiflora plant on which

The eternal arms race - butterflies, moths and their enemies

Stories of fairies and angels could have been born of perhaps the most beautiful insects: butterflies and moths (Lepidoptera). Behind the myth and beauty lies a biology marvellous and near-miraculous, but at the same time somewhat sinister. Lepidoptera metamorphose from larva to pupa to adult, so the first phase of life is spent as a caterpillar. Its sole purpose is to accumulate enough food and energy to complete pupation, making it little more than an 'eating machine'.

Caterpillars generally feed only on one or two plant species. They specialise because most rainforest plants produce toxic, sticky or indigestible substances, which deter herbivorous insects. So as not to starve, the caterpillar has counter-measures - an array of toxin-neutralising enzymes. But these are expensive on energy: the caterpillar simply can't make enough enzymes to neutralise the defences of more than a few different plants. As one plant evolves greater defences, the caterpillar must produce more and more enzymes to deal with it. Inevitably, the caterpillar evolves to become increasingly specialised to feed from one or two plants, creating a natural arms race between the plant and caterpillar. Such runaway co-evolution is believed to be an important speciation-promoting mechanism. In terms of diversity, Lepidoptera comprise about 100,000 described species worldwide.

As the caterpillar munches away out in the open, it cannot help leaving evidence of its activities. These eventually catch the watchful eye of a bird or predator. Now begins the second arms race, as the caterpillar tries to avoid becoming a meal itself. Two basic strategies are used.

Deception is one strategy, more properly called mimicry: relying on deceiving a curious predator. Mimicry is a common defence. Some mimicking species copy a particular natural object. Many look like twigs. Other species mimic eyes,

to lay her eggs. To defend itself from an army of hungry caterpillars, the plant produces tiny protuberances that look like eggs. Fooled into thinking that the plant already has real eggs, the female moves on to look elsewhere. The plant has saved itself from a horde of ravenous caterpillars.

But of course, there is strong selection for the female who is not easily deceived. When she tells the difference she lays the eggs. Selection favours the plant that produces a more realistic fake egg, and the butterfly evolves to get better at detecting the deception – an evolutionary arms race unfolds. Some passion vines produce nectar to or other parts of bigger animals. *Caligo* butterflies (see page 106) have owl's eyes on their wings' underside and the hairy thorax mimics the owl's beak. One species of moth caterpillar resembles the whole head of a snake, complete with wiggling, tongue-like appendage. Another appears exactly like a bird dropping.

To get a meal, predators must become better and better at spotting deception. To avoid detection the caterpillar must become more and more like the object it mimics – epitomising the art of camouflage in the eternal battle between hunter and hunted.

Some caterpillar species opt for a second strategy by using poison and bright warning colours to defend themselves, often acquiring their toxins from the host plant. Rather than starve, predators evolve ways to deal with poisons so, in turn, the caterpillar becomes ever more poisonous. This chemical warfare spirals as each species stakes its survival on the next generation improving on the last. In recent years, more research has been devoted to insect pharmacopoeias, a natural laboratory of chemical experiments.

One form of mimicry is when a non-poisonous butterfly has almost the exact appearance of another related but genuinely toxic species. In comparison, another type of mimicry is when a series of toxic species hedge their bets by all looking similar, so a predator learns that a distinctive pattern tastes bad.

Another lepidopteran arms race involves aerial warfare. Bats emit clicks to detect their environment at night and hunt aerial insects. Some poisonous moths respond by emitting a warning click to announce their unpalatability. So how do non-poisonous moths protect themselves? When tiny hairs on the moth detect air vibrated by the bat's click, the moth instantly drops from the sky, beyond the bat's flight path. Of course, over time the bat's sonar gets better and better; it's one explanation for why bats have such huge ears. Who knows the end result of these life-and-death struggles? One thing is certain: as long as plants and caterpillars, butterflies, moths and their predators exist, nature's 'arms race' will continue.

attract ants and wasps that attack butterfly eggs and caterpillars, but many longwings are highly poisonous, 'a flying cyanide capsule', in the words of butterfly expert Diane Murawski. Toxins produced by the host plant are ingested by the caterpillar, and sequestered for later use. Now it gets really interesting. Different species of poisonous heliconiids (longwings) have evolved to mimic each other, sharing similar wing patterns. In the late 19th century, German naturalist Fritz Müller first described the phenomenon, which bears his name: Müllerian mimicry. The benefit of this type of mimicry is that predators associate with poison the 'search image' used to recognise food. Subsequently

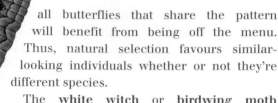

all butterflies that share the pattern will benefit from being off the menu. Thus, natural selection favours similar-looking individuals whether or not they're different species.

The **white witch** or **birdwing moth** has among the widest wingspan of any insect, up to 12 inches (30cm) across.

Occurring throughout much of the Americas and Europe, **hawk moths** closely resemble a hummingbird in form and size. The biggest hawk moths are sometimes called hummingbird moths because they 'hum' due to rapid wing beats while hovering as they feed on flowers at night. If you catch it in the light of your torch, its eyes might reflect orange. This is the nocturnal equivalent of the hummingbird's ecological niche and, to attract the moth, flowers are usually white and pungent.

Caligo butterflies have markings that resemble owl eyes, to put off predators
(IS/IB/FLPA)

Other insects

Most of us see **cockroaches** as revolting, but they have a distinguished lineage, having existed on the planet for some 300 million years. Commonly seen as cosmopolitan pests, they are persistent and hardy. The Amazon boasts the world's largest, *Megaloblatta longipennis*, which is longer than a credit card.

It is said that some people have been driven mad by the ever-present electronic rasping of **cicadas**. These insects superficially resemble huge flies. Like the rest of their order (Hemiptera), they possess a sharp, hypodermic proboscis to suck plant fluids. They sound out different songs according to species, to mark territory and attract mates. Most hemipterans are plant feeders, as you might see if you closely examine a green stem or leaf. Here, you will also find aphids, greenfly and plant-lice; leaf-hoppers, which jump as you go to touch them; scale insects, which look like tiny shields; and mealy bugs, which are fluffy or spiky, covered with a whitish, woolly substance. Most sedentary **plant-suckers** produce some type of defensive chemical as protection against predators and parasites. **Assassin bugs** (one of which causes Chagas disease) use a similar implement to suck animal fluids, usually from other insects.

Many insects are masters of disguise. Suddenly, a twig moves without a breeze, and then you see it is a 12-inch (30cm)-long stick insect, another twist in evolution's game of hide and seek. Stick insects are related to leaf insects, which evolved to mimic a different part of the plant. **Praying mantises** (Mantodea) are voracious predators of other insects and mimic leaves, sticks or even flowers in order to ambush prospective prey as well as hide from their own predators.

Flies need no introduction – irritatingly zipping around your food and rubbish tips – and mosquitoes are probably the most troublesome members of

The praying mantis is a voracious predator of other insects, with camouflage that allows it to ambush prey (WWL/GT)

this order. But some flies serve a useful purpose. Parasitoid flies attack insects like leaf-cutter ants, blowflies hasten the decomposition of dead animals and fruit-flies help break down rotting flowers, fruit and fungi. Flies and their larvae are food for birds, reptiles and other insects.

Grasshoppers, **katydids** and **crickets** are abundant and highly diverse. These plant eaters do not swarm locust-like, but can strip whole fields overnight to satisfy their voracious appetites. Katydids are nocturnal and have long, whisker-like antennae. Most are cryptically camouflaged and emerge after dark. Go on a walk at night to look for them; you'll be astonished at the abundance and variety.

We have touched on the best-known insect groups here, but these are only the tip of the iceberg, with dozens of other insect orders. Mostly, these are inhabitants of places biologists have difficulty reaching, such

Specimen insects

You'll often see hawkers hanging around hotels and airports selling displays of mounted insects. Most of the native insects in the trays are wild-caught. Specimens are usually unlabelled so have no significant scientific value and are not treated with preservative, so fall apart a few months after you return home. Some insects, such as the iridescent blue morpho butterflies and the Hercules and rhinoceros beetles, are threatened with extinction from over-collection for commercial sale. Please don't buy them.

The thorny devil katydid is only one of many thousands of katydid species in the Amazon (SS)

as the high canopy, the middle of swamps or dark, dank places. The true diversity of these cryptobugs is anyone's guess. One could start looking at tiny soil insects, such as springtails or thrips, or look for bigger ones: earwigs, mayflies or scorpionflies. These are just a few orders of insects that are under the scrutiny of tropical entomologists, whose task to catalogue and name but a fraction will surely never be done.

Biological riches

Most Amazon products we hear about are plants, such as açai berry or cat's claw. But bio-prospectors suspect that much of the Amazon's economic value may lie in the unexplored realms of invertebrate species. Such creatures, engaged in interactions with plants, predators and symbiotic relationships, harbour complex, poorly understood chemistry. This natural laboratory can't be equalled by human endeavour. *Medicine Man*, a 1992 film starring Sean Connery, culminated in the discovery of a cancer cure in a species of ant that dwelled within the roots of an orchid. If we can look past Hollywood's dramatisation, such an outcome is not pure make-believe.

Arachnids

The Amazon endlessly fascinates arachnophiles – those who admire spiders. We do not all share a love for spiders but we ought to respect these eight-legged arthropods. Spiders are major predators of pest insects and an important food source for many birds.

On jungle walks or canoe rides you will notice huge webs, up to 3ft (1m) across. Groups of thousands of communal spiders (*Anelosimus* spp) weave the structures. These spiders are thankfully much smaller than their web size implies! The funnel-shaped webs catch prey dropping from the canopy. Collectively, dozens of tiny spiders dash out, inject the victim, then suck out its juices.

Orb-weaver spiders build large circular webs, sometimes big enough to ensnare a hummingbird or poison a frog (MPF/MP/FLPA)

Communal spiders would not get the prize for the most beautiful webs, however. This is awarded to the orb-weaving spiders, like those you see in your house and garden. But the rainforest, in characteristic profligacy, harbours orbweavers much bigger and more striking. The elegant **golden orbweaver**, with an elongated black and silver body and long black legs, spins a giant web of strong gold silk that stretches across forest gaps and trails. (Don't walk into one – it takes a while to pull off all that sticky thread.) Orbweaver webs catch large insects, and the biggest webs, up to 8ft (2.5m) across, can snare small birds and bats.

Think of a rainforest spider. What picture comes to mind? Something big and hairy? That's the description of a tarantula. These spiders fit our preconception of a jungle spider, but despite their fearsome appearance tarantulas are mostly harmless: their bite is no more painful than a bee sting. However, their bodies should not be handled because their hairs detach and irritate skin, though it's quite safe to let one walk across your hand or arm. **Tarantulas** do not catch prey in a

Pinktoe tarantulas, such as this one photographed near the Pacaya River, Peru, inhabit crevices and holes in trees (SS)

web, but actively hunt for prey in swamp vegetation or other damp habitats. Many tarantulas prey on tree frogs, but the **Peruvian pinktoe** hunts moths. A number of tarantulas, the so-called bird-eating spiders, also prey on tiny birds. The world's biggest spider is the **Goliath birdeater**. It can weigh over six ounces (170g) and measures 12 inches (30cm) across. Scholars dismissed early reports of spiders big enough to eat birds as the stuff of legend.

Some other spiders are dangerous because their cytolytic venom dissolves cells, which break down and die, hindering the healing process. Untreated, the wound spreads and ulcerates. Indeed, the venom from two or three species can be life-threatening without prompt treatment. One of these is considered to be the world's most venomous arachnid: the **Brazilian wandering spider**, which lives in the thatch or walls of jungle huts.

The **funnel web spiders** may also be potentially venomous. They produce neatly spun funnel-shaped webs between clumps of grass, against tree trunks or among leaf litter: the spiders' lairs. Here they wait patiently for feckless insects to wander by. Then, almost too fast to see, the spider leaps out, grabs the prey, injects it with venom and drags it back into the funnel, all in one swift, smooth move.

Scorpions tend to prefer drier climates, but many inhabit rainforest. Most will give a mild sting, but some species are potentially dangerous. Despite the scary signs, the **tailless whip scorpion**'s appearance is all bluff: it is harmless and lacks a sting.

Millipedes and centipedes (myriapods)

Myriapods look like long armoured caterpillars. Millipedes are usually round in cross-section, like a cylinder. In contrast, *Barydesmus* spp, a common rainforest species, greyish and up to five inches (13cm) long, is flattened, with horizontal projections from each segment. Millipedes have two pairs of legs per segment, of which there may be as many as 60. They feed on dead vegetation. If threatened, they eject an unpleasant-smelling fluid and roll up, but they are harmless. Centipedes are flattened in cross-section and have only one pair of legs per segment. They prey on small insects and other invertebrates. All species have a venomous bite, but most are harmless to humans.

Aquatic life

The Amazon's mouth is so big that early explorers thought they had discovered a giant lake. Now we know it's the world's biggest river with the most diverse freshwater fauna on the planet. Amazonia is home to at least 2,000 fish species, with perhaps 1,000 more to be described. By comparison, only about 150 fish species are known from all of Europe's rivers.

Aquatic mammals

Freshwater dolphins

Although Amazon dolphins do not take as much interest in people as their open-water relatives, they occasionally tolerate humans and often allow people close. To this day, dolphins thrive across much of the Amazon. They're mostly left alone by people, particularly the indigenous people, who have taboos against killing them. Fishermen occasionally do kill them by accident, or deliberately when dolphins become entangled in nets. They are also killed for medicinal extracts or shamanistic rituals.

Worldwide, there are five freshwater cetaceans, of which the Amazon has two. The Amazon species are found in most lowland rainforest rivers and lakes. They are smaller than their marine relatives, and differ in details of anatomy and behaviour. River dolphins are commonest at the mouths of rivers where fish are abundant. They are more often seen in blackwater rivers and murky whitewater rivers.

Natives call the **pink dolphin** *bôto* in Brazil, and *bufeo colorado* in Peru and Colombia. It doesn't have a dorsal fin, but instead has a low ridge along its back. Its wide, triangular pectoral fins lie horizontally away from its body. It swims slowly along the river bottom, where it feeds using sonar to search for fish, crabs and small river turtles. According to experts, the dolphin stuns prey with sound bursts from the 'melon' organ in its bulging forehead. Early morning seems to be when they're most active; at this time of day you will often see a bachelor male, or sometimes a family pod of three or four, swim by. When they leap, their bodies do not clear the water, giving the impression that they

Pink river dolphins are often completely undaunted by tourist boats (WWL/GT)

are less agile than their saltwater relatives. Pink dolphins are common and incautious, although not friendly, and are easy to spot from the top of a riverboat.

The **grey dolphin** (*tucuxi* in Brazil) is smaller than the pink one. Juveniles are pinkish, but turn dark grey to black with adulthood. These colours make it easy to confuse a young grey dolphin with a pink dolphin. Grey dolphins are shaped more like their marine cousins, with a curved dorsal fin and small, down-pointing pectoral fins. When they jump, their bodies clear the water. Grey dolphins feed on fast-swimming fish close to the surface. This food source reduces competition for feeding between the two species. Found throughout the Amazon and in the lower reaches of the Orinoco, grey dolphins also venture along the Atlantic coast of South America into the southern Caribbean.

Manatee

The Amazonian manatee is the region's largest mammal, weighing more than 70 stone (450kg). But this creature wins no beauty contests. Its squarish, whiskered muzzle bears nostrils at the top to allow breathing while the barrel-shaped body and head remain mostly submerged. Broad up-and-down sweeps of its powerful, paddle-like tail move it ponderously, through the water.

These huge, gentle herbivores consume a tenth of their body weight a day in aquatic vegetation. In the absence of grazing pressure from manatees, waterweeds quickly clog rivers and streams. Unfortunately, they are now an endangered species due to hunting.

Otters

The **Brazilian or giant otter** is the world's largest freshwater otter. Highly social and gregarious, their loud playful antics do little to disguise their whereabouts. The **southern river otter** is dark brown above, with creamy-coloured underparts. It feeds on fish and crustaceans in clear rivers and fast streams, and can be found throughout the Amazon and Orinoco basins. Once common and widespread, both species are now endangered as a result of hunting. Fishermen also kill them in the belief that the otters are eating their fishing stocks.

Giant otters fish in the shallow water of lakes and rivers. In this photo a caiman approaches a feeding otter (TA/MP/FLPA)

Crab-eating racoon

The crab-eating racoon relies on aquatic food. It resembles its North American relative with a black mask over the eyes, ringed tail and similar body proportions, but its lifestyle is quite different. The crab-eater has specialised to prey on crabs and other aquatic animals, including fish, molluscs and amphibians.

Water opossum

The water opossum or *yapok* is the only opossum species to occupy an aquatic niche. It feeds on fish, crabs and insects. This species' gestation is less than two weeks from conception to birth – the shortest of any mammal. Being a marsupial, its young are born at an earlier stage than placental mammals.

Aquatic reptiles

Warm and stocked with tasty prey, tropical fresh water is ideal for aquatic reptiles. The two main groups are crocodilians and turtles. Their Amazon representatives are unique and mostly endemic species, which evolved from ancestors isolated when South America became an island continent.

Caiman

Caiman are South American crocodilians, and the biggest, the **black caiman**, rivals the world's other larger crocodiles in size and killing power. This is an awesome creature, reaching up to 16ft (5m) or so in length. That's big enough to take on a villager's livestock, as well as any native Amazon animal.

Your tour is likely to include a night boat ride, often with the purpose of finding a caiman. You sail parallel to the riverside, shining your torch into the reeds. With any luck, you will see the red eyes of a caiman reflecting back at you. The caiman you're most likely to find this way will be the **common or spectacled caiman**. This species grows up to 8ft (2.5m). The ones you'll find in the river will probably be considerably smaller. If so, your guide will reach from the edge of the skiff and try to grab the creature. If you manage to see one close-up, you will see that the bony ridge above the eyes conveys a bespectacled appearance.

These caiman are found throughout the Amazon and Orinoco basins. They make nests of vegetation like other crocodilians and lay 30 to 60 eggs at a time. These attract many predators, such as wading birds, iguanas and tegu lizards, so egg mortality is high, and up to four-fifths of the young do not survive. Even after hatching, juveniles have a slim chance – perhaps just one or two individuals in a clutch will survive to adulthood.

Caiman eat not only fish but also turtles, frogs and other reptiles. Populations throughout the Amazon Basin are under severe pressure due to hunting.

Spectacled caiman are the most common of four crocodilian species in the Amazon and often found during night excursions along rivers (SE/MP/FLPA)

Among the largest Amazon turtles, the yellow spotted Amazon river turtle is named after the yellow spots on the side of its head (IB/FLPA)

River turtles

An abundance of ideal habitats and food makes the Amazon perfect for freshwater turtles, locally called *tortugas*. The 13 Amazon species of river turtle are all side-necked turtles: they retract their head sideways into the shell. It's a primitive group; its fossils date back to the Cretaceous period, over 140 million years ago. Until recently, river turtles were abundant.

Traditionally, Indian tribes kept turtles and farmed them for their oil, eggs and meat. Turtles still occur in many parts of the Amazon, but are rare in most places. They tend to be shy but you may catch a glimpse of one on a rock or branch before it sees you and quietly slips into the water. Your best chance of seeing turtles in the wild is in remote, protected areas, with lots of lakes and rivers. Where left alone, they may even come to tolerate human presence, allowing you close enough to take a good photograph.

The largest species is the **giant river turtle**, at almost 3¼ft (1m) long. These prehistoric creatures continue to be over-exploited in the wild, but nevertheless may become farmed for meat, eggs and shell, as projected meat yields far exceed those of conventional cattle ranching.

The bizarre-looking **matamata** has a neck longer than its backbone;

The matamata is an oddity in the turtle world, with a neck as long as its body and a carapace with protuberances from the scales (SS)

the snout is long and tube-like to act as a snorkel, and its carapace has pointed peaks on the top – camouflage to hide it among floating leaves in wait of prey. It feeds on fish by opening its wide mouth suddenly to draw in small fish like a vacuum cleaner.

Fish

Over 2,000 endemic Amazon fish species have been catalogued – making the Amazon's fishes the most diverse freshwater fauna in the world. By a process called adaptive radiation, Amazon fishes have evolved and diversified into a multitude of niches. Around two-fifths are characins, the largest family of neotropical freshwater fish, which includes such groups as catfish, lungfish, gaudy aquarium fishes and the infamous piranha.

Piranha

If we believed B-movies, we would think there is only one type of Amazon fish: the deadly and vicious piranha. In fact, some 25 species of piranha lurk in lowland rivers: a few are specialist carnivores, one type feeds exclusively on fish fins and some are even vegetarian. Piranha attacks have injured people, but not a single fatality has been reliably recorded.

Nevertheless, piranhas do partly deserve their reputation as aggressive, ferocious fish – proven by the number of fishermen in the Amazon missing toes and fingers.

Of the various species, the piranha is the red-bellied (or *paña roja*). Its best-known attribute is extremely sharp teeth. These are serrated and triangular, just like a shark's, but no more than 1/5 inch (6mm) long. **Red-bellied piranhas** grow to 12 inches (30cm) long. They have an orange-red underside, which is more brightly coloured in males.

Piranha detect the splash of potential food as it falls into a stream or lake, as they sense the electrical signals and scent in the water. They attack prey only if it is bleeding and moving erratically. The famous flesh-stripping abilities depend on fish numbers, carcass size and season. Low water levels reduce food availability and increase competition, and tourists fishing for piranha in this season invariably catch more than those fishing during high water. It's a standard activity on jungle tours.

Piranha are easy to catch. A piece of raw meat on a hook and line work very well. If you catch one, let your local guide take it off the hook for you. With the excitement and a slippery fish, it's all too easy for a finger to get within biting distance. I've seen someone lose the end of a finger by such carelessness. With seemingly hundreds of tiny bones, piranha are time-consuming to eat off the bone. Locals, who consider them delicious, throw several into a pot for a fish stew.

In blackwater lakes, some piranha attain impressive size. The biggest species, the **piraya piranha**, reaches almost 20 inches (50cm). Found only in a remote area of Brazil, it's mostly omnivorous but will actively seek live prey when it is hungry.

The black piranha commonly preys on other fish but is just as aggressive as the better-known red-bellied piranha (RH)

Electric eel

Several well-documented cases report fatalities caused by the electric eel. This long, grey, slimy fish discharges a shock of up to 1,000V to knock out or kill prey. The shock also wards off predators. This level is non-lethal for humans, but it's powerful enough to cause temporary paralysis. Death occurs because most encounters are in water. The immobilised victim is drowned, rather than killed by electrocution.

The electric eel is common but rarely encountered, being a bottom-dweller in sluggish channels and streams. It surfaces every now and then to breathe air, or rather absorb it through specialised filaments in its mouth. Able to move backwards is the knife fish, a relative of the electric eel and an electro-navigator but without significant current.

Characins

Characins make up the largest family of neotropical freshwater fish. Many of these are catfish, which comprise much of Amazonia's aquatic biodiversity. Most of the hundred or more species are bottom-feeders, using their long whiskers (barbels) to search the river mud for worms, crustaceans and snails.

The largest catfish, and one of Amazonia's biggest fish with a scientific name to match, is *Brachyplatystoma filamentosum*, which thankfully has a shorter common name, *piraiba*. Individuals grow up to 10ft (3m) long. Good to eat and a popular catch, their huge jaws can easily wound the careless fisherman, but size is no indication of danger where catfish are concerned. Small squeakers (*cunchi* in Peru) squeak when caught. They possess long, toxic spines on the dorsal and pectoral fins.

The **dorado** is a common catfish, reaching 3ft (1m) long. Coloured pale gold along its flanks, with a silvery back, it is a staple food fish for people along the river, and often served at tourist lodges and on riverboats. Species in the *Doradidae* family have fat bodies and four to six barbels (whiskers). The **talking catfish** makes grunting sounds in and out of water. Species exploited for the aquarium trade include the **arch-backed catfish** and the **armoured catfish** or hassar.

In fish markets, you may see the **suckermouth catfish** (or *carachama* in Peru), dark brown and up to a foot (30cm) long. Its heavy scales bear ornate horns and each pectoral fin has a long, curved, bony-toothed projection. The fish probably uses these as an anti-predator defence; locals use them in handicrafts. Also popular with fishermen is the **thorny catfish**. Other heavily armoured catfish include several species of *Plecostomus*, which have a variety of common names. Some of these species are popular aquarium fish.

The Amazon is the source for many popular freshwater fish species including the cardinal tetra (FNS/FLPA)

Living gems of murky *igapó* waters, **jewel tetras** are among the most sought-after fish for aquaria. Under lights these tiny specimens glow brilliant primary colours, giving rise to names like cardinal tetra, neon tetra and glo-lite tetra.

Shaped like a miniature barracuda, the **dogfish**, about a foot (30cm) long, is coloured silvery-yellow and possesses two long, canine-like teeth. It uses these weapons to stab prey, typically other fish, up to half its size. Unrelated to small sharks of the same name found only in oceans, dogfish are often seen in a fisherman's catch or on sale at city fish markets.

Flying **hatchet fish** use their pectoral fins as wings to propel them through the air. This seems to be a defence against predatory fish. They will often fly high and far enough to land in a speeding canoe. Others behave equally strangely. **Headstanders** spend most of their lives with their tail up in the air, whereas **pencil fish** live mostly head-up.

Parasitic catfishes

The **candiru** is beloved of those who love to titillate with lurid tales. This tiny fish lives in the gill filaments of larger fish, feeding off the blood supply. It has a supposed propensity to wriggle up urogenital orifices of human swimmers. Urine attracts the candiru, which mistakes the pee for water discharged from gills. It barges into the body opening, where its sharp spines project into tender flesh, causing indescribable agony. That's the story, anyway. In reality, there has only been a single reliably documented attack – the victim of which had to undergo surgery to have the animal removed. In areas where candiru are present, natives wear protective garments and menstruating women do not swim because they believe blood attracts the fish. Just to be safe, wear a bathing suit and don't pee in the water while swimming.

The name candiru also applies to several species of small, scaleless fish. Some attach themselves to other fish, using spines on their gill openings, and rasp away at scales and flesh like fishy leeches. An afflicted fish might be infested with half a dozen or more wriggling, slimy candiru.

Fruit-eating fish

Flooded forests are important habitat for fruit-eating fish. Best known is the **tambaqui** or pacu (*gamitana* in Brazil). It is said to be the best-flavoured of fishes, with the result that it has been over-fished, especially around Manaus. This and other frugivorous fish disperse the seeds of

The tambaqui's mouth is oriented upward to better grab the fruits and seeds upon which it specialises (SS)

numerous tree species. We can only guess at the consequences of the loss of wild fish. The species has proven suitable for aquaculture – a development sure to relieve pressure on wild populations.

Bony-tongued fish

With fossils dating back to the Cretaceous era, Osteoglossidae are South America's most primitive fishes. They're represented by relatively few species. The diagnostic features are a hard, stiff, bony tongue, stiff scales and dorsal and anal fins continuing almost to the tail.

The Amazon boasts one of the world's largest freshwater fish, **arapaima** (*paiche* in Peru, or *pirarucú* in Brazil). Shaped like a huge pike, these are predators of other fish. Records show specimens up to 15ft (4.6m) long and weighing 550lb (250kg). Its size and tasty flesh have led to its rapid decline. Most caught today are much smaller. Their greenish-bronze scales turn white when removed. As big as your palm and hard as plastic, they evolved as armour-plating against caiman or dolphin attack, and are used as decoration or jewellery. The scales also make good nail files, and natives employ the arapaima's rough, bony tongue as coarse-grade sandpaper. When water warms up, oxygen levels drop, which forces the fish to gulp air. This is absorbed through a modified air bladder. Arapaima hibernate through warm, dry periods, burrowing deep in mud, curling into a ball and staying cocooned until the water returns.

The **water monkey**, locally called the *arowana*, doesn't depend on a chance meal to fall from overhanging vegetation or float by on the current. Instead, it jumps after prey. Up to 3ft (1m) long, it leaps a full body length out of the water to gulp unsuspecting meals perched on a leaf or branch. Given the opportunity, it will catch small reptiles, birds or even baby sloths. The arowana is a mouth brooder. After the eggs hatch, the male scoops the tiny larvae into his mouth to protect them. When the yolk sac is consumed, he releases fry for sporadic feeding and guides them back to safety by waving barbels on his lower jaw. It's a successful strategy to protect the young against natural predators but it's no protection against fishermen who capture fry for sale to foreign aquaria. Considered a premium aquarium species, arowana is a threatened species in the wild.

Cichlids

Cichlids are tropical freshwater fish with some 150 species described from the Amazon. Many are commercially important as food or sport fish, or for the aquarium trade.

Of greatest economic significance is the **peacock bass**, the biggest neotropical cichlid. Found in blackwater rivers, it grows to about 3 feet (1m) and weighs up to 66lb (30kg). It is golden-yellow with black dorsal bars and a prominent eyespot on the tail. The eyespot redirects a predator's attack towards the tail where damage is less likely than an assault on the head. Several other cichlids also have eyespots, so this must be a successful adaptation.

Discus fish have a round, compressed body. Their attractive markings make them popular with aquarium hobbyists. Two species are found in tributaries of the main stream. Their skin produces mucus on which the young feed, a unique form of parental care.

Leaf fish mimic floating leaves to avoid predators (RD/FLPA)

Other Amazon fishes

The **leaf fish** mimics a dead leaf floating on water. Drifting around, pointing downward, it preys on other fish as they swim by oblivious to the danger. A transparent tail and pectoral fins allow it to move without being detected.

Found in quiet streams with overhanging vegetation in tidal reaches of eastern Amazonia, the **four-eyed fish** is uniquely equipped to spot danger in or out of the water. Each of its two eyes is divided in two so that one half is above water and the other half below.

Tiny **killifish** spend most of their lives as tough, drought-resistant eggs in shallow, ephemeral ponds. Some killifish have adapted to hatch, grow, mate, lay eggs and die in places where water persists for a mere two or three weeks.

Amazon **stingrays**, or dasytid rays, are the only freshwater cartilaginous fishes (although sharks roam upriver from the ocean).

The 'sting' is a venomous barbed fin at the base of the tail. Rays are bottom-dwellers, resting half-covered in sand on the beds of shallow rivers.

There are several species of Amazon rays, including a stingray that can inflict a painful wound like its seagoing cousins (WWL/GT)

Aquatic Arthropods

Amazonia's rivers, streams and lakes are among the least biologically explored habitats. Ecologists lament how few land arthropods are studied relative to their diversity, but many forget there is a community of largely unknown species among the weeds and floating meadows. Lift up a mat of floating vegetation and you see water snails, diving beetles, water boatmen, aquatic stages of flying insects, paleomonid shrimp and other crustaceans.

4 Planning a Tour

A journey in the Amazon is the trip of a lifetime... at least, that's what the brochures and websites say. But there are so many options that it's difficult to know where to start. First and foremost, you should begin by asking why you want to go. If you're a birdwatcher or nature enthusiast, that might help you decide when, where and how to travel. Maybe you're interested in the cultures and people or the history and legends. Whatever your interest, this chapter will help you decide. We cover important considerations such as timing your trip, what to look for in a tour operator, the kinds of opportunities available and the basics of preparation, such as gear to take, vaccinations and finances. With a bit of forethought and planning, your Amazon adventure will indeed be the trip of a lifetime.

When to visit

For other destinations, you might use seasonal weather to decide the best time to go. But when deciding the ideal time to go to the Amazon, weather is not the best criterion. Throughout much of the region weather does not differ from month to month. There is generally no well-defined dry or rainy season. Humidity is high all year round. Temperatures are warm, around 75–86°F (24–30°C), but not unbearable.

What else can help you time your visit? Perhaps most important is the rise and fall in river level (see the diagram opposite, which shows the best times for visiting the Amazon, depending on the wildlife that you most want to see). Every year, around the same time, floods permeate the watershed. Floodwaters advance and then recede, with profound effects on the flora, fauna and human inhabitants. The river level rises and falls by as much as 40ft (12.5m). Your experience of the forest and river is very different at low water compared with high water. (See *Chapter 2*, page 22 for details on seasonal floods.)

In the central Amazon Basin, the lowest water period is from October to November. The level begins to rise between December and January, reaching high water during April and May. After several weeks the floodwaters begin to recede. This timing varies slightly from year to year. Recently the timing of floods has become less predictable: some areas have been subject to bad droughts.

An Amazon river dolphin jumping out of the Rio Negro, Brazil (KS/MP/FLPA)

If aquatic life is your main interest, the low water period (July to February) is best. River channels are narrow and shallow, so fish, caiman and dolphins are more abundant, and angling is better, while land trails are drier at this time. Insects also tend to be less bothersome.

On the other hand, small channels get clogged with vegetation. Your boat may run into submerged sandbanks, although this is usually just an occasional irritation, rather than a real hindrance. Animals disperse during low water, which may reduce sightings of arboreal wildlife. However, lakes and pools become more attractive to animals and may be excellent sites to spot game. The time of lowest water, from October to November, is often the hottest time of year.

For forest life, the time of maximum flood – high water – is best. Tree-dwelling animals are crowded into less space and you tend to see more monkeys, sloths and birds. Many riverside plants flower at high water – notably acacias, cecropias and morning glory. Boat rides along tree-lined tributaries bring you closer to the rainforest canopy, but land trails and footpaths may be cut short or totally inaccessible. Aquatic life is more dispersed at this time. Dolphins, caiman and piranha are locally less abundant.

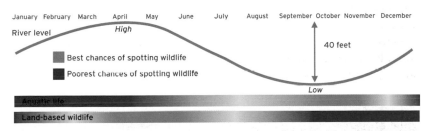

As river levels rise, muddy banks erode and flooded meadows are flushed out. Debris floats downstream, often in spectacular log-jams.

So there's no ideal time to visit, but a month or two before high water is a good compromise. Weather tends to be less cloudy then and it's not too warm. Fish are still moving upstream into newly flooded areas so plenty of aquatic life can usually be seen.

Organising your trip

Types of tours

Look online or through tour operator brochures, and the choices may seem overwhelming. In order to decide between the vast array of options on offer, ask yourself why you want to go to the Amazon.

Exploring the Amazon from source to mouth

Want to travel the full length of the Amazon? You're not alone. It's the ambition of many travellers; for some a lifelong goal, for others an interesting foray into another way of life. Perhaps unkindly, one travel journalist dubbed the journey 'the most boring trip in South America'. If you are a hardcore adventurer, such a title might be apt. Voyaging down the main stream will not provide the intimacy and excitement of canoeing down a remote tributary, but a trip along Amazon proper will impress upon you the river's vastness. Travelling this route also allows you to experience the working river; the people of the Amazon travel vast distances to trade, visit relatives and search for work. Cargo and people are transported in organised chaos, but the river flows impassively on.

Boat-hopping

Going by local riverboat will enable you to follow the main stream for the longest distance. With planning and foresight, you can plan excursions on your route downstream. Stop off at towns along the river, and tour down the smaller tributaries to less disturbed areas.

The best starting point is Pucallpa in Peru. Boats regularly leave Pucallpa from La Hoyada docks for the three- to four-day journey to Iquitos. You will need to change boats at Iquitos then Leticia, Manaus and Santarém before arriving in Belém. The whole journey may take around three weeks, or longer if you go sightseeing. Smaller boats also tend to stop at smaller villages en route. They also take a little longer. The cost will vary according to the type of boat and the time spent in cities. Figure on a minimum US$750 for transport and another US$250 for food and spending money. You'll need a hammock; it may be possible to get cabin accommodation but don't rely on it. Take your own supplies of food – essential if you're a vegetarian. Budget to buy bottled water; don't stock up for the whole journey as you can buy supplies along the way.

Whatever the reason, choose your trip wisely: this might be the only chance you get to visit.

Although tours may be lodge- or boat-based, or tailored towards adventurous types or wildlife aficionados, most itineraries offer several of a set of standard activities. Jungle **walks**, including night walks, are common, along trails through more or less intact forest. River-based

A convenient solution is offered by a consortium of companies based in Peru and Brazil. Start at Chiclayo in Peru, over the Andes and along the Amazon from Yurimaguas, then to Iquitos, Leticia, Manaus and ending in Belém. The trip takes 25 days. The basic option uses buses overland and provides hammock or dormitory accommodation on board; cost is US$730, or about US$30 per day. The 'deluxe' option – at around US$2,900 for the entire trip – uses private 4x4s for land portions and private cabins on the river portions. Enquire through Swallows and Amazons (see page 136).

Adventure cruises

Adventure cruise vessels cater to cruise passengers accustomed to tourist or luxury standards. This type of 'expedition' cruise is more experiential than a typical 'sun and sand' cruise. You get close to the local environment, feel, see and learn about the area's culture and nature. It's not the non-stop party of large cruise ships. Excursions on expedition cruises allow all passengers to visit local villages, lakes and tributaries, which the larger ships cannot. These side trips are usually in rubber inflatables (Zodiacs), which may not suit less mobile passengers. Itineraries are variable. These cruise vessels typically carry 80 to 200 passengers. They're much smaller than the megacruise liners, but still offer luxury amenities including five-star cabins, international food, high-quality educational content and a high staff-to-passenger ratio. It's the best way to travel to remote areas in comfort. The best cruises offer the same experiences you get with a lodge-based tour. You get to visit the Indian or *mestizo* villages, go on birding excursions, and take night trips to experience the river at night.

Cruises are the fastest and most comfortable way to visit the Amazon's larger cities, including Belém, Manaus, Leticia and Iquitos. For a typical cruise, count on 14 days from Belém to Iquitos, or nine for Manaus to Iquitos. These usually include a highly qualified expedition team, including a botanist, ornithologist and historian, who accompany the full length of the cruise. These experts give invaluable commentary, adding to the educational value of the trip.

Some itineraries focus on the Amazon proper; others include cruises from the Caribbean to Amazon cities. The business is in flux, so research your options carefully before you book anything.

activities include piranha fishing, with a simple rod and line provided, and caiman spotting by night. Motorised **canoe rides** may form part of the transfer to lodge or boat, and you may also be able to go on your own excursions in a dugout canoe. Most lodges have **swimming** opportunities, usually in a nearby river or lake; only luxury lodges offer a swimming pool with treated water. River cruises normally offer you

A river cruise on the Rio Negro, Brazil (SS)

the chance to swim from the boat. Tours also often include a **visit to an indigenous village**. Tribal groups vary in degrees of acculturation: while some riverside villages have preserved very little in the way of traditional customs, others have relatively little contact with the outside world.

Boat cruises

Boat cruises allow a leisurely exploration of the wildlife and ecosystems. International cruise lines provide luxury cruises that cater to those who want a high level of comfort. The ship docks only at major towns. Passengers take shore and nature excursions by inflatables operated by the ship's crew. Cruise vessels mostly ply routes in Brazil, from Belém to Manaus.

The widest choice of cruises is on locally operated vessels contracted by tour operators. These offer simple, tourist-level facilities, but more personal service. Encounters with nature and local people provide a more 'authentic' Amazon experience. Popular destinations to begin a boat cruise are Iquitos (in Peru) and Manaus (in Brazil). A typical trip is between large towns, or ventures into a wilderness area, and most boats include English-speaking naturalist-guides. A third type of trip is on local boats used for transport by local people. Few tour operators book such trips, which are only for hardy travellers on a budget. Some of the tour operators in this guide may be able to point you in the right direction for such trips, but would be more likely to recommend their tried-and-trusted itineraries and facilities.

Lodge-based stays

Lodges are typically built of locally available materials, with similar techniques and tools as local dwellings. Most facilities cater to the needs of foreign tourists. Consider access to natural areas, quality of accommodation and food, and English-speaking naturalist-guides who can lead field trips.

Adventure expeditions

For hardier souls, an adventure expedition takes you to remote areas rarely visited by outsiders. Travel is typically along small tributaries, all supplies are brought along for the trip and sleep may be in a covered canoe or in village dwellings. These are a great

A covered canoe departs for an expedition upriver along the Río Ampiyacu, near Pevas, Peru (RH)

way to see the 'authentic' Amazon, but you need a strong constitution. The tour companies that offer organised adventure tours provide all logistical support and transport with a local guide and boat crew, including a cook. They also arrange accommodation with villagers.

Birding

Birding trips may be either lodge-based or on a tourist-standard cruise. If you are a keen birder, ensure that your tour operator includes protected areas outside of major cities and settlements. This would include nature preserves or national parks.

Angling

Keen anglers have a range of destinations and trips to choose from. The best angling trips are on specially equipped boats that maximise chances of catching fish such as peacock bass. Some species are under severe pressure from over-fishing. The eco-conscious angler should ensure that fishing trips are conducted with a view to sustainable

Visiting Amazon tribes

A member of the Tukano tribe, Colombia (SS)

Many guidebooks, tour brochures and coffee table books show indigenous tribes as Westerners often want them to be. The 'noble savage' is untouched by civilisation and still bonded with nature. But this reflects our own desires and dreams more than reality. Most tours offer visits to tribal people, but these people are usually accustomed to visitors. For the occasion, villagers may don traditional clothing and demonstrate using a blowgun, or a tribal dance. Performances given for tourists can be lacklustre and rote, but it's a way for them to earn income and avoid migrating to the teeming cities. After the performance, the people go back to their preferred dress – Western-style clothing, often donated by charity or traded from tourists and other outsiders. Some tour operators recommend that you avoid visiting these people; others include them as part of the tour. I recommend that you take the opportunity if it is there, as you will get an insight into a way of life that is transitioning. That said, avoid tours that specifically focus on visits to relatively unacculturated tribes. Some unscrupulous tour operators (none of those featured in this guide) offer trips from Iquitos to see the Matses tribe, also known as the Cat People. According to Dr James Pantone, an American ecologist and conservationist, 'The simple truth is that Matses people do not want outsiders entering their territory and have fiercely fought against outsiders for their entire history. Simply said, the Matses tribe is not hospitable to tourists and visiting them is not secure.'

fishing practices, such as catch and release. You can book specialist fishing tours with a number of tour operators. Be sure to check with the tour operator regarding their catch-and-release policy.

Natural history

The best natural history trips offer destinations that are remote from human habitation, such as national parks and protected areas. Some tour operators emphasise specific plants or animals on their natural history trips. You can choose trips that focus on looking for reptiles or butterflies, as well as birds. On these trips be sure that the accompanying naturalist guides have specialist knowledge.

Photography

Any standard tour will provide ample opportunities for photographing wildlife, landscapes and local people. For a specialist photography tour, ensure the guide is an accomplished photographer who will provide hints and tips on getting the best photos.

Ethnobotany

Ethnobotanical tours emphasise indigenous uses of plants. You will visit a local shaman who can educate on how species are used. The guides on such trips have specialist knowledge on the use of plants.

Volunteering

Various organisations offer volunteer opportunities. You can participate in research projects, or support local communities, education, medical programmes and religious projects. The volunteer usually pays travel expenses. Accommodation and meals may be provided.

Guides

Seasoned travellers often baulk at the idea of using a guide. Overcome this phobia! A guide is essential for your safety and a deeper understanding of the jungle. The guide leads you along trails, takes you on canoe rides and helps you spot wildlife. For any trip to remote areas, a local or native guide is essential. All the recommended tour operators will provide a local guide as part of the tour. The guide's main job is to accompany you on jungle walks, canoe rides, visits to villages and so on.

Native/local guides

The average local guide knows the area well, can identify most animals and some plants and can talk with the indigenous Indians in the area. The quality of local guides varies considerably. The best are knowledgeable and able to talk at length on rainforest flora and fauna, and native cultures. The worst guides drink on duty, promote their own business, speak little English, and have poor knowledge of wildlife and a nonchalant attitude to clients' well-being. You will, of course, avoid

What to look for in a tour operator

Here's what to look for in a reputable, trustworthy firm:

Good online reviews Check independent reviews of tour operators. Look on websites such as ⌖ www.tripadvisor.co.uk or ⌖ www.tripadvisor.com. Search forums and blogs. No one is perfect and mistakes do happen, but if there have been problems, consider how the tour operator dealt with them.

Social media presence Check the tour operator's Facebook page to see how they engage customers. A presence on Twitter and LinkedIn or a blog suggests they value feedback.

Length of time in the business Poor tour operators do not last long in this competitive market.

Quality of sales materials High-quality sales materials (brochures, websites, etc) shows attention to detail and a willingness to invest in the business.

Availability by email and phone Ensure you can contact them through multiple channels and that you can get a human at the other end.

Responsiveness Shoot them a quick email. If they don't respond within 48 hours, that's a red flag.

Cost Cheapest or most expensive might not be best. Simply choose what's within your budget. Most of the time you get what you pay for.

Special interests If you have a special interest, choose a tour operator that focuses on your speciality. If you're into reptiles, for example, you don't want to go with a specialist birding or fishing outfit.

Licensing Look for licensing, certification and memberships. If you have doubts, check with the relevant organisation. In-country regulations and licensing tend to be less rigorous than in developed countries.

Referrals and testimonials A good tour operator will provide testimonials. Ask to call and speak with previous customers to get an independent assessment.

Guides A guide can make or break your trip. Is the trip fully escorted? Is the guide local? Ask about the quality of guides - training, experience, language ability and reviews or testimonials.

See pages 134-7 for details of recommended tour operators.

guides with this level of unprofessionalism if you book through one of the recommended tour operators in this book.

Escorted group tour guides

Some travel companies offer escorted group tours. Usually this is a qualified naturalist-guide who complements the local guide. They may have expert knowledge in specific fields, such as ecology, ornithology

Water planes floating on a pontoon bridge on the Rio Negro, Brazil. Water planes are used to take travellers to the starting point for tours in the remotest parts of the Amazon (GF/IB/FLPA)

or entomology. As with local guides, the experience and background of biologist-guides or tour leaders is highly variable. The best are university-trained, have experience of travelling in the area and knowledge of tropical biology, and speak Spanish or Portuguese.

Booking

(See pages 134–7 for details of our recommended tour operators.)

Trip of a lifetime or a week from hell? Your tour operator can make all the difference. Most tour operators strive to meet their obligations and provide what you paid for; they are in the business of keeping you happy. The tour operators featured in this guide are at the top of their game, and are exemplars of this approach. At the other end of the spectrum, there are tour operators that are willing to cut corners. A few are fly-by-night operations, ready to leave you in the cold if things go awry. It has happened!

Make a checklist of your requirements and then a list of prospective operators. Then make a short list to help you towards a final decision. Does the tour operator go the extra mile to get your business? Take your time, do your research and you'll greatly increase your chances of a wonderful trip.

US- and UK-based tour operators

Adventure Life

☎ (US) 800 344 6118 (intl) +1 406 541 2677
✉ trip.center@adventure-life.com 🖱 www.Adventure-Life.com

We specialise in quality small-group travel to the Ecuadorian, Peruvian and Bolivian Amazon and throughout Latin America, with a positive impact on the local culture and environment. On tours, group size is kept to a minimum, encouraging a friendly atmosphere. Every trip is designed to present the best of the region, while also allowing freedom and flexibility. Offices in the US.

Andean Trails

☎ +44 (0)131 467 7086
✉ info@andeantrails.co.uk 🖱 www.andeantrails.co.uk

We are a specialist tour operator offering trekking, biking and jungle expeditions in the Amazon and the Andes. We offer both small group fixed-departure tours and bespoke itineraries to experience the indigenous cultures and wildlife and explore mountain landscapes. We work as much as possible with locally owned businesses and support several local community projects. Offices in the UK.

crees

☎ (UK office) +44 (0)20 7581 2932 (Peru office)
+51 (0)84 262433 ✉ info@crees-manu.org 🖱 www.crees-manu.org

crees is a leading non-profit company focused on conservation, environmental sustainability and community development in the Peruvian Amazon. We are pioneers in sustainable eco-tourism and volunteer adventures, which exist to support non-profit initiatives. Join crees today to experience the wonders of the rainforest and help safeguard its future! Offices in the UK and Peru.

Explorations Inc

☎ +1 (239) 992 9660 ✉ info@GoExploring.com
🖱 www.GoExploring.com

Since 1992 we have offered fun and educational adventures in the Peruvian Amazon and throughout Peru, introducing indigenous cultures and the natural world. Our personalised safaris use premier rainforest lodges for excellent birding and wildlife viewing, including the ACTS Canopy Walkway. Our small ship cruises explore both up and down the Amazon River from Iquitos. Offices in the US.

LADATCO Tours
📞 +1 800 327 6162 or 305 854 8422 ✉ tailor@ladatco.com
🖰 www.ladatco.com

We have been introducing travellers to the intriguing places, special lodgings and rewarding experiences of the Amazon for 45 years. Ladatco custom-designs every programme based on your 'wish list' and trip parameters. We've been there, done that. Let us put our more than 45 years of destination expertise to work for your trip of a lifetime. Offices in the US.

Rainbow Tours
📞 +44 (0)20 7704 3931 ✉ info@rainbowtours.co.uk
🖰 www.rainbowtours.co.uk

At Rainbow Tours Latin America our specialists have been providing expert advice and bespoke tours to the region for over a decade. Focusing on comfortable adventure, our trips are aimed at allowing travellers to get to the heart of the Amazon through their contact with local communities and accompaniment by specialist naturalist guides. Offices in the UK.

Reef and Rainforest
📞 +44 (0)1803 866965

✉ mail@reefandrainforest.co.uk 🖰 www.reefandrainforest.co.uk

We specialise in escorted group and tailor-made tours to the Brazilian, Ecuadorian and Peruvian Amazon. Our reputation has been built over 22 years upon an ability to translate clients' individual requirements into stimulating itineraries. Our consultants share a love of natural history, and travel widely to seek out the best wildlife viewing. Offices in Devon, England.

Southern Explorations
📞 (US/ Canada) +1 877 784 5400 (intl) 001 206 784 8111
✉ info@southernexplorations.com 🖰 www.southernexplorations.com

Southern Explorations is dedicated to providing high quality travel experiences that preserve the fragile lands we visit. We cater to active, independent travellers seeking tours with an adventurous slant. Groups are small, and we strive to provide an authentic experience of the Amazon, using bilingual guides on our in-country coordinated and guided trips. US and local offices.

Steppes Discovery
📞 +44 (0)1285 643 333
✉ enquiry@steppesdiscovery.co.uk 🖰 www.steppesdiscovery.co.uk

For over 20 years we have been taking travellers to see fascinating places that are off the tourist track. By joining forces with local research projects and carefully chosen wildlife charities, we give travellers privileged insight into the natural world while supporting conservation and local communities. We offer tailor-made and group trips to Brazil, Ecuador and Peru. Offices in the UK.

Other US-based tour operators

Amazon Voyages ⚓ www.amazon-voyages.com Cruises on restored historic riverboats.

Field Guides Incorporated [web] www.fieldguides.com. Specialists in birding tours.

Fishquest ⚓ www.fishquest.com. Fishing in the Brazilian Amazon.

GreenTracks ⚓ www.GreenTracks.com. Riverboat cruises and reptile tours.

Last Frontiers ⚓ www.lastfrontiers.com. Tailor-made travel to Latin America.

Southwind Adventures ⚓ www.southwindadventures.com. River cruises and nature tours.

Tara Tours Inc ⚓ www.taratours.com. Cultural and nature tours from South America specialist.

Tucan Travel ⚓ www.tucantravel.com. Amazon–Machu Picchu combined tours.

Wildlife Worldwide ⚓ www.wildlifeworldwide.com. Tailor-made wildlife tours in Brazil and Ecuador.

Other UK-based tour operators

Journey Latin America ⚓ www.journeylatinamerica.co.uk. Options for families, active, wildlife or cruise holidays.

Tribes Travel ⚓ www.tribes.co.uk. Jungle lodges for walks, treks and boat trips.

Naturetrek ⚓ www.naturetrek.co.uk. Expert-led wildlife trips.

Peruvian tour operators

Amazon Trails ⚓ www.amazontrailsperu.com. Tours from Cusco to Manú National Park or to Manú Biosphere Reserve.

Manú Expeditions ⚓ www.ManuExpeditions.com. Long-established operator in the Manú Biosphere Reserve.

Muyuna Lodge ⚓ www.muyuna.com. Itineraries for specific-interest groups (biologists, birdwatchers, etc).

Tropical Nature Travel ⚓ www.tropicalnaturetravel.com. Offers tours to wildlife lodges in Peru.

Wasai Lodge & Expeditions ⚓ www.wasai.com. Operates a lodge in Puerto Maldonado and another located in the Tambopata-Candamo National Reserve.

Brazilian tour operators

Amazon Tree Climbing ⚓ www.AmazonTreeClimbing.com. Specialists offering a wide variety of day climbs and multi-day expeditions, including Rio Negro cruises.

Swallows and Amazons ⚓ www.swallowsandamazonstours.com. Offers bespoke tours in and around Manaus.

Tropical Tree Climbing ⚓ www.tropicaltreeclimbing.com. Week-long expeditions with master tree climbing instructor Tim Kovar (see page 226).

Locally based tour operators

Machete Tours
📞 (Lima) +51 1 992987202 (Cusco) +51 8 422 4829
✉ info@machetetours.com 🖰 www.machetetours.com

With over a decade of experience in offering tours throughout Peru, we have a strong focus on ecotourism and making visitors aware of local customs and Peruvian history, so that they are immersed in the life of the Amazon and Inca heritage. Our guides are all bilingual and licensed, and we have a very high level of environmental care. Offices in Lima and Cusco, Peru.

Nomadtrek
📞 +593 2 290 2670, +593 2 290 6036
✉ info@nomadtrek.com 🖰 www.nomadtrek.com

We are a family-run tour operator with 30 years' experience under our belts, offering a variety of tours in mainland Ecuador and the Galápagos Islands. Our aim is to offer well designed and attractive tourism and ecotourism packages with a personalised touch, and we respond to all enquiries and requests very rapidly. Office in Quito.

Trek Ecuador
📞 +593 2 227 7916, +593 9 775 6340
✉ info@trekecuador.com 🖰 www.trekecuador.com

We believe that travel is about investing in an unforgettable natural and cultural experience, so we specialise in small-group journeys and adventures to two destinations: the Amazon Rainforest and the Galápagos Islands. On group or individual itineraries you can participate in activities that promote biodiversity conservation, cultural preservation and sustainable development. Office in Quito.

Colombian tour operators
Amazon Holidays 🖰 www.amazon-holidays.com. Longer and more upmarket adventures based in Leticia.

Ecuadorian tour operators
Neblina Forest 🖰 www.neblinaforest.com. Based in Ecuador, and does tours to other Amazon countries. Guides are birding and plant experts.
Salsa Reisen 🖰 www.salsareisen.com. Tailored packages throughout Ecuador for couples and families.

Your tour: 10 top Amazon experiences

One of your first steps in planning a tour should be to decide which activities you absolutely must try, perhaps starting with the brief synopsis of our top ten Amazon experiences. Once you've identified what you want to do, your operator can discuss with you how to best accommodate your interests.

1 Cruise the world's biggest river

As your riverboat leaves the noise, smells and bustle of a city port, a calm settles about you. The rhythmic chugging of the engine, the smooth passage of the boat and a gentle river breeze lull you into a sense of peace rarely found on other kinds of excursions or holidays. Scant river traffic passes by. Passengers on other boats might wave in a shared camaraderie. The dark forest edges the river, a brooding promise of mystery.

(SS)

2 Experience the rainforest canopy

Climb a tower, stroll along a walkway, even spend a night in the treetops – a hundred feet above the ground. The canopy is where the action is. Birds, small mammals, reptiles and countless insects call this home.

3 Explore a miniature world

The forest is quiet, humid, shaded. Dappled sunlight rays break the gloom. If you disturb the leaf litter, dozens of tiny creatures scurry away: a beetle, a small worm, an odd-looking arachnid. You reach out and touch a moss-encrusted branch, festooned with its own community of plants, and accompanying miniature creatures. Here is a forest within a forest.

4 See a pink dolphin

We think of dolphins as quintessential sea creatures, so a dolphin swimming in the murky waters of an obscure Amazon tributary seems absurd. You're making your way up a tree-lined river, cicadas' shrill notes broken by calls of hidden birds. You hear a ripple, then a blowing sound. The ripple disappears and you see the wake of a dolphin. Keep looking and you'll spot the creature – its bright pink a seeming paradox of nature.

(CTB)

5 Catch a piranha

The dreaded piranha's fearsome reputation is well-deserved, so why would you want to catch one and risk those razor-sharp teeth? They're not the tastiest fare, after all. 'I caught a piranha' is a great party line, of course. But more than that, you are introduced to the richness of the Amazon's fish life. The piranha is but one of 2,000 species of fish, many of which are less vicious and better to eat.

(DB/DT)

6 Hold an Amazon alligator in your hand

At first glance the Amazon's alligator, the caiman, is a scaly, toothy brute. But at night as you cruise in a small canoe, you shine your flashlight at the river's edge. A bright spot of red reflects the caiman's eye. Keep the light trained on the eye, mesmerising the animal. As you approach nearer your guide leaps forward to grab the caiman – if it's a youngster. Now you see its beauty. It resents the intrusion, but you connect with its raw wildness as the guide lets it go, back into the night.

7

Climb tropical trees

Climbing trees might seem like a risky business, but new techniques have been developed to create a unique way to explore the rainforest canopy. With special equipment you are safely hoisted high into the treetops, where you can experience the richness of bird life, small mammals and epiphytic plants closer than ever before. (ATC)

8

Meet indigenous tribes

An encounter with indigenous tribes will open your mind to a different way of life and new ways of thinking about the world. It's dark and muggy in the village hut. A villager offers you a mildly alcoholic slimy gruel as a welcome drink. It is *masato*, says your guide, brewed from chewed manioc and fermented with the yeast from women's saliva. It's an honour to be offered it and you'll offend your hosts if you refuse. What do you do?

9

Taste tropical fruits

Maracuya, aguaje, ungurahuí: their names seem almost unpronounceable, but bite into one of the Amazon's hundreds of kinds of exotic fruits and you'll be struck by the flavour and texture. Street vendors and market stalls sell fresh fruits of all sizes, shapes and colours.

10

Listen to the sounds at night

The evening brings a moment to relax in your lodge. As the tropical night envelops the trees, sounds from frogs, katydids, night birds and mammals chorus through the darkness. Nature's symphony fills the air, and you feel part of the forest.

(DE/DT)

Red tape

Travel to Amazon countries is straightforward for passport holders from the UK, US and other English-speaking countries. However, visa requirements can change, so be sure to check with the embassies of the countries of your intended destination. Your tour operator will tell you what travel documents you'll need. At the time of writing, most visitors from the UK, Australia and New Zealand can obtain a temporary visitor's permit at the point of entry to all Amazon countries; no advance visa is needed. US visitors to Brazil do require a visa, which must be obtained in advance from the Brazilian embassy or consulate nearest to the traveller's place of residence. There are no 'airport visas', and immigration authorities will refuse entry to Brazil to any US passport holder not possessing a valid visa.

If you are travelling from another country within the Amazon, you may need a valid yellow fever inoculation. Check with your tour operator or the country's consulate for the most recent travel regulations. Embassy information changes frequently, so please check the book's companion website ([✲] www.amazontravelbook.com) for up-to-date information.

Getting there

Numerous options are available for travelling to the Amazon. A typical tour package will include meet-and-greet at a major Amazon city such as Iquitos, Manaus or Belém. Your tour operator will either make arrangements or advise you on the best options for air travel to your Amazon destination.

In most cases, you will fly from your country of origin directly to a gateway city, usually the destination country's capital or another major city. If you are travelling to **Brazil**, there are direct flights to the Amazon from some US and European cities to Belém or Manaus. Your tour operator will advise you on the most convenient or economical flights. To reach the **Colombian Amazon** gateway of Leticia, you will need to fly to Bogotá, and then catch an onward flight. The **Ecuadorian Amazon** can be reached by flying to Quito, and then travelling by bus or plane to Amazon gateways including Lago Agrio and Coca. You should fly to Lima and catch a bus or plane to **Peru's Amazon gateways**, including Iquitos (though note that Iquitos is inaccessible by road).

Health and safety
with Dr Felicity Nicholson

Use common sense and you will stay safe and healthy on your Amazon trip. You don't need a medical kit full of drugs and bandages. A typical tour is very safe. Your tour operator will provide information and advice on how to balance sensible caution with a realistic risk of travel.

Inoculations

On a typical tour (ten to 14 days), immunisations such as typhoid and rabies are overkill. Malaria is rare in most places and the side-effects of preventatives are almost as unpleasant as the illness. For more information visit ⌁ www.traveldoctor.co.uk/malaria.htm and ⌁ www. preventingmalaria.info. Unless you are on an extended trip, you won't encounter pathogens that pose significant risk. If you are in an 'at-risk' category (elderly, immune-compromised) or are taking young children, consult with a travel specialist, doctor or travel clinic for advice. At the time of writing, no inoculations are required for entry to Amazon countries if you are travelling direct from Europe or the US, but if your trip includes travel between countries you may be required to have a yellow fever vaccination. Check with your tour operator if you are planning to travel extensively between two or more Amazon countries.

Deep-vein thrombosis (DVT)

Prolonged immobility on long-haul flights can result in deep-vein thrombosis (DVT), which can be dangerous if the clot travels to the lungs to cause pulmonary embolus. The risk increases with age, and

Personal first-aid kit

Most lodges and tourist riverboats have first-aid kits for routine scrapes and bruises. But to make life comfortable, pack some basic items:

Painkillers such as aspirin, mostly for headaches or hangovers

Sticky plasters for minor cuts

Insect repellent to deter pesky critters, mostly encountered on jungle walks

Anti-diarrhoeal medicine such as Peptobismol

Antiseptic gel to minimise chance of infection when treating wounds

Antifungal powder or cream especially if you are prone to fungal infections

Sunblock SPF 15 or higher will protect from sun exposure for several hours

Motion sickness medicine if you are prone

Travel clinics and health information

A full list of current travel clinic websites worldwide is available from the International Society of Travel Medicine (🌡 www.istm.org). For other journey preparation information, consult 🌡 www.tripprep.com or 🌡 www.nathnac.org. ds/map_world.aspx. Information about various medications may be found on 🌡 www.netdoctor.co.uk/travel or 🌡 www.emedicine.com. Other useful sites include 🌡 www.fitfortravel.scot.nhs.uk (a useful source of general travel health information) and 🌡 wwwnc.cdc.gov/travel (includes updates on specific destinations and information for those with limited mobility and those travelling with children). Both the US State Department (🌡 http://travel. state.gov/) and the British Department of Health (🌡 www.nhs.uk/nhsengland/ healthcare abroad) also provide dedicated travel information.

is higher in obese or pregnant travellers, heavy smokers, those taller than 5ft (1.5m), and anybody with a history of a clot, recent major operation or varicose veins surgery, cancer, a stroke or heart disease. If any of these criteria apply, consult a doctor before you travel. Ensuring that you are well hydrated, and moving around during long periods of travel, can help to reduce the risk.

Women travellers

Women travelling alone in the Amazon have few gender-specific challenges compared to travelling in some parts of the world. On an organised tour, guides and facilities staff are highly professional. Bear in mind, however, that the Latin culture is less sensitive to gender issues than Western society. You may encounter mild flirtation or wolf-whistles in public places, but rarely will this be truly bothersome. If your tour includes travel in crowded public transport, try to find a seat or at least have your back to the wall to avoid an exploratory bottom-pinching hand. Again, this is most unlikely, but use common sense and stay aware and you'll avoid any unwelcome encounters.

Toiletries are available in Amazon towns, but the selection is limited, particularly in more remote areas. If you have a favourite brand of products, plan accordingly and take what you need. Bear in mind that travelling in the tropics can induce heavier than normal periods.

Disabled travellers

Until recently there were few facilities for disabled travellers in the Amazon, but fortunately this is changing. More tour operators are conscious of meeting the needs of less-mobile or otherwise less-able travellers. However, in cities and towns, public places and streets rarely accommodate mobility- or sight-impaired travellers. Expect to need the help of a companion more than you might in a Western city.

Of course, in planning a trip, be sure to check with a tour operator about which facilities accommodate less-abled travellers. The recommended tour operators will be open about the challenges and how easily their itineraries, transport and facilities can accommodate you. Please check the book's companion website (🕮 www.amazontravelbook.com) for up-to-date information and lists of specialist tour operators catering to less-abled travellers.

What to take

Lugging around a suitcase you can barely lift is not the best start to your holiday. Consider the kinds of activities you'll be enjoying and where you'll be staying. Most hotels offer a laundry service, but it's not standard in many jungle lodges or on riverboats. Figure on a change of clothing per day, particularly underwear and T-shirts. Repackage items such as toiletries so you carry only as much as you need. For lotions and liquids, put the necessary amount in a small, used container. (Regulations limit the amount of liquids in carry-on luggage.)

Make a checklist before you go to make sure you don't leave anything behind. The companion website to this book provides a detailed checklist you can print and use for your trip (🕮 www.amazontravelbook.com).

Clothing

Clothing should be lightweight and quick-drying. A pair of synthetic or cotton trousers is ideal. Light enough to stop you getting hot and sweaty and long enough to keep the insects off, they reduce the chances of scratches and infections. If you want to stay cool, shorts are fine, but you'll need to apply insect repellent when on jungle trails. In any case, ensure the material is easy to wash and dries quickly. A lightweight cotton-mix shirt/blouse with long sleeves is a good bet. Short-sleeve tops are fine but, again, expect to need insect repellent during jungle walks. Take a lightweight jumper or sweatshirt in case of a chilly night, and a waterproof for jungle walks.

Footwear

You don't need heavy hiking or trekking boots; running or tennis shoes or trainers with lightweight socks are generally suitable but may get muddy and wet. Sandals are fine, but watch for ants and other bugs while you're on a trail. They're good for tramping around boats, towns and villages, though.

Photographic gear

In the jungle, wildlife is often too far off or too concealed for good pictures. Without a telephoto lens, a sloth, bird or monkey will appear as a blur or blob on most photos. For decent results, a good SLR camera and zoom lens (70–300mm) are best. A tripod is also useful for steadying the camera for the slow exposures needed with a long lens. A digital camera is versatile enough to overcome some of these restrictions, but you may find that you have less control over the final image than is possible with film.

An ultraviolet (UV) or daylight filter is useful for protecting the lens, while a polarising filter greatly improves scenic shots, reducing glare from the river and preventing over-exposure. Humidity can be a problem in the forest, and fungal growth on lenses may occur in very damp conditions. Put a sachet of silicon crystals beside the camera to absorb excessive moisture.

If you are using film, this may be difficult to obtain once you are on your tour, so bring as many rolls as you are likely to need. If you are using a digital camera, remember to bring all the batteries, plugs, connectors and storage devices that go with it.

Electricity

On an organised tour you won't often need to worry about electric power, aside from charging batteries for electronic equipment or for a hair dryer or electric shaver. Electric power in some Amazon countries is the same as the United States, 120V, whereas Peru is 220V. If you are using 220V equipment (from the UK, for example) you will need a transformer to step down the voltage. In any case, power outlets in Amazon countries have various fittings so take a universal adapter to accommodate your electrical equipment plugs.

At some lodges and on some cruise boats, the voltage may vary since it is provided by generators or solar panels. If you are using sensitive equipment, consider using a surge protector to avoid 'frying' your gear. Check with your guide or tour manager to make sure that the electricity supply is reliable enough to use with your equipment. For information on voltage and plug type, visit ⤷ www.kropla.com/electric2.htm.

Luggage

Take a hard case if you plan to bring back fragile souvenirs. If you're on a high-activity trip, a duffel bag is best because it will stand up to a battering. In any case, ensure luggage is lockable to deter casual pilfering. If you use a small luggage padlock, be sure it is TSA-compatible so that it can be easily opened by airport security. A small backpack is ideal for important things like passports, tickets and so on, when you're separated from your main luggage.

Other essentials

If you are on a budget tour, take a small padlock or combination lock to secure the doors of cheap hotels. However, this won't be necessary at reputable hotels and lodges provided on an organised tour. A money belt and luggage lock will also prevent easy access by pickpockets or opportunistic thieves. Other essentials include sunscreen, insect repellent, a basic first-aid kit and toiletries (see page 142). Your tour operator will provide a more comprehensive list of what you need to take. A printable checklist is provided on the book's companion website (⊕ www.amazontravelbook.com).

Organising your finances

One of the advantages of an organised tour is that you don't need to carry much money, since the major expenses are included in the package, but be sure to check with your tour operator exactly what is included and what is not. A typical package includes accommodation, airport and other transfers, ground transport, guide services, pre-booked flights, and park and other entrance fees. Most tours include breakfast, lunch and dinner (BLD in brochures) for all but the first and last days, which typically include dinner and breakfast respectively, so be sure to check with your tour operator so that you can budget accordingly.

Since you will have paid in advance you will need to budget only for **day-to-day expenses**. These include drinks, tips and souvenirs, which are likely to total less than US$500. This is best carried as cash in US dollars. Pounds, euros and other currencies are not widely accepted, and it is easy to change US dollars for local currency if needed. In Ecuador, US dollars are the official currency in any case. If you are planning on spending a large amount of local currency, check exchange rates online before you go – try ⊕ www.xe.com.

If you are leery of carrying a lot of cash, take a couple of hundred dollars and use your **ATM** card to get cash as needed. Bear in mind that cash machines usually dispense local currency only. Most lodges and cruise operators will accept debit or credit cards for incidentals. Restaurants and souvenir shops in larger cities also take debit or credit cards. Visa is most widely accepted, followed by MasterCard, but you might have trouble using other credit cards such as Maestro, Discover or American Express. However, for small purchases in towns and villages, you'll need cash. Take your dollars in small denomination notes: larger notes may be harder to spend and may even be refused because of rampant counterfeiting.

If you need larger sums of money or emergency funds, bear in mind that **travellers' cheques** are only accepted at large banks. American Express is most widely accepted. They can, however, be difficult to change in out-of-the-way places, and you'll need your passport when cashing them. Given the prevalence of ATMs, travellers' cheques are less practical than a bank card.

5 On the Ground

Most tour operators will provide information on local money, food, and shopping opportunities. The following details will help you plan the various facets of your trip. Travel in the Amazon is very safe, but it is worth familiarising yourself with the basic dos and don'ts. This chapter will help you feel more confident about coping with perceived and real risks (which are minimal, really). You'll need to organise your finances for your trip. The provided information will help you understand the local currencies and how to budget. You'll want to anticipate your needs for meals, communications and connecting with local communities and people. This chapter tells you the kinds of food to expect, how to communicate with the outside world, if you need to, and what to know about local customs and culture.

Health and safety in the Amazon
with Dr Felicity Nicholson

Overall, travel to the Amazon is relatively low risk. Crime rates are generally on a par with or lower than in industrialised countries. Diseases that we associate with tropical travel, such as malaria, do occur but are generally rare. For most travellers on a typical tour, exposure to pathogens such as typhoid, yellow fever and all the other nasties we dread is highly unlikely. Follow the simple common sense precautions outlined in this section and your trip will be trouble-free. That said, if you are in a high-risk category, be sure to consult your physician or a travel clinic.

Food and water

Be sure drinking water is from a safe source: drink only bottled or purified water. Most tourist riverboats and lodges provide free purified water. When you buy bottled water, choose a recognisable brand and make sure the seal is not broken. Don't drink tap water even in the best hotels and avoid ice unless it is made from purified water. Commercial soft drinks are safe.

You should also be scrupulous about what you eat. Most meals served to tourists at lodges or on tourist riverboats use sterilised water for preparation. Basic precautions include eating only fruit and vegetables prepared in a trustworthy kitchen or that you have peeled yourself, ensuring that any meat is cooked through and fresh from the kitchen.

One trip too many

Diarrhoea commonly strikes the Amazon visitor. One trip too many to the toilet is often caused by contaminated food or water. But just a change of diet can upset your tummy; on a week-long Amazon trip, diarrhoea may afflict one in ten people. Anti-diarrhoeal medication usually relieves symptoms. Diarrhoea 'blockers' are good when you need a quick fix, but they retain the diarrhoea microbes in your system. Replenish fluids lost through diarrhoea with a rehydration salts mixture; these can be purchased in sachets (*oro suero*). Alternatively, mix a few tablespoons of sugar and a teaspoon of salt in a litre of water. Avoid milk, fatty foods and alcohol, and get plenty of rest. Most cases of diarrhoea clear up in a day or two. Should symptoms continue for more than a few days, consult a doctor.

Sunburn, heatstroke and dehydration

Use sunblock when you expect to be out in the sun: SPF 15–30 is best. The equatorial sun is stronger than the summer sun at high latitudes. Fair-skinned people need a higher SPF than those with darker complexions.

High humidity hinders the body's cooling mechanisms so heatstroke is a risk, and can be dangerous. It occurs when the core body temperature rises too high. Watch for headache accompanied by faintness, dizziness and nausea. Don't tough it out: anyone with these symptoms should move into a cool place and drink plenty of non-alcoholic fluids.

Excessive loss of body fluids through perspiration can also lead to dehydration. Drink plenty of water throughout the day. Alcohol doesn't rehydrate, so even if a beer feels refreshing, balance it with a glass of water. Thirst is the first sign of dehydration, so drink right away if you feel thirsty. Take a pinch more salt on food than you normally would to help balance electrolytes. If you are feeling low due to dehydration, fruit juice or non-caffeinated soda will help you rehydrate and provide some extra energy.

Minor cuts and bruises

Treat small cuts or insect bites right away, as they are prone to infection given the tropical warmth and humidity. Wash with clean water, rinse and allow to dry, before applying disinfectant cream. Cover with a sticking plaster and replace the dressing daily. If a wound reddens and weeps, clean thoroughly with a drying antiseptic and apply antibiotic powder or ointment.

Fungal infections

High humidity and warm temperatures foster fungal infections. Symptoms include itchiness and flaking skin around the armpits, crotch and between the toes, but symptoms can occur anywhere on the body. Treat with fungicidal cream and powder.

Altitude sickness

If you spend time in an Andes gateway city, the elevation may be high enough to cause altitude sickness. Travellers to La Paz, Quito or Bogotá should be careful.

Motion sickness

Motion sickness is rarely a problem on riverboats on the Amazon. However, rides in small motorboats used for transit to lodges can be bouncy, and bus rides and flights in small planes will be bumpy. Some motion sickness pills may cause drowsiness and do not interact well with alcohol. Ginger sweets or candy may also be effective.

Allergies

If you suffer from pollen- or dust-based allergies remember to pack your preferred medicine. Be aware that insect bites come with the territory, and mosquito bites are commonest. Stings from bees, ants or wasps are possible, but usually avoidable. If you are especially prone to severe allergic reactions or at risk of anaphylactic shock, consult a medical travel professional for advice before you travel.

The bushmaster is the Amazon's largest venomous snake, but rarely encountered (WWL/GT)

Snakebites

Most snakes are non-poisonous and not at all aggressive. You are unlikely even to see a snake, and exceedingly unlikely to be bitten. Most species warily slither off as soon as they sense ground vibrations from human footsteps. Few cases of snakebite are life-threatening. In the extremely

Safety on jungle walks

Forest trails are safe but present minor hazards as in any natural area. Here are some simple precautions for safe jungle walking.

- Do not grab at vegetation to steady yourself. Many plants have thorns or spines, or harbour stinging ants.
- Take care where you step on the trail. You can slip on mud, trip on tree roots or tread on a column of army ants. Stay on the trail to avoid potential hazards and minimise your impact on the surrounding forest.
- Take a bottle of water and perhaps a small snack. It is easy to get dehydrated with the humidity and heat.
- Wear appropriate shoes. You do not need hiking boots. Some lodges and tour operators supply guests with rubber boots, which keep your feet dry. Trainers or tennis shoes are fine but will get wet and muddy. Sandals are OK too, if you don't mind having to wash mud off your feet, but you'll have to be more diligent to avoid stinging ants.

unlikely event that you are bitten, identify the snake if possible and get professional medical help immediately.

Insect and other bites

Sandflies, chiggers and ticks

These pests are abundant in pasture and inhabited areas. If you walk around grassy areas, apply repellent to bare skin, particularly legs and ankles. Treat shoes and socks to deter the critters. During an excursion, check your clothing and any exposed skin regularly for them. In the privacy of your lodge room or riverboat cabin, check particularly for ticks, which love to explore your body's intimate parts.

Spiders

Most spiders are harmless. The scary-looking tarantula is common in Amazonia, but is not a threat. However, some Amazon species are venomous. The most dangerous are the wandering and recluse spiders. These species frequent houses, clothes, shoes, boxes and log piles. A spider bite is most likely in bed (check the bedding and mattress) or in clothing left overnight (shake thoroughly before dressing). You can sometimes recognise a spider bite by the presence of two small spots close together. (Most insect bites leave only a single spot.) If a spider bite fails to heal, get professional medical attention.

- Wear loose-fitting clothes. You do not need an Indiana Jones-style outfit. A long-sleeved shirt and long trousers will minimise the amount of repellent you need. Otherwise, shorts and a T-shirt are fine.
- Be sure to apply insect repellent to exposed body parts before and during a jungle walk. Mosquitoes will attack unprotected bits.
- Take a waterproof. A sunny day can turn to a tropical deluge in minutes. A poncho is good because it also covers your daypack.
- On jungle walks at night, take a torch (flashlight). Don't wear a headband-mounted torch for walking in the jungle at night – it attracts insects to the light beam and thus to your face.
- You're very unlikely to encounter dangerous wildlife. Animals are invariably terrified of humans and only attack if they feel threatened. If you encounter a potentially dangerous animal, back off and make as much noise as you can.

Scorpions

Most scorpions can sting, but only a few are dangerous. These species are rare and generally restricted to dry areas. To avoid being stung, don't put your hands or feet in dark nooks or areas.

Ants, bees and wasps

On jungle walks, watch out for huge bullet ants, which can grow to over an inch (25mm) long. Insect repellent does not deter these gargantuans, which wield an excruciating sting. The area goes red and throbs for a day or so, but there's no lasting damage. The same goes for bites from tree-dwelling ants, which swarm out of holes in the trunk. If you suffer from severe allergic reactions, consult your doctor for appropriate medication before your trip. Around lodges or on jungle walks, you might see bee or wasp nests. Leave them alone, and they'll usually ignore you. Should you knock into one accidentally, try to get low to the ground and move away slowly. If you run, they'll chase you. If that happens try heading for water and fling yourself in.

Safe swimming

Don't miss your once-in-a-lifetime opportunity to swim in the Amazon! No, you won't get attacked by piranhas. That said, keep your swim brief if you have an open wound or are menstruating. Stingrays, electric eels and the notorious candiru – which allegedly lodges itself in body orifices (see page 118) – are not significant threats. One risk of swimming is strong currents; if the water is flowing at or close to walking pace it is too fast for swimming. Water-borne microbes are another risk. To avoid infection, do not swim near villages and towns, particularly downstream. Most parasites are orally ingested, so if the site is not ideal, avoid swallowing river water.

Boat safety

You will usually be provided with a lifejacket on tourist-standard riverboats and on canoe excursions. Operators differ on whether they require you to wear a life jacket on canoe excursions, so if you have the option, use common sense, and judge the weather and river conditions. Below are a few basic precautions.

- When getting into a canoe, make sure only one person boards at a time. Step into the middle of the canoe and get seated before the next person boards.
- Once under way, never stand up. Always have your life jacket to hand and wear it on open water or in rough weather.

Piranha fishing

It's easy to get carried away with excitement at the prospect of catching this most notorious of fishes. The equipment is simple – stick, line, hook, bait. No float or reel is needed. But when there are a dozen tourists in a small boat flailing at the water, watch out! A line can snap back, sending the hook towards someone's tender flesh. When you catch a piranha don't try to remove the hook yourself – those teeth can easily remove a chunk of your finger. Your guide will remove the hook for you. See also page 117.

- Only one person should get out at a time. Take care if you are disembarking onto a muddy riverbank or unsteady floating pier.
- As your canoe manoeuvres through overhanging vegetation along narrow streams, watch out for projecting branches. Besides possibly poking you in the eye, they harbour biting or stinging insects, which may drop into the boat or swarm around the occupants.

Crime

Keep the threat of petty crime in perspective: travel in the Amazon is relatively safe. Peru's per capita murder rate is a third of New York City's. If you are in a tour group, the chances of serious crime are small. Remember though, that bag-snatchers and pickpockets target tourists. Theft is commonest in airports, among crowds, close to money-changing facilities, tourist attractions or in other settings where you might let down your guard. On an organised tour there is safety in numbers and you will have a guide to keep you alert and advise if you are entering a risky area where, for example, pickpockets might be active. However, you may have free time, particularly at the beginning or end of a trip, where you have the chance to roam. This is where most novice travellers get into trouble, often lulled into a false sense of security from having been in the security of the group with its protective chaperone. Most of the tips below are more relevant at these times, but use common sense and you'll have a trouble-free trip.

Here are some basic precautions.

- Use a hotel safe for valuables when there is one, and take a small padlock or combination lock to secure doors of cheap hotels. Lock your luggage to stop opportunistic thieves rummaging through the contents.

- Leave expensive jewellery and watches at home.
- Take a money belt or keep your wallet away from easy access by pickpockets.
- Keep a little cash close at hand for casual spending. Avoid getting out your money belt or wallet in public areas. Where possible, use a credit card for transactions.
- Keep a few low-denomination bills and expired credit cards in a cheap wallet should you need to give something to an opportunistic thief.
- Take copies of essential travel documents. Keep copies separate from the originals. Note down ticket and travellers' cheque numbers along with serial numbers of any electronic or camera equipment for insurance purposes.
- Carry your camera, mobile phone and similar items in a daypack that is resistant to cutting. If you have a high-end camera, use a generic shoulder strap that doesn't advertise the brand. Don't take your eyes off your camera bag!
- At night, stay with your fellow travellers. Stay in brightly lit, busy areas with easy transit back to your hotel. Take a taxi at night instead of the bus.
- If using long-distance public bus transport, check that your luggage is loaded before boarding. Keep your carry-ons under your seat. Some companies provide luggage receipts. Most organised tours will provide transport, so this needn't be a worry.
- Report theft to the police or a local authority right away. The police will provide you with a report – essential for an insurance claim.
- Be wary of unusual activity. Criminals try to distract you by dropping items in your path, or applying mud or lotion to your clothes. While you are distracted, a member of the team relieves you of your valuables. Tour groups are especially noticeable and may be targeted by pickpockets, who take advantage of the greater sense of safety in numbers.
- Thieves may impersonate police officers. The villains accuse victims of drug possession and demand an on-the-spot fine. Bona fide police will provide identification and be happy to accompany you to a police station. On an organised tour this type of scam is unlikely, but be cautious if you are free before or after a trip.

Drugs

The usual drug laws apply in all South American countries. If you are indicted on drug charges, your embassy will not support your case. Don't accept offers of any intoxicants, legal or not. Travellers have been drugged and awoken to find all their personal belongings have disappeared, or worse. Don't accept medicine or drinks from any unfamiliar person. Coca leaf is legally cultivated in several Andean countries for its medicinal and cultural uses, but it may be illegal to bring back it to your home country.

Banking and foreign exchange

US dollars are the best currency to use while in the Amazon. If you're in a tour group, most of your costs are prepaid, but you will still need cash to pay for drinks, some meals, souvenirs, tips and airport taxes. Small denomination bills – fives, tens and twenties – are most useful. Notes should be pristine. Moneychangers and exchange bureaux often refuse notes damaged with just a small tear.

Credit cards are widely used in larger stores and hotels in cities. ATMs are increasingly common, allowing you to get cash in some of the most remote places. If using your credit card to withdraw cash from a bank you'll need to show identification. When in cities, use a money belt or pouch for cash and passports.

Ecuador's official currency is the US dollar, but in Peru, Colombia and Brazil you will need local currency to shop at stores in town. Peru uses the Nuevo soles, Colombia uses pesos, and Brazil uses reais (singular *real*). In remote villages some people will accept dollars as well, but you should carry some local currency just in case. You can withdraw local currency from an ATM before you head into rural areas. Alternatively, bureaux de change are common in the main gateway cities. Bear in mind that exchange rates at bureaux de change are less favourable and they charge a transaction fee, which ATMs do not. Check online for the latest rates; ⌨ www.xe.com is a useful resource.

Tipping

Airport porters and hotel and restaurant staff rely on income from tipping: a tip of 10–15% is acceptable in most situations. Taxi drivers do not generally expect a tip, but a few will probably encourage you. Agree on a price before you travel so that any tip is a bonus. If you're on an organised tour, it's customary to tip for good service. Usually the tip is given at the end of your trip, and is commensurate with services rendered. For an exceptional guide, consider 10% of your trip price (ground cost). For average service 5% is reasonable.

Viewing wildlife

Of course you want to see the Amazon's wildlife. But the spectacular animals you see in nature magazines and on television shows are rare and elusive. The fact is that if you're planning to see a jaguar or anaconda you're likely to be disappointed. To get the most from your trip, shift your perspective. You can stroll for an hour along an Amazon trail and see nothing but plants. But pause a moment. Look around and you'll see each plant is different. Delve into the vegetation and you'll find dozens of insects and spiders, each unique, with its own role in this complex ecosystem. Consider the small and seemingly insignificant; this is the beauty and wonder of the Amazon. Another time, on a different trail, you'll again see dozens of different kinds of invertebrates – none the same as those you encountered previously. Appreciate the details, and anything else you see – birds, monkeys or, if you're lucky, a snake or lizard – will be a bonus.

On a week-long trip, you'll be lucky to see more than two or three common species. Several factors make it hard to spot wild mammals in the Amazon. First, most rainforest mammals are inconspicuous, being small, well camouflaged, shy and nocturnal. Second, populations are patchily distributed – you have to be in the right place at the right time. Third, dense vegetation easily obscures even sizeable creatures. Fourth, you will probably be spending your time near inhabited areas, where most mammals have been over-hunted. So they're entirely absent or, if in the vicinity, will slink off into cover without you ever being aware of their presence. Get off the beaten track and with luck, patience and a good naturalist-guide, you will increase your chances of seeing some of the species described in this book. See the tips in the box opposite to maximise your chances.

Butterflies are great subjects for close-up photographs (BC)

Photography

(See also *Photographic gear, Chapter 4*, page 145, for more about camera equipment to bring with you.)

To be pleased with your results, you should keep your expectations in proportion. Photos of nature magazine standards are

Spotting wildlife

Most large animals and birds you expect to see in the Amazon are rare, elusive and wary. If you want to catch a glimpse, remember the following:

Be quiet Wild animals usually sense us long before we are aware of their presence. Talk in low tones. Tread quietly.

Be attentive Many Amazon creatures are masters of disguise. In the forest, dense vegetation and low light make it hard to see well-camouflaged animals such as sloths and tree-snakes. Keep your eyes (and ears) wide open.

Look and listen closely The rainforest is a treasure chest of nature's smaller jewels. Observe closely a fallen rotting log, under leaf litter or among the leaves of a shrub and you are bound to find something.

Stay together In the forest, many eyes are better than two. In a group you are more likely to see interesting wildlife. People spread out across a distance scare away animals more than a compact group. Keep up with your guide, who is more likely to spot animals.

Avoid perfumes Animals are often spooked by an unusual scent. Your favourite after-shave or cologne will put more distance between you and what you have come to see.

Early to rise Birds and monkeys are more active around dawn.

Wear 'quiet' clothes Subdued colours such as khaki, greens or browns are less visible to animals (but avoid camouflage gear: locals will wonder if you are with the military!). Primates and birds see colour, so bright objects may frighten them off. On the other hand, red attracts hummingbirds, so you might want to tie a red cloth where it can be easily seen.

Bring binoculars These will literally bring the world of the rainforest considerably closer to you. Most birds and other wildlife will be a distance away and hard to see with the naked eye. Small, compact binoculars are very light. If you've not used binoculars before, be sure to practise a bit before setting off on your trip.

unlikely on your first foray into the jungle. Professionals use expensive equipment, and spend hundreds of arduous hours in blinds and tree houses. But with planning and care, wonderful images can record memories that will last a lifetime.

Whatever film or camera you use and whatever your experience, it's impossible to capture the forest's grandeur on film. Nevertheless, the rainforest offers endless opportunities for photographers. If you're lucky you may have that thrilling moment when you encounter a wild animal, but most wildlife is too fast, far off or well concealed for good pictures. When you do see some interesting wildlife, it is often better to enjoy the animals with binoculars rather than waste time fumbling with a camera.

Even with an inexpensive camera you can get good photos of scenic views or close-ups of flowers and leaves. Beetles, leaf insects and butterflies also make good topics. Brightly coloured and relatively fearless, poison frogs can be approached quite closely. Unfortunately, their minute size makes it hard to get well-lit and well-composed photographs. Don't touch poison frogs or any amphibian, to be on the safe side. Handling easily damages them, and there is a danger of poisoning from the toxic compounds that their skin secretes.

For the best natural light, dawn and dusk give ideal conditions. The low-angle light adds contrast and atmosphere to photographs. Close to

Dawn in the Amazon is an ideal time for taking atmospheric photos (CM/MP/FLPA)

the horizon, the low sun bathes the subject in a soft, golden glow and enhances contrast as it casts deep shadows.

When you go outside from an air-conditioned room or cabin, your camera lens will fog up. Leave a bit of time for your camera to warm to the ambient temperature. Use a lens cloth to wipe off any moisture in the meantime.

Photography etiquette

When photographing local people, respectfully ask permission. If you don't speak the language, point to your camera in a querying gesture. Spontaneity is great, but not at the expense of offending local people.

To break the ice, let the subject look through the viewfinder first, or even take a picture of you. Children and even adults love the image preview available on digital cameras. Most people do not mind being photographed and rarely ask to be paid, but courtesy dictates that you do ask. Respect demands that you honour the person's wishes. Tour operators prefer you not to offer money simply for a photograph. To thank someone, offer to send them a copy of the photograph, and of course remember to do so.

Eating and drinking

Food

Food served on Amazon tours typically features lots of fruit and fish, and is low in fat. Local foods are generally inexpensive and nutritious: rice, bread and eggs are staples. Most vegetables are grown locally, although some are imported, and some foods are not widely available. Whole wheat is uncommon, so bread is normally white, but you could try asking for *pan integral* (Spanish) or *pão integral* (Portuguese) (wholemeal/whole wheat bread). Fresh dairy produce is rarely offered – evaporated or powdered milk is used instead. Diet menus or drinks are rarely available. If you have dietary restrictions be sure to let your tour operator know; most facilities will be happy to accommodate your needs if they have advance notice. Make sure that you are very specific and check and double-check that the food you are given does not contain ingredients that are off-limits.

Since most of your meals while on your trip are prepaid, you usually needn't worry about arranging meals in advance. (See *Planning a tour, Chapter 4*, page 123 for details of what is typically included in the tour price.) The meals served at lodges and on riverboats tend to be somewhat similar. Meat stews, fried fish, rice, simple salads and various tropical fruits are standard fare. Wild-caught meat is eschewed in most lodges, so don't worry that you'll be served endangered turtle or monkey meat. The quality and presentation may vary depending on the lodge or cruise standard, but lodge staff and riverboat crews are invariably anxious to keep you happy, and they know that fresh, tasty food is a relatively easy way to do that. Keep your expectations realistic (you're in the middle of the Amazon, right?) and you'll be unlikely to be disappointed.

In larger cities you can satisfy your urge for fast food. Sometimes it is convenient to dine at hotel restaurants, but you might want to look elsewhere if your tour itinerary and budget allow.

Marvellous manioc

Versatile and easy to grow, manioc is a multi-purpose vegetable, and farmers cultivate more than 140 varieties. Manioc, or *yuca* as it is called within the Amazon (or *cassava* in Africa), is the principal ingredient in more than a dozen foods and beverages. It is ground into a coarse flour, and this *farinha* is sprinkled on food. Manioc flour is the staple starch. People bake a bland and rubbery flat bread made from it, similar to a tortilla or pancake. Manioc is toxic if eaten without preparation: the root must be soaked for two days before being pounded and dried. Many indigenous groups believe the plant seeks the souls of children for nourishment, and it needs to be carefully tended to keep the spirit of the plant under control. It is said that if you dig up a manioc root following the death of a young child you will see red in the veins of the tuber.

Brazilian woman making farinha (OCS/A)

Meat served at hotels and lodges is usually beef or pork. Villagers hunt wild animals for meat, but it's not served at tourist facilities. Widely hunted species include iguana, turtle, tapir and peccary. Only tribal Indians are legally allowed to hunt these, but a lot of poaching goes on. Chickens are ubiquitous, and villagers often keep forest birds such as curassows. Vegetarians can ask tour operators to arrange non-meat dishes; bear in mind that South Americans often don't consider chicken to be meat.

Fish is the chief source of animal protein in the region. Usually it's baked, and then eaten off the bone; sometimes it's filleted and fried. At restaurants and lodges fish is sometimes cooked in batter – along with manioc 'fries': this makes a delicious 'fish and chips'. Pirarucú and tambaqui are tasty but should be avoided, as over-fishing has reduced their wild populations. The dorado catfish or large silver dollar fish make a good alternative. Piranha are high on the traveller's list of 'must-try' Amazon foods: somewhat bony and oily, they are most often eaten in broth.

Breakfast (*desayuno* in the Spanish-speaking countries, *pequeno almoço* in Brazil) in restaurants or cafés tends to be simple: you often get bread and jam with coffee. In a lodge or hotel, eggs, bread and tea or coffee are typical – perhaps with some fruit.

Lunch (*almuerzo/almoço*) is usually the main meal. At jungle lodges and on tourist riverboats it might include salad or soup to start, and a beef and vegetable stir-fry, with corn tamales wrapped in banana leaves. A delicious dish is fresh heart of palm salad. Usually served on its own, the palm heart is shaved into thin ribbons from an ivory-coloured cylinder about 3ft (1m) long. This dish is safe, because the vegetable is peeled and does not need to be washed. Restaurants or hotels typically serve a pre-set three-course meal such as soup, a meat dish and something for dessert. If you're eating out, you can often find lunch for less than US$10.

The **evening meal** (*cena/ceia*) is usually light, perhaps fish and rice with a small dessert. Some restaurants or hotels may not serve any evening meal.

The variety of fruits provides you with many choices for dessert. Ice cream and iced drinks are also popular, and from street vendors you can buy pastries or sugared popcorn. You can also get bread, cakes and cookies topped with powdered sugar from most food stores and markets.

Drinks

Drink only purified, bottled water, and never drink untreated tap or river water. Most lodges and hotels provide purified water around the clock. Some charge for the bottled water in your room, but often it's provided free. Given the heat, be sure to drink more water than usual. Fizzy drinks and beer are widely available, but alcohol dehydrates, so hold back on booze if you're planning to participate in activities.

A great variety of fruits, some of them wild-harvested, are used in alcoholic or soft drinks. Hundreds of different beverages are made from exotic-sounding fruits such as naranjilla, guayaba, uvilla, obos, taxi, and morete from the fruit of the moriche palm. The popular guaraná is made from a small fruit about the size of a coffee bean. Raspberry-coloured, it is high in caffeine. Locals swear it has magical and aphrodisiac properties. Whatever its powers, guaraná is an alternative to the ubiquitous Coke and Fanta. If you like fizzy drinks, Incakola is Peru's answer to Coca-Cola and in Peru is almost as popular.

Guanábana, also known as soursop or custard apple, is related to the pawpaw or papaya. It's the size of a grapefruit, with a hard skin and covered in blunt spines. The firm flesh is yellowish with a few large, black seeds. It's also eaten fresh or in ice cream. The oval, dull-yellow *cupuaçu* fruit belongs to the chocolate tree family. Its whitish, creamy flesh is made into fruit juice, which tastes distinctly of citrus. Locals drink it before a hunt or a day's fishing for its energising properties.

Locally known as *maracuya*, passion fruit or grenadilla mixes well with alcoholic drinks. Tree tomato, or *tomate de árbol*, grows on what looks like a giant tomato plant. The tangerine-sized fruit yields a tart, delicious juice. It tastes better with some honey or sugar. *Camu-camu's* plum-sized fruits are natural vitamin pills – each has ten times the

A local delicacy

'When in Rome', right? Then you'll want to sample palm grubs – a native Indian delicacy. The whitish, thumb-sized grubs are beetle larvae harvested from the heartwood of rotting palms. Locals chop down a palm, which is then colonised by the beetle larvae. They're fried and eaten, although the chitinous head of the grub is usually removed.

Freshly cooked palm grubs at Iquitos market (SS)

Masato - a drink for special occasions

Masato is Amazonian champagne imbibed on special occasions. Village women chew wads of manioc, then spit them into a container. Natural yeast in the women's saliva ferments the manioc's sugars. Water is added; and the mix ferments for a few days. Given the effort to make it, and the high esteem in which the locals hold the soupy brew, don't risk offending your hosts by refusing an offer of *masato*.

vitamin C content of a lemon. They have a high caffeine content, too – just a few fruits will keep you awake all night! Although the juice of the açai berry, made from the fruit of the heart of the palm tree, is popular among Western health food fans, it is not widely offered in Amazonia.

Roots of various plants are soaked in rum to create various alcoholic root tonics, such as *seite reis* ('seven roots'). The resulting brew packs a punch.

Wine available at tourist lodges and on riverboats is pricey (about US$10–15 a bottle) for the quality. Try Tacama, from the Ica region of Peru. Given the influence of German beer makers immigrating to South America, local beer is usually good and cheap.

Coffee is widely grown in the Colombian and Brazilian highlands and rates among the world's best. But both countries export most of their produce. Most restaurants, lodges and hotels serve only instant coffee – decaffeinated is rarely served. Black or herbal tea is usually available.

Shopping

The most popular souvenirs are native-made handicrafts. Woodcarvings are widely available, from city shops to remote forest villages. The commonest woods are mahogany, genipa or balsa. Other local handicrafts include palm-fibre baskets, mats and hats, woven goods, pottery and simple adornments made out of collected wild seeds, shells and insect parts. Animal teeth, feathers, claws and skin are sometimes used. Do not buy items with animal parts or wood from rare or endangered trees. Ecological considerations aside, such products may be confiscated by customs upon arriving in your home country.

Except in town shops, bartering is commonplace, if not expected, when purchasing souvenirs, but if you like something and are happy to

Numerous potions, salves and ointments are made from herbs, roots and oils from the rainforest and sold at local markets (IB/FLPA)

pay the asking price, no-one is likely to complain. Other good buys are 'naive' paintings on postcards and woven goods. Gold and gemstones, such as emerald, sapphire and topaz, are good value. However, some mining operations can cause significant habitat destruction.

Media and communications

Amazonia is increasingly wired and online. The bigger cities have internet cafés where you can log on to catch up with email and news. Free wireless is still scarce, but may be available in better hotels and Western chains. Using the internet is a great way to research a trip by checking rates, comparing tour operators and so on, but do most of your research before leaving home – that way you can focus on the experience. A mobile phone signal is available in most of the big cities: check with your provider before leaving to see if they cover where you're visiting. On an organised tour, your guides will provide you with up-to-date information about internet access and speed, where it is cheapest to use it, as well as public phones, buying local SIM cards and major phone networks.

Most high-end city hotels have television with CNN or BBC, so you can catch up on news that you might have missed while you were in the jungle. Most lodges and riverboats do not have any internet, telephone or television. They do have a radio connection for emergencies, but aside from that you are more or less cut off from the outside world.

Business and time

Opening hours
Most shops, businesses and public facilities such as museums in Amazon countries tend to keep slightly different hours from what you might be

used to. Typically, shopkeepers and workers try to avoid the heat of the day, so they open early, around 07.30, and close for a long lunch break from about midday to mid-afternoon, in some cases reopening as late as 16.00. Stores then stay open until late, often to 20.00 or 21.00. Your tour schedule will take into account opening and closing times of museums and stores, but if you're exploring on your own when you have free time, you should be sure to check ahead if you want to visit a museum, gallery or specialist store.

Time zones

South America is so big that it covers three time zones. Brazil itself is big enough to be split into two time zones, three hours and four hours behind GMT respectively. Peru, Ecuador and Colombia are five hours behind GMT (the equivalent of Central Time in the US). Bear in mind that only Brazil observes daylight saving time (equivalent to British Summer Time).

Language

Spanish is the lingua franca throughout most of South America, with the notable exception of Brazil, where Portuguese is spoken. South American Spanish is rather different from European Spanish, but the differences are manageable. With the expansion of tourism and industry in recent years, most tour guides in the Amazon's popular tourist areas speak some English. If you don't want to struggle with understanding a heavy accent, make sure your tour operator guarantees a bilingual guide.

In rural Amazonia, the Spanish is more or less different from that used in more populated areas. The introduction of slang, slight changes in accent developments in the concept of grammar – and a host of other influences – can make it sound like a new language.

The most widely spoken native language in the western Amazon is Quechua. Given the difficulty of pronouncing Quechua, with its many guttural rasps, you're unlikely to benefit from linguistic experiments. But try a few words; don't feel embarrassed about making a fool of yourself. You'll get closer to people's hearts than by not trying at all.

Berlitz and Lonely Planet publish compact travellers' dictionaries specifically for Latin American Spanish and Portuguese, with useful phrases and a phonetic pronunciation guide. Portable electronic translators also ease communication. Numerous models are available from as little as US$15; popular brands include Nyrius, Franklin and Lingo. Check online reviews before buying.

Cultural etiquette

The Latino (a Spanish-speaking person from the Americas; the feminine form is Latina) is typically less reserved and more voluble than the North American or north European. A quick hug (*abrazo/abraço*) is a normal gesture among men who know each other. A handshake is considered formal and is suitable for most occasions, including greeting and parting. When men and women greet, they hug with a quick kiss on the cheek, or just hold hands and touch cheeks. For strangers, this becomes a shoulder grasp, leaning forward, first to the left, then the right. Beckoning is opposite to the northern European gesture: Latinos typically beckon with one hand palm down, waving the fingers.

Amazonia's culture focuses on getting things done tomorrow (*mañana*). This attitude may seem like a lack of concern, and the indifference to haste can easily frustrate Westerners, but you'll enjoy your visit more if you accept the local pace of life. People throughout the Amazon enjoy a **siesta**, a Mediterranean custom. This nap during the heat of the day means that shops close, and activities cease or slow down – frustrating for Westerners who expect services to continue dawn to dusk.

Not long into your trip, you'll be confronted with **begging**. When you visit more remote towns and villages, throngs of kids surround you, their hands outstretched. In this situation you should exercise common sense. Gift-giving by tourists, in whatever form, creates a dependency culture. Especially undesirable effects arise if you give out sweets, as most of these children have little or no access to dental care. Likewise, gimmicky gadgets or toys serve no real purpose other than to gratify the giver. Simply saying 'no' usually stops the begging. If the reason for giving gifts is to create temporary friendships, then use the time on your hands and be creative. You can devise ways to share experiences across cultures that don't relegate one half to the status of beggars. Photographs of family and postcards of home are always interesting. If you want to help with cash, seek out local schools or hospitals. Back home, donate to conservation or health organisations that work locally.

Bartering is common outside cities. You can purchase items with cash (dollars) but barter is appreciated as it can meet immediate needs. Bartering is a good way to engage more closely with the local people. If you're visiting indigenous communities, consider bringing along a few items for barter. Things in daily use are most desirable, such as fishhooks, children's clothing, school materials and women's makeup. Your tour operator can advise what would be most suitable.

Amazon Highlights

6 The Peruvian Amazon

The big advantage of the Peruvian Amazon is that primary rainforest (never logged) is within a couple of hours by river from Iquitos, the gateway city, and it is also on the main stream of the Amazon River, so if you have to say, 'I've done the Amazon,' Peru has it all. Several tour operators offer trips up remote tributaries in the area south of Iquitos, to the Pacaya-Samiria Reserve, Peru's only officially protected area in the Amazon lowlands. From Lima or Machu Picchu/Cusco, the nearest place to visit the Amazon is Manú National Park and Tambopata-Candamo National Reserve. Rolling hills divided by snaking river valleys comprise habitat quite distinct from the lowland rainforest. Besides the rainforest areas covered in this guide, visitors come to experience the rich pre-Colombian history west of the Andes. You could spend several months in Peru and still feel as if you've left important bits out.

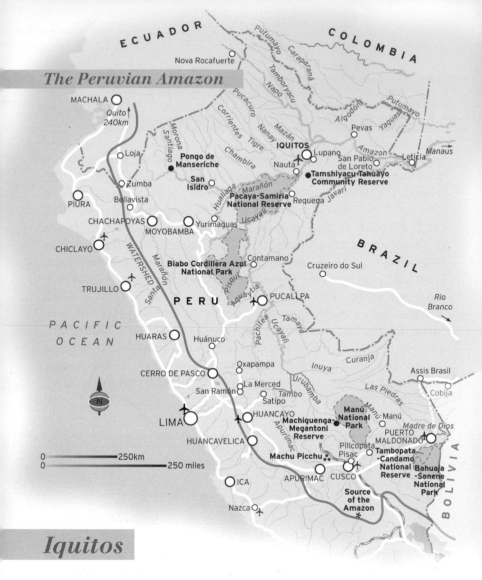

The Peruvian Amazon

(map labels)

ECUADOR

COLOMBIA

Nova Rocafuerte

MACHALA

Quito↑ 240km

Putumayo
Caraparaná
Tamboryacu
Napo
Pucacuro
Mazán
Nanay
Tigre
Corrientes
Chambira
Huallaga
Marañón
Algodón
Putumayo
Yaguas

Loja

Morona
Santiago

Pongo de
Manseriche

IQUITOS
Lupana
Nauta
San Pablo
de Loreto

Pevas

Leticia

Manaus

Amazon

Zumba

San
Isidro

Pacaya-Samiria
National Reserve

Tamshiyacu-Tahuayo
Community Reserve

Bellavista

Requena

Javari

Ucayali

PIURA

CHACHAPOYAS

Yurimaguas

MOYOBAMBA

CHICLAYO

WATERSHED

Marañón

Santa

Biabo Cordillera Azul
National Park

Contamano

Cruzeiro do Sul

BRAZIL

TRUJILLO

PERU

Pisqui

Aguaytía

PUCALLPA

Rio
Branco

PACIFIC
OCEAN

HUARAS

Huánuco

Pachitea

Ucayali

Tamaya

N

Oxapampa

Inuya

Curanja

Assis Brasil

CERRO DE PASCO

La Merced

Urubamba

Las Piedras

Cobija

San Ramón

Tambo

Satipo

Manú
National
Park

Manú

LIMA

HUANCAYO

Machiguenga-
Megantoni
Reserve

Madre de Dios

PUERTO
MALDONADO

HUANCAVELICA

Apurímac

Pillcopata
Pisac

Tambopata-
Candamo
National Reserve

BOLIVIA

0   250km
0   250 miles

Machu Picchu

APURÍMAC

CUSCO

Bahuaja
-Sonene
National
Park

ICA

Source
of the
Amazon

Nazca

Iquitos

Most people have never heard of Iquitos, yet it is the largest city in the
Peruvian Amazon, and the third largest in the Amazon as a whole. It is
brash and noisy, but its unique allure grows on you.

Iquitos is the world's largest city inaccessible by road; the only access
is by air or ship. It is the world's most inland river port and naval base.
Ships must sail 2,300 miles (3,700km) upstream from the Amazon's
mouth to reach the city; this is the world's longest stretch of navigable
river. Despite being so far upstream, Iquitos is only 380ft (115m) above
sea level. And it is still another 1,770 miles (2,848km) to the Amazon's
source. The sprawl covers most of a large rise at the confluence of the
Amazon, Nanay and Itaya rivers. To the west is Isla Padre, a large island
in the main stream of the Amazon River.

Founded as the Jesuit mission of Santa Maria de Iquitos in the 1750s, Iquitos remained a remote backwater trading post. During the rubber boom from the 1880s to the early 1890s it grew rapidly and huge fortunes were made and lost almost overnight. The city's older buildings reflect the prosperity of this past; look for fine tile and ironwork imported from Europe. In 1864, three years after President Ramón Castilla established the Departamento de Loreto (State of Loreto), port facilities were built. This is considered to be the founding date of Iquitos.

The discovery of oil has led the latest boom. Oil, combined with ecotourism, has driven the city's population from 250,000 in the 1970s to 600,000 today. Iquitos is now an important commercial centre and its large influx of foreign visitors and status as a busy port give it a cosmopolitan feel. This is the starting point for the thousands of visitors who embark on rainforest tours from here every year. Hotels are adequate and shopping for souvenirs, food and travel supplies is good, but increasingly expensive. Iquitos has an airport and dock facilities.

Besides oil and tourism, Iquitos's economic activities include small shipbuilding, fisheries and lumber. The most important exported woods are mahogany and Spanish cedar. Jute is exported for use in fibre products. Fish are exported to markets in Lima and dozens of species are exported the world over for the aquarium trade. Natural rubber is still exported from Iquitos and worth several million dollars annually.

Iquitos highlights

The waterfront

The town's Malecón (boulevard) gives a window onto local life. Locals looking to relax after the city's bustle stroll the waterfront, overlooking the Itaya River. On weekend evenings, it's packed with families, onlookers and street performers. Street vendors sell plastic toys, handicrafts and snacks; kids ride around in miniature *motocarros*; Indians dance with snakes; and mimes and magicians practise their craft.

Museo Amazónico

Malecón Tarapacá 386 ℓ (065) 23 4221

Also on the boulevard, housed in the former Loreto State government building dating from 1863, the Museo Amazónico is worth an hour and the US$1 admission fee. The main attraction is 50 plaster statues cast by the late Felipe Lettersten from living Indians. Also featured are pottery displays, various photos of Iquitos, a portrait of Julio César Arana (notorious for his treatment of Indian rubber tappers) and military memorabilia. Nearby is the regional **military headquarters**, housed

Practicalities

As you're on an organised tour you should be provided with **transport** in a minibus or a chartered local bus. If you're on your own, transport around town is mostly by *motocarros*, three-wheeled motorised rickshaws – motorcycles with two-wheel cabs behind. Agree on a price before you get in. The usual cost is 1.50 to 2.00 soles (about US$0.70) from A to B in the city.

Accommodation

The tour operators featured within this guide will be able to recommend accommodation if you are staying in Iquitos. Here follows a few further suggestions from the author.

El Dorado Plaza Hotel Napo 254 ✆ 65 222 555 🖰 www.grupo-dorado.com
Doral Inn Raymondi 220 ✆ 65 241 970
Hotel El Dorado Napo 362 ✆ 65 237 326 🖰 www.hoteldoradoiquitos.com
Hotel Réal Malécon Tarapacá ✆ 65 231 011
Hotel Victoria Regia Ricardo Palma 252 ✆ 65 231 983
🖰 www.victoriaregiahotel.com
Rio Grande Hotel Aguirre 793 ✆ 65 243 530 🖰 www.riograndehotel.com

Eating out and nightlife

Acarahuazu (fish) Kilometer 1, Zugarococha Highway
Antica Pizzeria (Italian) Jr Napo 159

in a 1912 building that was the Hotel Palacio. It's arguably the city's finest example of early 20th-century rubber-boom architecture. Note the wrought-iron balustrades outside each balcony and the blue-and-pink wall tiles.

Belén Market

Just about everything is sold here, from fluorescent pink plastic shoes and bootleg tapes or CDs to unidentifiable animal parts awaiting the pot. The market can be exhausting. It is crowded, noisy, smelly and dirty, but to see how local people live, this is the best one or two hours you can spend. Near to the market is the **Floating City**, or Ciudad Flotante, made

Travel beyond Iquitos is not for the faint-hearted. When you're booking a lodge, make sure your tour operator will make arrangements for travel to and from there, and check whether the lodge uses its own boats. If you're striking out on your own for a day trip to Nauta, you can get a taxi. For most other places, the riverboats that run between Iquitos and other cities are the only option.

If you must contact the outside world, there are numerous **internet** services. Most are open from early to late and cost US$1-2 per hour. Almost every block has one or more internet service stores. Try Cyber Coffee (Raymondi 142).

El Nuevo Meson (local dishes) Malecón Maldonado 153
La Quinta de Abtao (local dishes) Abtao 527 ☎ 65 267 998
Maria's Café (coffee and pastries) Nauta 292 ☎ 65 231 388
Parrilladas Al Carbón (local) La Condamine 115 ☎ 65 223 292
Polleria El Kikiriki (chicken) corner of Napo and Condamine ☎ 65 232 020
Pollos El Rancho (chicken) corner of Huallaga and Napo ☎ 65 221 937
Taberna del Cauchero (bar and restaurant) Raymondi 449

Iquitos's tourism boom has resulted in numerous nightclubs and dance halls. Clubs feature a wide variety of music, including the local chicha or technocumbia, merengue, Colombian vallenato, Brazilian toada, pop and salsa.

The Lounge (rock) 3rd block of Putumayo
Noa (salsa & cumbia) Pevas with Fitzcarraldo
El Refugio (bar) Moronacocha Lake
Adonis (gay) EJercito 1333
Arandu (bar) Malecón Maldonado

up of several thousand shacks, hovels and huts that float, rising and falling with the river. From the market, a long flight of crumbling concrete stairs leads down to the shanty town. It's safe during the day but muggers prowl the area at night.

Looking up towards Belén Market the, Ciudad Flotante is made up of floating houses and shops, both areas providing a fascinating insight into local life (SS)

Map: Iquitos

Boats ↑

Tavara

Yavari

La Condamine

Malecón Tarapacá

Flow ⇧

Amazon

Loreto

Fitzcarraldo

Pevas

Av Grau

✕ **Taberna del Cauchero**

Pucallpa

Raymondi

Nauta

Nanay

Maria's Café ✕

🏠 **Doral Inn**

Callao

Parrilladas al Carbón ✕

Napo

Polleria **El Kikiriki** ✕

✕ **El Dorado**

🏠 **El Dorado Plaza**

El Nuevo Meson ✕

ℹ

Antica Pizzeria

Pollos El Rancho ✕

Putumayo

Ariburger ✕

Plaza de Armas

X 🏠 **Hotel Réal**

🏛 **Iron House**

Huallaga

✝

🅔 Colombian Consulate

ℹ • **Military HQ**

Calva

Calva de Araujo

Sargento Lores

🅔 **Brazilian Consulate**

Morona

Museo Amazónica ♨

N

Av Grau

Brasil

✉

Arica

0 ——— 200m
0 ——— 200yds

ℹ

🏠 **Victoria Regia**

Ricardo Palma

Malecón Tarapacá

Av Cáceres

Bolognesi

San Martín

• **Miniature locomotive**

← Santa Fe Aquarium

✝ **Cathedral**

Airport (5km), Acarahuazu, ✈ La Quinta de Abtao ↓

Plaza 28 de Julio

Ucayali

Local buses ↓ Rio Grand (200m) ↓ Hotel Aguirre

Belén Market ↓

Plaza de Armas

Close by the waterfront is the Plaza de Armas. On one corner of the square is **La Casa Fierro (the Iron House)**, a two-storey edifice with iron panels painted silver-grey, designed by Gustav Eiffel and imported to the city during the rubber-boom days. A wealthy rubber baron bought it after the Paris Exposition of 1889 and had it shipped over in pieces. It was destined for Pucallpa, but the river dropped and the vessel reached no further than Iquitos. The Iron House's second floor houses the Amazon Café, run by an American.

Iquitos's largest building is unnamed and incomplete due to severe instability of the foundations. It has been mostly derelict since its beginning. The huge concrete edifice looms over Plaza de Armas, and dominates the city's skyline. Originally built by cocaine dealers in the 1970s as an apartment and hotel complex, money ran out after the main shell was completed. Later plans were to convert the building to a hospital, hence the faded sign: 'More health for more Peruvians'. These were abandoned after the design was found unsuitable for such a function. Today, it is occupied by a few squatters and is used for telecom and cellular antennas. One television station has a control room two-thirds of the way up, and social security uses a couple of the lower floors. Sporadic rumours circulate of buyers who are aiming to turn it into a five-star hotel. Locals say it is collapsing. The roof swimming pool is ideal for breeding millions of mosquitoes, but otherwise it

Colourful tiles can be seen all over Iquitos, such as these on a building near the Plaza de Armas (RH)

remains only a monument to yet another faded dream.

Plaza 28 de Julio

The **miniature locomotive** in Plaza 28 de Julio was once used to haul raw rubber to the river, from where it could be floated to market for sale. In later years, the engine pulled street cars. The same square has a modern **church**, with geometric architecture and a bold mosaic. An appropriate last spot to visit in Iquitos is the **city cemetery** nearby for the eccentric tombstones and mausoleums.

Santa Fe Aquarium

Calle Abtao 1474 ✆ 652 659 904 ✆ www.acuariosantafe.com

This aquarium has dozens of different kinds of Amazon fish. Visit to get an idea of the amazing variety of species inhabiting the waters of the region.

Shopping in and around Iquitos

There is some good shopping in Iquitos besides jungle souvenirs, which you can buy or barter for at Indian villages. Basketware and bark paintings are light and easy to pack. Tonics prepared from plant roots infused in rum are *siete raices* (seven roots) and *viente-un raices* (21 roots). The numbers signify how many different plants are used to make the brew. Vendors claim the tonics have aphrodisiac or healing properties. These are alcoholic beverages so you might be restricted on taking them out of Peru or back to your home country.

The local herbalists know the properties of hundreds of plants. They have a remedy for anything from an upset tummy (*yerba luisa*, lemon grass) to skin tumours (*uña de gato*, cat's claw).

Other skills are alive and well, including pottery. At Padre Cocha on the Nanay River, the potters mix clay with charcoal to create distinctive, dark pieces. Delicate, intricately painted Shipibo Indian pottery features mystical geometric designs. Around Plaza de Armas, Shipibo women sell embroidered cloths with similar patterns for around US$20. Shipibo pieces such as plates, bowls and vases can be bought in Iquitos souvenir stores for US$5-20; larger pieces are available for US$100 or more.

Further afield

Pilpintuwasi Butterfly Farm
℡ 623 232 665 📶 www.amazonanimalorphanage.org ⏱ 09.00–16.00 Tue–Sun
Half a day here introduces you to some of the region's butterfly species and to some endangered animals, including red uakari monkeys. At the entrance, a pair of macaws greet visitors with loud caws of 'Ola!' The owner gives a brief orientation, followed by a tour of the flight area, a screened with a variety of plants. Butterflies include morpho, caligo, glasswings, heliconius and swallowtails. In the pupa room, larvae hatch out of eggs and are raised until they metamorphose into pupae, whereupon they are transferred to the flight area or released into the jungle. The owner is lobbying the Peruvian government to ease restrictions on the export of live pupa.

Pilpintuwasi is also an animal orphanage. Its rescued animals include monkeys, a jaguar, an ocelot, capybaras, a coati, agoutis, parrots and other Amazonian birds, an anaconda and tortoises. In a small lake there are caimans, turtles, fish and a manatee. Most tour operators offer excursions to the farm. Guided tours start at 09.30, 11.00, 12.30, 13.30 and 15.00. If it's rainy, don't go, because the butterflies won't be active.

Acobia Manatee Rescue Centre

🖱 www.acobia-dwazoo.org

Here you get to see these gentle giants up close, and since you are unlikely to see them in the wild it's an opportunity not to pass up. The centre is located at IIAP, the Peruvian Amazon Research Institute, on the Nauta road. This is also a good place to get maps. The ride by *motocarro* costs 10–15 soles. Ask for the 'ee-ee-ah-pay' – most *motocarro* drivers know the location. The centre works closely with the Dallas World Aquarium in the US. Admission is free so a donation is much appreciated.

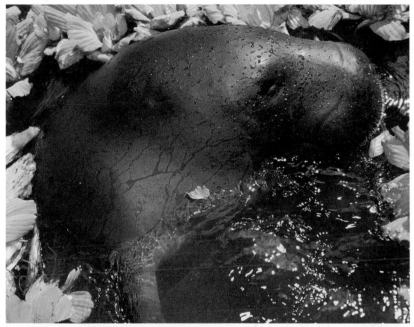

Although protected, the Amazonian manatee remains under pressure from hunting and habitat loss (LC/MP/FLPA)

Institute of Traditional Medicine

🕘 09.00–15.00 Mon–Fri, 09.00–12.00 Sat

The botanic gardens here feature more than 600 species of plants used by local people. It's a relatively new facility so your tour may not include it as part of a city tour. If you have a day on your own, you can get there by *motocarro*; ask to be dropped off before Orvisa, in Pasaje San Lorenzo on Quiñonez. Admission is free.

Grippa's Art Gallery, Pevas

This is worth a morning's excursion to Nauta. Some river cruise itineraries stop here on the way to or from Pacaya-Samiria Reserve. One

In Conversation with...

Which Amazon cruise ships would you recommend?

Mostly the *Jungle Discovery* and the *Arapaima*. These ships offer comfy, air-conditioned cabins with private baths, accommodating about 20 travellers. They are excellent value for the service provided and the quantity and quality of educational programmes. Accompanied by knowledgeable guides, they cruise both up and down the Amazon River  from Iquitos. Upriver, we explore the 'mirrored-forest' of the Pacaya-Samiria National Reserve, and a longer voyage downriver explores from Iquitos to Tres Fronteras, where the borders of Peru, Colombia and Brazil meet. Meals onboard are healthy and delicious and there is ample deck area for a leisurely look at life on the river. Small excursion boats provide an even closer look at the Amazon rainforest and its peoples.

What is your favourite Amazon lodge?

 We use those operated by Amazon Explorama Lodges! We have worked with Explorama for over 20 years, not because their name is similar (although it's a nice coincidence), but rather because they have the most to offer. Simply put, their facilities and guides are the best in the region. Being in protected reserves for many years, the lodges offer rainforest and wildlife viewing opportunities at your doorstep and on the miles of hiking trails. With Explorations' custom itinerary, the **Amazon Jungle Safari**, you overnight in four different lodges, allowing for a diversity of activities. Your naturalist guide accompanies you throughout the week, so they can tailor the excursions to better suit your interests. The final night is at Ceiba Tops, complete with air-conditioned rooms and even a swimming pool. Our itinerary includes an overnight at the remote ACTS field station where the world's longest canopy walkway of its type is located. You can experience dawn and sunset in the treetops and get a birds-eye view of the rainforest. If the weather is good, you can even explore the canopy at night! For those looking for more adventure and rustic accommodations, we arrange camping in the jungle. For clients touring Cusco, we recommend lodges in the Tambopata region of the upper Amazon, home to impressive clay licks along the river banks which attract a multitude of macaws.

Explorations Inc.

What is your favourite itinerary?

Excluding itineraries customised for private groups, we have two favourite itineraries. Our **Amazon Frontiers Cruise** provides for incredible cultural interactions along with the natural history content. Sailing to Tres Fronteras, you explore Leticia, Colombia and Tabatinga, Brazil. En route, you visit several villages typical of the region and some that retain their tribal cultures. You witness the ancient traditions and skills of the Yagua, Bora and Huitoto tribes. In Pevas you may visit the flamboyant artist, Francisco Grippa. You may also visit one of the last remaining leper colonies; although it may sound strange, many customers consider it one of the best parts of their trip. Our other favourite itinerary is our **Amazon Jungle Safari**, which is like luxury camping. You stay in remote rainforest lodges enveloped in the sea of green that is the Amazon. Spending time on the Canopy Walkway also adds a special dimension to exploring the rainforest. Combining one or both of these Amazon tours with a visit to Cusco and Machu Picchu in the Andes makes Peru one of the world's very best cultural and nature destinations.

What are some of the highlights of an Amazon tour?

The Amazon provides more than one expects. In addition to the grand scenery of the rivers and rainforest, it is often the subtle things that amaze visitors. When reading client's trip critiques, besides being pleased with the high level of satisfaction, it has been interesting to note the lasting impressions that the indigenous people leave. While life in Amazon villages may seem basic and hard, the people are resourceful, have a rich social life, a good sense of humour and a delightful outlook on life. Our main suggestion for planning an Amazon visit is simply to go and explore, whether you go with us or not! Go test your courage by swimming with pink dolphins and piranha, learn how to use a blowgun, or touch a caiman or tarantula. As always, we will do our best to provide you with a superior, educational travel experience for a good value.

Founded in 1992, Explorations Inc. offers fun and educational adventures of discovery in the Peruvian Amazon and throughout Peru, introducing discerning travellers to indigenous cultures and the natural world. Explorations' staff are knowledgeable, sincere and reliable. We spoke with Charlie Strader, President.

☏ +1 (239) 992 9660 ✉ info@GoExploring.com
🖰 www.GoExploring.com

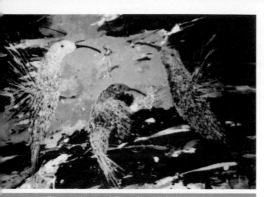

The subjects of Francisco Grippa's paintings often include the region's wildlife such as this trio of hummingbirds (RH)

of Peru's most accomplished artists, Francisco Grippa has dedicated his career to depicting the scenery, wildlife and people of the region. The gallery showcases Grippa's own works as well as various artists from the region. Grippa trained in Paris, London and New York and exhibits in the US. Besides board and conventional canvas, Grippa paints on a cloth made of tree bark, unique among established artists, and works in oils and acrylics. His style combines impressionist depiction with the techniques of Jackson Pollock. But, as he says, 'Grippa is Grippa, and no-one else'. He makes guests welcome without an appointment, whether or not they buy a painting. There is something here for everyone. Tapes of specially composed music, postcards and prints range from US$1–100. Original paintings are priced from US$500–5,000, about half of what they sell for in US galleries.

Monkey Island

Not to be confused with the eponymous island in Colombia, Monkey Island is a private reserve located on the Amazon River near Explorama's Ceiba Tops. The monkeys on the island are free-roaming. Most are not afraid of people and therefore make good subjects for photos, but any physical contact with the animals is strongly discouraged. The island's residents include woolly, saki and titi monkeys as well as tamarins and marmosets. Visits to Monkey Island are available as day excursions from nearby lodges or from Iquitos.

Pacaya-Samiria National Reserve

⌗ www.pacayasamiria.com.pe

Located 114 miles (183km) southwest of Iquitos, Pacaya-Samiria is the only officially protected area entirely within Peru's lowland Amazon. It is the country's second-largest protected area. Rounding a bend in the blackwater Samiria River, your riverboat chugs gently past densely packed vegetation, with chaotic lianas tying everything together in an impenetrable mass. Giant kapok trees poke from the canopy, while countless egrets roost along the riverbank. They take flight as you intrude further into their world, soon settling back down as you pass. Pink dolphins break the water surface, oblivious to the newcomers.

During low-water season access to some areas can be difficult, but this is the time to come here if you're keen on spotting aquatic species, because caiman and otters are more readily seen. During high-water season (April to August), on the other hand, you can reach smaller rivers and increase your chances of seeing primates and other mammals.

The nearest significant town is Nauta, about 70 miles (110km) from Iquitos. Some trips leave from Iquitos, while others depart from Nauta after a two-hour drive from Iquitos (the road has recently been surfaced). Given the remoteness of the park and the red tape involved in visiting it, you will need to arrange visits with a tour operator.

Huge flocks of water birds accompany your voyage along the Pacaya River in the Pacaya-Samiria National Reserve (RH)

Don'ts in the Peruvian Amazon

When in Peru, please don't...

... visit the small zoo in Iquitos, Quistococha Park Most animals are in kept in tiny enclosures. It's a long ride out of town for a disappointing and depressing visit.

... give money or food to street kids It is likely to go to their parents or to buy drugs. It sends the message that street begging is an easy way to make a living, and is better than attending school. Do not give them sweets either, since the street kids have little to no access to dental care.

... order turtle for lunch or dinner These animals are diminishing fast due to over-hunting and population pressure.

... change money with street vendors The exchange rates seem good, but you run the risk of being short-changed.

... buy souvenirs with animal parts Some species are endangered and you risk confiscation of pieces by customs.

Warning While looking for a jungle tour you might be offered a special kind of 'trip' with *ayahuasca*. This powerful hallucinogen is not a recreational drug. Entheogenic (the proper term) drugs are important and interesting, but potentially dangerous. We do not endorse self-diagnosis and medication.

crees itineraries have an emphasis on eco-friendly accommodation. What are your favourite Amazon lodges, and what do they have to offer?

Lodges play such an important role in introducing people to the rainforest, and my favourite one is the Manú Learning Centre. It started as a basic research centre welcoming scientists to explore the biodiversity and forest, but in recent years it has evolved into a fantastic lodge that mixes research, education and sustainable projects with responsible tourism, wonderful staff and delicious food. Plus, for me, it's still a place of learning before anything else, and every time I go it seems I meet scientists exploring new species or locals developing new sustainable projects (they've recently built a great bio-garden with mushrooms, fish, and chillies!). If I could pick a second-favourite lodge, I would choose Romero Rainforest Lodge, which is an old guard-post in the Amazon that's been retrofitted with hot showers and makes a great base for exploring the primary forest of Manú.

What makes Manú Biosphere Reserve so special, and how can you make the most of your experience there?

I think Manú is one of the last great natural reserves on the planet. Since it's a geographic bridge between the Amazon and the Andes, it's a unique space that spans over 3.5 million acres (1.5 million ha) ranges from 820ft (250m) to 13,100ft (4,000m) in elevation, and features such diversity as cloudforest, Andean grasslands, and lowland floodplain forest. In fact, one of the joys of visiting Manú is that as you head in overland across the Andes, you get to traverse the different ecosystems, experiencing both breathtaking mountain scenery and spectacular rainforest views. Additionally, the region's rich history of Inca invasions, rubber barons and Andean settlers has shaped much of its cultural landscape, and yet it's the local indigenous tribes, including some of the world's last non-contacted indigenous people, who serve as the most amazing example of the how people can live harmoniously with the environment.

What are your top tips for visiting and travelling within the Amazon?

My top tip is to choose the right company for you! Different companies offer different activities in different parts of the rainforest, so you want to make sure you don't end up with the wrong group or go to the wrong place. Ask the right questions before you go and make sure you're comfortable with your itinerary and other details of your stay. One question you might ask is, 'Besides employment, what does your company do to help the local community?' Another tip is to be prepared to wake up early once you're in the Amazon. It's  amazing how much life stirs from 05.00 to 08.00, and being out in the forest and watching the sun rise with hundreds of parrots and macaws feeding on clay cliffs is a truly unique experience.

What can visitors do to manage their environmental impact when visiting the Amazon, and is there any way in which they can give back?

I must first reiterate that you should choose your tour company carefully. Your company's behaviour and practices will end up being your behaviour and practices while you are in the Amazon. I personally prefer companies that give back locally, so I always ask about what local initiatives I can support. For example, crees offsets all carbon emissions generated by their tourism with local community agroforestry projects, which helps alleviate local poverty while helping tourists to act responsibly. Indeed, if you can be a tourist who truly helps locals, that's the best feeling you can get!

UK-based crees (Conservation, Research & Education towards Environmental Sustainability) operates the Manú Learning Centre in Manú's Cultural Zone. Ongoing research includes the endangered blue-headed macaw, local diets and reforestation models. All net proceeds from volunteering and tourism are used to provide scholarships for Peruvian and international researchers. The organisation has offices in the UK and in Cusco. We spoke to Quinn Meyer of the company.

☏ (UK office) +44 (0)20 7581 2932
(Peru office) +51 (0)84 262433
✉ info@crees-manu.org 🖰 www.crees-manu.org

Manú National Park and environs

The Manú conservation area in Peru offers some of the best cloudforest exploration opportunities in the country. Peru's largest protected area, it comprises almost 5,800 square miles (15,000km²) around the watershed of the Manú River. Habitats comprise lowland tropical forest, cloudforest and montane forest, and it has one of the highest levels of biodiversity of any park in the world. Visitors often see giant otter, black caiman, jaguar and ocelot. You are virtually guaranteed to see several of the 13 primate species. Manú is heaven for ornithologists: the bird species count tops 1,000. There are several macaw and parrot clay licks throughout the reserve.

Manú by numbers

159 mammal species recorded
250 tree species counted in
a single hectare
1,000 bird species recorded

15,000 plant species recorded so far
5,800 square miles (15,000km^2):
the area encompassed by Manú
National Park

The Biosphere Reserve comprises three zones in Peru's Madre de Dios Region: the National Park Zone, Reserve Zone and Cultural Zone. Entry to the park is only allowed with permits and a guide on an organised tour; otherwise, the Reserve Zone and National Park Zone are closed

Heavy rains wash silt into rivers, colouring the waters of the Manú River, Manú National Park (SS)

Manú practicalities

Travel to Manú starts from Cusco. Many visitors combine a Manú trip with Machu Picchu (see page 101). The **road route** from Cusco takes two full days and involves ascent to elevations considerably above 10,000ft (3000m). If you are at risk from altitude sickness, fly instead.

The **air taxi** from Cusco is a 45-minute flight to the Boca Manú airfield. Most tour operators offer this. Travel continues by boat for several hours depending on your destination.

The journey to Manú can be expensive and time-consuming, and accommodation may be reserved months in advance. To ensure that things go smoothly, book all-inclusive tours from the UK or US, or through a tour operator in Lima.

Accommodation

Most lodges in Peru's south cater for visitors to Manú National Park. These lodges also serve Bahuaja-Sonene National Park and Tambopata-Candamo National Reserve. Tour operators can also provide details of their recommended accommodation.

Las Piedras Biodiversity Station ✆ www.tambopataexpeditions.com
Manú Wildlife Center ✆ www.manu-wildlife-center.com
Pantiacolla Lodge ✆ www.pantiacolla.com
Tambopata Research Center ✆ www.perunature.com

to casual tourism. These areas are open only to indigenous people and scientists. Only the Cultural Zone is accessible without a permit.

Infrastructure for travel and accommodation provides more flexibility and options than in less-popular areas. Here, the opportunity to combine cloudforest with lowland rainforest gives you insights into the diversity of habitats that in turn underlie the exceptional species richness of this area.

The Manú Learning Centre
✆ www.crees-manu.org

Situated in the Amazon foothills, the Manú Learning Centre overlooks the Alto Madre de Dios River. It accommodates up to 18, offering internet access, full catering and a bar. Primarily a research and education centre, the centre offers excellent trails within its private reserve. The Centre also features a notable ethno-botanical and orchid garden. Over three years residents have recorded 365 species of birds, and the lodge provides easy access to macaw and clay licks.

Romero Rainforest Lodge

Although rare elsewhere, giant otters are commonly seen in Manú National Park (GL/FLPA)

✆ www.crees-manu.org

Romero Rainforest Lodge is among the newest facilities in Manú National Park. Located on the banks of the Manú River, it's a one-hour boat ride from Boca Manú Airport, which has connections to Cusco. Surrounded by pristine rainforest, the lodge's small capacity of 16 guests lessens its impact on the surrounding land. Nearby wildlife includes the giant river otters and black caiman that inhabit the three oxbow lakes close by. There are excellent birdwatching opportunities and a plethora of small mammals, reptiles and butterflies. The lodge was built with sustainability in mind, and offers above-average comfort.

Tambopata-Candamo National Reserve

Adjacent to Manú is the Tambopata-Candamo National Reserve, site of the world-famous macaw clay lick. The park lies alongside the Bahuaja-Sonene National Park, providing tourism facilities in a buffer zone. The Reserve can be reached by river or highway from Puerto Maldonado. Most tour operators with Manú itineraries can advise on the options for Tambopata-Candamo.

Macaws and parakeets supplement their diet by gnawing earth deposits at the clay lick in Tambopata-Candamo National Reserve (KW/MP/FLPA)

Do you have a favourite Machete Tours destination?

I love several Amazon destinations, but for me Manú National Park is the ultimate highlight because it starts high in the Andes Mountains. Once we enter the park from Cusco we drive down through the elf wood forest, cloudforest, subtropical rainforest and end by sailing in the Amazon Basin forest. In this way, you can observe several Amazon levels, each with its own characteristic flora and fauna.

Budget aside, what should you consider when choosing a tour to Manú and Tambopata?

You need to consider the different jungle levels as this can give you a wider experience of both the wildlife and ecosystems. As an example, the elf wood forest at over 8,200ft (2,500m) above sea level offers a multitude of orchids and fantastic biodiversity. The only place that you can spot a cock-of-the-rock bird is in cloudforest over 3,940ft (1,200m) above sea level, while jaguars, black caimans and giant otters can be observed down in the Amazon Basin.

Other tips would be to consider visiting a less inhabited area, and experiencing a tour that involves walking and camping.

Machu Picchu is one of the world's top tourism destinations. What do your tours to this site offer?

Our staff makes us special. Machu Picchu has a wonderful history and nature, and the cloudforest surrounding it is extraordinary too. Our licensed tour guides are experts in both archaeology and ecosystems. When on the Inca Trail, our cooks provide nutritional and balanced meals, our porters are highly motivated, and we use only professional camping gear.

Machete Tours is a Peruvian-Danish tour operator with offices in Cusco and Lima. It offers tours throughout Peru, with a strong focus on ecotourism and knowledge of local customs. We spoke with Ronald Rengifo of the company.

☎ (Lima) +51 1 992987202 (Cusco) +51 8 422 4829
✉ info@machetetours.com
🖰 www.machetetours.com

Peruvian cloudforests

Cloudforests (see also page 36) have had relatively little attention as a stand-alone destination, being overshadowed by opportunities to visit lowland rainforest, which is more accessible. However, options are increasing, particularly around Machu Picchu, which visitors are beginning to appreciate for its natural as well as archaeological heritage. In Peru, the best place to explore cloudforest is in Manú National Park, given the infrastructure for tourists. Other notable locations include the area around Machiguenga-Megantoni Reserve and Alto Rio Piedras in the Madre de Dios region.

Pongo de Manseriche

From high in the Andes, the Marañon River carves its way through the mountains to the lowlands. Before it begins its tumultuous descent, the river flows through its narrowest point, the Pongo de Manseriche. The gorge is about 3 miles (5km) long, and narrows to a mere 100ft (30m) in places. Cliffs tower 2,000ft (600m) above the river, seeming to enclose the traveller. It's one of the Amazon's great adventures to raft through the swirling rapids.

The area is remote and largely inaccessible. Few tour operators offer tours here, but it's worth the effort. There are no established lodges in the vicinity, and bear in mind that you need almost a week of travel just to get to the Pongo. Amazon Insects and Neotropic Turis offer speciality entomology and photography expeditions to the Santiago-Comaina Reserved Zone, including the area around the Pongo.

Machu Picchu

Machu Picchu is Peru's top tourist attraction. Most people visit the 'Lost City of the Incas' for its archaeology, but nature lovers will appreciate its cloudforests. Machu Picchu is situated in the Urubamba River valley, the uppermost tributary of the Amazon.

Most tour operators will arrange an extension to Machu Picchu before or after an Amazon trip. Machu Picchu is a destination in and of itself. All Peru country guides cover it in detail and there are several books that are dedicated to the area's archaeology, natural history and travel opportunities. (See *Selected reading*, page 269.)

The grounds of the **Inkaterra Machu Picchu Pueblo Hotel** embrace 12 acres (5ha) of cloudforest. Recorded species include 192 species of birds (including 18 hummingbirds), 111 species of butterflies and 372 native species of orchids, as well as ferns, bromeliads and other

The area around Machu Picchu is rich in natural history as well as cultural history (FL/FLPA)

epiphytes. Inkaterra also runs a rescue centre for spectacled or Andean bears, an endangered species. It's the only place you're likely to see these rare animals. If you like butterflies, be sure to visit the butterfly farm at the Mariposario Inkaterra, which supplies pupae to butterfly houses around the world.

Biabo Cordillera Azul National Park

Although it does not get much publicity, this beautiful area is well worth the effort for its wide range of habitats, including exceptional cloudforest. Formally protected in 2001, the park covers an area bigger than the state of Connecticut. It protects what may be Peru's most biodiverse habitats, according to a 2001 biological inventory. Indigenous communities in the area include the Lamas, Shipibos and Cacataibos. Pucallpa is the nearest large town close by the park. Tourism is prohibited within the protected area; however, tours are available to areas surrounding the park. Consult with Peru-based tour operators such as Machete Tours (see page 190) for travel opportunities and the latest news and updates.

Machiguenga-Megantoni Reserve

Created in 2004, this reserve protects an expanse of varied upland forest. The elevation range encompasses ten life zones. Orchids are especially diverse here and several species of endangered mammals are protected in the reserve, including jaguar, tapir and puma. Indigenous people include the Machiguenga and Yine Yami, who live in the Urubamba River watershed. Since this is a relatively new area, tour operators are not, at the time of writing, offering organised tours here. However, this is likely to change in the near future, and tour operators offering trips to Manú will be able to offer updates and advice.

Indigenous people use rainforest products for decorative items, such as this necklace of peccary teeth worn by a Machiguenga woman (SS)

Peruvian canopy experiences

Explorama ACTS

🖥 www.explorama.com

With a walkway reaching up to 115ft (35m), and stretching 550 yards (500m) long, Explorama's private reserves protect almost 5,000 acres (2,000ha) of rainforest near Iquitos. Community workshops provide information on environmental education, nutrition and sustainable practices for community leaders. Water treatment plants have been built in 14 communities. The Amazon Conservatory of Tropical Studies (ACTS) offers 20 rooms a short distance from the walkway. Alternatively, ExplorNapo Lodge is located a 25-minute walk from the canopy walkway. Bathroom and shower facilities are basic but acceptable and shared. Day trips to the canopy walkway are offered from Explorama Lodge, which has 50 rooms with private bathrooms, and Ceiba Tops – 75 rooms with air conditioning, private bathrooms and a pool.

Inkaterra's Reserva Amazonica Lodge

🖥 www.inkaterra.com

Opened in 2004 on the Madre de Dios River, adjacent to Tambopata-Candamo National Reserve, Inkaterra funds research with revenue from

Andean Trails offers tours to the Ecuadorian and Peruvian Amazon. What does each country have to offer the Amazon enthusiast?

Both Ecuador and Peru offer a variety of lodges and camping trips to suit all tastes and budgets, from two- or three-day taster trips to ten-day expeditions. You can go at any time of year; some months are a bit wetter than others, but the wildlife is always there. In Ecuador there are over a dozen lodges which are readily accessible from the highland city of Quito, by bus or plane and then river travel. Peru has three large protected Amazon areas with an excellent choice of tours: Manú Biosphere Reserve and the Tambopata-Candamo Reserve in Peru's southern jungle are accessed from Lima or Cusco, usually by bus or plane, while the Pacaya-Samiria National Reserve in the northern jungle is accessed by boat from Iquitos. On any trip into the Amazon you'll see some amazing wildlife: monkeys, river dolphins, capybara, caiman, macaws and dozens of other species of birds, butterflies and insects. You may also be lucky and spot the more elusive giant river otter, peccary, jaguar and tapir.

Are any of your tours particularly good for wildlife-spotting? Which animals might you see?

I've had some spectacular wildlife sightings in the Amazon on camping trips and lodge-based stays in Peru and Ecuador. I was lucky enough to see a jaguar at close range in the Tambopata-Candamo Reserve, on the way to a lodge, just lying on the river bank having a snooze, then later slowly lifting itself and wandering along, in no hurry to escape our prying eyes. The macaws in that area are also superb, and nothing is quite as impressive as the activity on a clay lick at dawn or dusk as thousands of multi-coloured birds come to eat clay. In the same area I've watched many a family of giant river otters feeding and playing. Several of the lodges are on lakes where otters live permanently. The longer you spend and the deeper into the forest you venture, the more you will see. If you are prepared to get out on early morning walks, go quietly and be patient. The chances of wildlife sightings are very good at any of the lodges and on all the camping trips we organise.

Andean Trails ANDEAN M TRAILS

What would you recommend for travellers who want to take a more adventurous approach to exploring the Amazon?

Longer camping trips allow you to really feel the forest and to be up close to the sights and sounds of the Amazon. You need to be prepared for the discomforts associated with camping in hot, steamy jungle and the insects, especially mosquitoes, that are inherent to that sort of environment – but you will increase your chances of close encounters with the wildlife.

If you had time to spare at the beginning or end of your Amazon trip, would you recommend combining it with another trip elsewhere in South America?

Oh yes, the Amazon combines really well with a trip to see the other highlights of Peru or Ecuador, or some other part of the continent altogether. Most people visit the Amazon for a few days at the end of a longer tour taking in the highlands, a trek such as the Inca Trail or climb such as Cotopaxi, and perhaps a Galápagos cruise.

Andean Trails is a specialist tour operator offering small-group trekking, mountain biking and jungle expeditions in the Amazon and the Andes. They offer both fixed-departure tours and bespoke itineraries to discover the indigenous cultures and wildlife of the area, with a commitment to sensitive travel. We spoke to the company's manager, Kathy Jarvis.

☏ +44 (0)131 467 7086 ✉ info@andeantrails.co.uk
🖰 www.andeantrails.co.uk

A stand of aguaje palms at Sandoval Lake, Tambopata (KW/MP/FLPA)

ecotourism, and was the first Peruvian company to fight against carbon dioxide emissions. Inkaterra's tourism facilities provide local jobs, train people for new jobs and promote sustainable development based on conservation. The facility comprises two towers, eight platforms and seven bridges, with the walkway reaching up to 150ft (45m). The Inkaterra Canopy Tree House, with room for only two, is built on a platform and adjoins the Inkaterra Canopy Walkway 90ft (27m) above the forest floor below. Guests can take a canopy night walk.

Camungo Lake

✉ info@amazontrailsperu.com 🌐 www.amazontrailsperu.com

At 140ft (42m) above the forest floor, Camungo Lake employs local people, including boatmen, guides and lodge staff, for tours of the Manú Biosphere Reserve. The private reserve maintains valuable primary forest, including habitat for tapirs visiting the clay lick.

Refugio Amazonas

✉ info@rainforest.com.pe 🌐 http://perunature.com

Opened in 2005, Refugio Amazonas is a lodge constructed 100ft (30m) up in the canopy, four hours upriver from Puerto Maldonado on the 500 acre (200ha) Tambopata-Candamo National Reserve. It works with the local Brazil nut concessions to limit hunting in exchange for hosting groups during forest visits.

Tamshiyacu-Tahuayo Community Reserve

🌐 www.perujungle.com

This reserve is located upriver from Iquitos, about four hours by speedboat. In 1991 the Peruvian government designated the area as a reserve to protect the red uakari, one of the Amazon's rarest primates. Its boundaries marked by the Tamshiyacu and Tahuayo rivers, the reserve has among the world's highest plant and vertebrate diversity. One reason for the region's diversity is that it never lost its forest cover during the last ice age, when much of the Amazon was savannah grassland. Combined with Brazil's Vale do Javarí Indigenous Reserve, it is now part of the largest contiguously protected zone in the Amazon – over 15 million acres (6 million ha). To explore the canopy, visitors use a zipline near Tahuayo Lodge. You are secured in a harness and then pulled through the treetops along a cable suspended between the trees. It's the closest you'll get to flying through the canopy. Accommodation is at the Tahuayo Lodge.

In Conversation with...

Can you describe one of Southern Explorations' itineraries that gives a good range of experiences in the Amazon rainforest?

With so many options, that's a tough question. It's hard to beat Yasuní, Ecuador's largest national park. The accommodation in the park is all indigenous-owned, from camping-style to eco-lodges. You can hike, kayak and explore both *igapó* and *várzea* forests and learn about life in the rainforest from the indigenous Huaoranis. The Yasuní really has everything except a lot of tourists. We include the Yasuní in two of our Ecuador tours, plus three tour extensions that can be added to any of our trips.

What kinds of opportunities do you offer for exploring cloudforest areas?

Most of South America's cloudforests are located on either side of the Andes. That makes a trip to the Amazon a great opportunity to see the rare, rapidly disappearing, bio-diverse cloudforests which ecotourism helps sustain. Nature lovers with a penchant for hummingbirds, butterflies and orchids will find that the cooler-than-jungle temperatures and misty landscapes makes them a most memorable destination. We offer cloudforest lodgings and/or hiking excursions on several of our tours from Costa Rica to Peru. Two of our Ecuador trips and a tour extension spend time in the aptly named Bellavista Cloud Forest Reserve. Being so close to Quito makes Bellavista an easy day trip, but staying overnight is much better.

Can you suggest, aside from budget alone, how someone might decide what kind of trip they should choose?

All but one of our trips to the Peruvian and Ecuadorian Amazon are eco-lodge based. There is no experience quite like staying in the Amazon Rainforest, surrounded by the sights and sounds of nature, and where your accommodation doubles as a wildlife observation area. But if your fantasy is an Amazon riverboat odyssey, we also offer a luxury sleep-aboard Peruvian Amazon riverboat trip from Iquitos.

Southern Explorations

> *South America has so much to offer. Time and budget allowing, would you spend more time exploring the Amazon, or would you also go somewhere completely different?*

Though they may dream otherwise, many people only get to South America once. This means that pairing an Amazon trip with another top destination makes sense, but most people prefer not to eat up too much vacation time getting from one place to another. One of the first things to think about when planning your Amazon trip is, 'Where else do I want to go?' If your answer is Machu Picchu, then your choice of an Amazon base is easy: go next door to the Peruvian Amazon, either Manú Wildlife Center, in the most bio-diverse region in the world, or the Madre de Dios and Tambopata tributaries near Puerto Maldonado. If you'd like to squeeze in the Galápagos Islands, then you should go to the Ecuadorian Amazon.

Southern Explorations caters to independent travellers seeking tours with an adventurous slant. Groups are small, and the company strives to provide as authentic an experience of the Amazon as possible with in-country coordinated and guided trips. We spoke with Justin Laycob of the company.

☏ From within the US and Canada:
+1 877 784 5400;
from outside the US and Canada:
001 206 784 8111
✉ info@southernexplorations.com
🖰 www.southernexplorations.com

7 The Brazilian Amazon

Even today, as globalisation puts adventure travel within reach of the masses, the Brazilian Amazon's potential for nature tourism is largely untapped. The country encompasses three-quarters of the Amazon Basin. Most visitors go to Manaus, where the Rio Negro joins the Amazon. This is the biggest lowland Amazon city, with over a million inhabitants.

From poverty-ridden slums to beach paradises, from idyllic river cruises to bone-rattling road journeys, from relaxing in hammocks in the canopy to exploring the unknown, Brazil's passion, rhythm and drama have inspired generations of adventurous travellers.

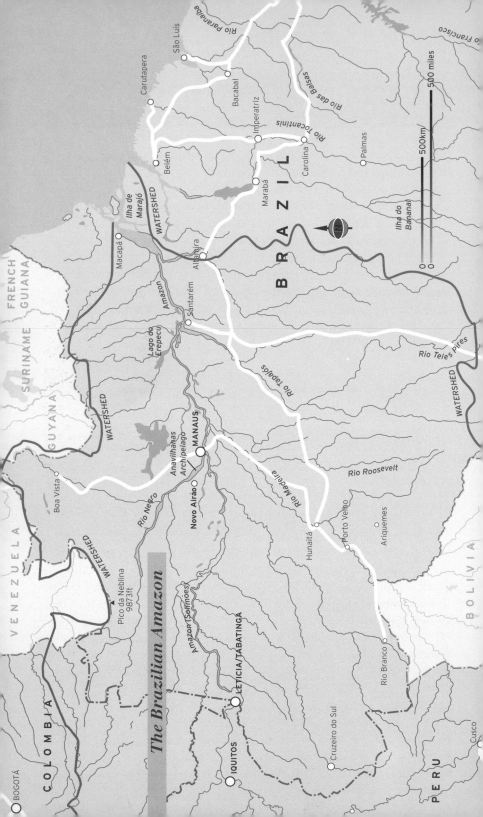

The Brazilian Amazon

Manaus

In essence the capital of Amazonia, Manaus is a booming, modern metropolis in the centre of the world's largest tropical rainforest. It's the most populous city in the Amazon watershed.

Most visitors to Brazil's Amazon begin their travels in Manaus. It serves as a waypoint for some – a stop on the journey to remote jungle areas, other parts of Brazil or to other countries in South America. You'll most appreciate Manaus after a jungle trip when you can relax in one of its many hotels, enjoy the good food and nightlife, shop for souvenirs or visit a variety of tourist attractions.

Favelas such as this one on the outskirts of Manaus are best avoided unless you are accompanied by a knowledgeable guide (ss)

Manaus is so far west from Brazil's coast that it is in a different time zone (one hour behind). The city is a focus for regional trade, tourism and administration. Although 820 miles (1,320km) from the Amazon River's mouth, Manaus lies barely 100ft (30m) above sea level. Located at the confluence of the Negro and the Amazon main stream, the city's most popular natural attraction is the Meeting of Waters (see page 217), where the dark, tea-coloured Negro runs into the caramel-coloured Amazon. The flora and fauna along these rivers differ markedly. Along the Negro the characteristic flooded forest is termed *igapó*. Along the Amazon, it is called *várzea*. For the visitor, either habitat is equally rewarding in terms of biodiversity and wildlife opportunities.

Brazilians generally refer to the Amazon upstream of Manaus as the Solimões and downstream as the Amazonas. Other countries, notably Peru, also recognise the upper stretch of the river as the Amazonas, up to the confluence of the Ucayali and Marañón rivers near Iquitos.

History

Manaus was founded on the site of Barra, a fort built by the Portuguese in 1669. The settlement's fortunes initially waxed and waned with demand for products such as brazilwood and quinine, but the population mushroomed in the 1850s because of the rubber boom. In 1856, the town was renamed Manaus and became the capital of the new Brazilian state of Amazonas.

Fuelled by the Industrial Revolution, new ways of using natural rubber dramatically increased demand. By 1870, 3,000 tons of rubber were being exported annually, and the population grew to 50,000. By the end of the 19th century, Manaus was shipping 20,000 tons of rubber to the point where global industry depended on Amazonian rubber in the early 20th century, and Brazil had an almost complete monopoly on the commodity.

The resulting wealth financed explosive further growth of the city, which came to be known as 'the Paris of the Tropics'. Manaus's excesses became a byword for extravagance; according to historian Anthony Smith, spendthrifts even sent their clothes and linens back to Europe just to be laundered!

The rubber barons imported Portuguese stone to pave marshy areas, along with work crews to lay the slabs. In 1896, financiers erected an opera house to rival those in Europe and America. Along with the arts, Manaus's nouveaux riches were enamoured with technology. Electric

Manaus Opera House ranks among the most architecturally elaborate and well-known buildings in Amazonia (WWL/GT)

trolleycars were rattling through the streets by 1897, and in the same year a telephone exchange was installed to serve 300 phones.

Together with a huge floating dock, in 1902 the British built the Customs House entirely of stone imported from England. Both are still in use today (see page 217). The splendid Municipal Market (see page 209), constructed of glass and wrought iron, was copied from Les Halles in Paris. Yet such luxury came at a price in human lives. To work the plantations, rubber companies enslaved thousands of indigenous people and imported Chinese work gangs. Workers were treated appallingly – whipping, torture and mutilations were reliably documented.

Economics, rather than workers' rights, closed down the Amazonian rubber industry. Rubber plantations in British Malaya flourished, developed from seeds smuggled out of South America. With this cheaper product, demand for Amazon rubber slumped and by 1923 the collapse was complete.

It was not until the middle of the 20th century that prospects perked up. Amazon rubber's high quality sustained a small market that prevented the city's total disappearance. During World War II, Japanese forces occupied Malaysia, cutting off rubber supplies. The Amazon became the Allies' only reliable source of rubber, essential to the war effort, and the town emerged from its generation-long depression.

Manaus's tax-free status, established in 1967, and growth in tourism, have boosted local fortunes. As the city has grown, so too has investment. Industry and commerce have expanded, with companies attracted by easy access to raw materials and cheap labour. Today much new construction is under way, including a complete restoration of the old Municipal Market. Away from the busy traffic, the historic centre remains. It's safe and walkable, comprising wide boulevards, tree-lined parks and elegant historic buildings.

Manaus highlights

The majority of interesting sights in Manaus are within 25 minutes' walk of the central area. This busy, bustling part of town has lots of shops, a couple of museums and floating dock. The area is quite safe to walk around during daytime, if you keep a close eye on the unstoppable traffic. After dark, caution is required: walk around only with companions, dress casually and conceal any valuables, purses and so on. Going any distance is best done by taxi.

Porto Flutuante

Formerly a dingy backwater trading post, Manaus owes much of its success and status to the huge floating docks, completed in 1902 by

Practicalities

Eduardo Gomes International Airport is 11 miles (18km) from Manaus city. Of the two terminals, Terminal One serves both international and domestic **flights**, while Terminal Two serves regional flights. If you're on a pre-booked tour, your tour operator usually provides transport to your hotel. Otherwise you will pay about US$30 for the 30-minute **taxi ride into town**. Buy a set-price ticket for your destination from a booth in the airport near the exits. On the way back, get a ticket at your hotel. Never leave luggage in a taxi alone with the driver.

Dollars are accepted in places aimed at tourists, but if you are on your own for meals or accommodation you will have to use *reais*. The best places to **change money** are at branches of Banco do Brasil and foreign exchange houses. ATMs are common in Manaus, but they do not always work and sometimes the machines will not accept non-Brazilian cards.

It's easy and safe to explore the city centre on foot although you should keep an eye out for traffic. If you want to do a lot of **sightseeing**, transport in Manaus can be a nightmare. The easiest way to see one or two attractions

Accommodation

Lodgings in Manaus tend to be oriented to the tourist, but there are now also several international business hotel chains in the city. There's a wide range of price and quality. Hotels tend to fill at busy times of year so book in advance. Business hotels are clustered near the city's industrial district and shopping centres. Your tour operator will be able to arrange quality accommodation in Manaus. Here are a few suggestions from the author:

Atlantica Go Inn Rua Monsenhor Coutinho 560 ⌂ www.atlanticahotels.com.br
Hotel Brasil Av Getúlio Vargas 657
Hotel do Largo Rua Monsenhor Coutinho 790
⌂ www.hoteldolargomanaus.com.br
St Paul Hotel Rua Ramos Ferreira 1115
Taj Mahal Av Getúlio Vargas 741 ⌂ www.grupotajmahal.com.br
Tropical Hotel Av Coronel Teixeira, 1320-Ponta Negra
⌂ www.tropicalhotel.com.br

Eating out and nightlife

Restaurants, mostly clean and inexpensive, offer a wide range of international dishes. Of course, fresh fish is the regional speciality.

Like the rest of Brazil, Manaus celebrates carnival season with fervour and vivacity (ss)

outside the centre is by taxi. Make sure the meter is turned on when you start off. Larger travel agencies offer **guided city tours** of Manaus. A twice-daily, double-decker bus tour of Manaus city departs at 09.00 and 14.00 daily. It leaves from the Amazonastur information booth (CAT) on the south (lower) side of the São Sebastião/Opera House Square.

Allegro Bar (buffet) Amazonas Shopping Center, Av Djalma Batista 482
Choupana (fish) Rua Recife 790
Churrascaria Búfalo (Brazilian barbecue) Av Joaquim Nabuco 628
Confeitaria Alemã (fast food) Rua Jose Paranaguá 126
Galo Carijó (fish) Rua dos Andradas 536
Glacial Ice Crème (desserts) Av Getúlio Vargas 161
Mandarin (Chinese) Av Eduardo Ribeiro 650
Suzuran (Japanese) Av Djalma Batista 3694
Ristorante Fiorentina (bistro) Av Djalma Batista 482
Splash (pizza) Rua José Clemente 500
Tarumã Restaurant (international and local) Tropical Hotel (see opposite)

If the heat of the jungle makes you doubt Brazil's reputation for vitality and love of music and dancing, visit Manaus's nightclubs. Most of the newer dance clubs are congregated on the stretch of road between the Ponta Negra/Tropical Hotel and the airport. Most open around 21.00 and stay open for longer than you'll be able to party. (Most of these places do not have websites, but your local guide can provide details. Check on Tripadvisor for reviews of larger establishments.)

Coração Blue (pop, modern jazz) Tropical Hotel, Estrada da Ponta Negra
Hype (techno-pop) Estrada da Jonasa 100
Tukannu's (disco) Estrada do Turismo 121

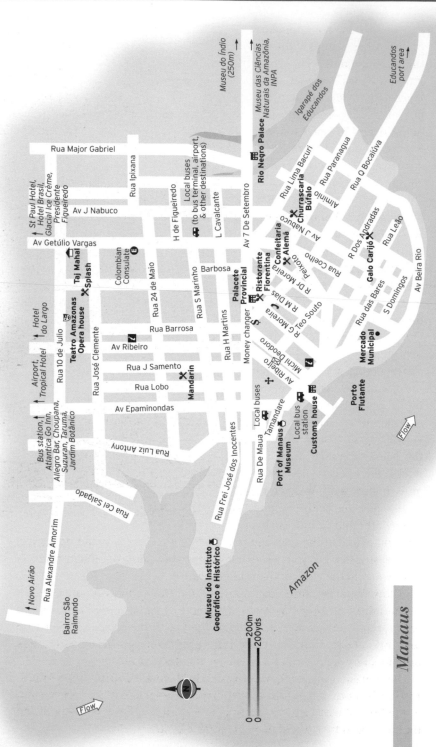

Manaus

the British to accommodate ocean-going ships during the rubber boom. The Porto Flutuante was essential to increasing trade through the port of Manaus. Today, despite being over 100 years old and having suffered ship collisions and fire, this ageing edifice continues to serve the city's shipping. Construction began in Glasgow before pieces were shipped to Manaus and assembled in situ. The docks are 165 yards (150m) long and designed to rise and fall with the annual flooding of the river, accommodating a change in water level up to 40ft (12m).

It remains an engineering marvel and, even if you are not interested in tonnage capacity or shipping schedules, is worth a visit just to observe the press of human life. The docks have been revamped and are now more welcoming to the passing cruise visitor. In turn, the hustle and bustle,

The Port of Manaus is a fascinating place to watch the rhythm and flow of river traffic (SS)

grit and grime of the working port have gone. Access to the docks has been restricted, but you can reach the viewing platform and bars along a walkway to the right of the main entrance.

In low water season, you can see what the chaos was once like a few hundred yards downstream of the main dock, where riverboats and cargo ships, tourists and local people flock to the riverfront. If your ship or riverboat doesn't actually berth there and you come into town by bus or plane, any local can tell you where the dock, is located.

The Parisian-inspired, high-vaulted **Mercado Municipal Adolfo Lisboa** deserves a mention. It formerly housed the Manaus fish market. At the time of writing it was closed for restoration, but if it's open by the time you read this, it will be well worth a visit.

The builders of Manaus Opera House spared no expense lavishing the building with sumptuous decoration (SS)

Teatro Amazonas (Opera House)

Praça São Sebastião ⏱ 09.00–16.00 for tours

You can walk here from the floating dock, a short but hair-raising stroll – be careful of the traffic. From the dock's main gates head straight up the hill past the post office and across Avenida 7 de Setembro, then along Avenida Eduardo Ribeiro a couple of blocks, and the Teatro Amazonas, on Praça São Sebastião, will be right in front of you: unmissable in both senses of the word. A resplendent monument to past glory, the Teatro

Amazonas is surely among the most splendid edifices in the Amazon. Today, more than 110 years after it opened, the building, atop a small bluff, dominates its surroundings. The luxurious features were paid for with profits generated by the trade in natural rubber. Its pink-and-white-wedding cake style is surely testament to its sponsors' confidence and arrogance, if not taste. Over the four years it took to erect, the opera house was adorned with no expense spared: marble from Italy, a massive, four-storey dome covered with glass tiles imported from Alsace in France, and gold plating elsewhere. The inside is decorated with English china and Baroque French furniture. Enthusiastic guides will tell you that the opera house, which opened in 1896, hosted the world's greatest artistes at the time, such as the dancer Anna Pavlova and, allegedly, the famous Caruso. Margot Fonteyn and Mikhail Baryshnikov also once danced here.

Built as it was with profits made from rubber, the opera house was an early victim as the rubber barons' empires crumbled. The price of rubber collapsed in 1910, and in 1912 the doors of the opera house closed, 16 years after they had so proudly opened. The building itself remained, but without a company to perform there it was mute testimony to a bygone age.

In imminent danger of collapse, restoration began in 1974, and it reopened in March 1990. There are almost daily shows, including dance, theatre and music. During the year it hosts international opera, jazz, dance, theatre and even film festivals.

Instituto Nacional de Pesquisas da Amazônia (National Institute for Amazon Research)

Estrada do Aleixo 1756 ᣔ www.inpa.gov.br

The headquarters of the INPA is the centre for much of Brazil's rainforest research. There are pleasant botanical gardens and a public park with labelled trees and plants. In study tanks you can see manatees, otters, caimans and lots of birds. You can also stroll along the short though well-constructed walkway through the treetops.

The **Casa das Ciências** (Science House) showcases the INPA's world-class research on Amazon ecology, with projects on practical applications. Especially interesting are displays on the effects of development on the rainforest – notably dams and mining.

Jardim Botânico (Botanical Gardens)

Avenida André Araujo ᗉ 08.00-12.00 & 14.00-17.00 daily

The botanical garden is a small garden dedicated to Chico Mendez, the martyred rubber tapper and trade union leader. It's a pleasant retreat

Food and drink in Manaus

Local staples are rice, beef, chicken and beans. The Brazilian speciality *feijoada* consists of cuts of salted or smoked meats with seasoned black beans, eaten with dried manioc (*farinha*), hot sauce and grated kale and orange slices as a relish. Many buffet-style (*por kilo*) restaurants in Manaus now include *feijoada* in their daily menus. Many eateries close late on Sunday and all day Monday, or all weekend. Meat sold by street vendors is called *churrasco*; this is usually grilled steak, sausage or chicken with roasted manioc. Another popular street food is *empanadas de camarão* (shrimp pastries with heart of palm and olives).

Tacacá is shrimp with manioc juice (*goma*), hot sauce and *jambu* leaves. Pirarucu is heavily over-fished and an endangered species, but it remains the most popular filleted fish. *Gamitana* (*tambaqui* in Peru) has also been seriously over-fished, although some restaurants may serve gamitana from commercial fish farms. *Tucunare* (peacock bass) is a popular choice. All over Manaus small, simple neighbourhood restaurants serve fresh fish with side orders of mixed rice and beans (called *baião*).

Perhaps not for the faint-hearted, the fish market in Manaus gives an idea of the biological riches of the surrounding area (SS)

In terms of **drinks**, cold, Pilsner-style beer is ubiquitous. For a change, ask for *chopp*, lager beer on tap served by many bars. Sugarcane rum is the traditional spirit, called *cachaça* or less formally *pinga*. It's the basis of *caipirinha*, a potent mix of crushed limes, sugar and fiery *cachaça*, and the national cocktail of Brazil. A good bottle of Brazilian wine costs US$25–30.

Popular non-alcoholic drinks include cupuaçu juice and guaraná, which has enough caffeine (7%) to satisfy even the most dedicated coffee drinker. Other fruit juices are cashew, guava, passion fruit and the lesser-known *chirimoya* and *sapote*.

from Manaus's bustle, with a fine selection of Amazon plants, including many species that gardeners will recognise.

Museu do Instituto Geográfico e Histórico (Geographical and Historical Institute Museum)

Rua Bernardo Ramos ◷ 08.00-12.00 Mon-Fri

From the floating dock, turn left (if facing away from the water) along Rua M de Santa then left again all the way to the west end of Avenida 7 de Setembro and the Praça Dom Pedro II. Follow the road to the right of the old municipal palace (under restoration) to this museum. Exhibits include mounted animals, locally crafted artefacts, fossils and a history of Manaus from its earliest colonial days.

Museu das Ciêncas Naturais da Amazônia (Amazonian Natural Sciences Museum)

Estrada Aleixo (beyond INPA) ◷ 09.00-17.00 Mon-Sat

A visit to this museum will give you some idea of rainforest biodiversity, with displays of butterflies and a huge variety of beetles and ants. A large pirarucu is on show at the aquarium. Of particular interest to entomologists is the world-famous **insect collection** (Coleção Sistemática de Entomologia). A visit here will give you some idea of how much you are missing if you don't think much of insects. Post-tour, you can head for the museum shop to buy handicrafts. It's best combined with a trip to INPA (see page 211) by bus, after which you can continue to the museum by taxi. It's worth the effort.

Museu do Índio (Indian Museum)

Rua Duque de Caxias, near Avenida 7 Setembro ◷ 08.00-12.00 & 14.00-17.00 Mon-Fri, 08.00-12.00 Sat

Run by the Salesian Mission, this ethnic museum is one of Manaus's most popular repositories of memorabilia, including pottery, woven goods, traditional dress and art objects. Best represented are the Tikuna and Waiwai peoples, with some material from the Yanomami along the upper Negro, including paintings by contemporary artist-explorer Roland Stevenson, the 'discoverer' of El Dorado. A small gift shop sells postcards, books and crafts.

Other places of interest in Manaus

Other museums include the **Museu Amazônico**, a small archaeology museum opposite the Saint Paul Hotel on Rua Ramos Ferreira, and the **Palacete Provincial** on the Praça da Polícia (Police Park), Avenida 7 de Setembro and Avenida Getúlio Vargas. The old military headquarters

In Conversation with...

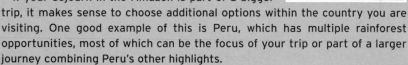

LADATCO covers a wide range of different options in the Amazon. Can you help readers choose between them?

Yes, we certainly can once we have the traveller's wish list. It's important to remember that, as mere mortals, our rainforest experience is likely to be different to the stuff of TV specials.

Your first decision is whether the rainforest is the primary purpose for your trip; if it is the reason for travel, then choose how you wish to experience it – on a lodge-based tour in a biosphere reserve, a cruise along the Amazon River, or perhaps a combination.

If your sojourn in the Amazon is part of a bigger trip, it makes sense to choose additional options within the country you are visiting. One good example of this is Peru, which has multiple rainforest opportunities, most of which can be the focus of your trip or part of a larger journey combining Peru's other highlights.

The next decision is how active you want to be. Do you want to walk, hike or explore by skiff? Is encountering the peoples of the Amazon as important to you as seeing its flora and fauna? Are you willing to expend time and effort to get to your rainforest experience or is ease of access mandatory?

In the end it comes down to you finding out what interests you as much as researching the rainforest opportunities.

What are your top tips for travel to the Amazon?

Our top travel tip is to adopt a flexible attitude. You should also make sure that you take the right gear. Ziplock bags are vital for film, wet shoes, damp clothing and to protect your camera from that sudden downpour. Other items to consider are a black bag to line your suitcase, lightweight, long-sleeved shirts and trousers, flip flops and hat with both brim and chin strap.

The success of your trip will also be largely dependent on your tour operator making sure that you and the rainforest experience you choose are the right fit. Be sure to give an honest profile of your likes and dislikes , and what your expectations are. With your input, your tour operator's destination expertise can assure the right rainforest trip for you.

Out of your trips to Brazil, Peru, and Ecuador, which offers the best wildlife opportunities?

It is important to be realistic. All rainforests teem with life but while often easy to hear, it is not always easy to see. Life in the rainforest is often 'up there' in the canopy or impossibly small and camouflaged on the forest floor. Not all signature rainforest wildlife is everywhere: lodges may not be close to a parrot lick or a lake with otters, and not all rivers and tributaries have dolphins.

In general, the more pristine and bio-diverse areas will always offer more wildlife simply because they are less influenced by man. I have not met a rainforest yet that did not wow me with plenty of opportunities to view birds, monkeys, alligators and creepy-crawlies.

It's also important to realise that wildlife alone does not make the Amazon, or any rainforest, special: this also comes from its flora, the indigenous people, and even the weather.

If you had only ten days, would you combine two Amazon tours to make the most of your time there, or combine the Amazon with another country highlight?

If the focus of your trip is a rainforest experience in Peru, for example, we can combine a lodge in the south that offers a canopy walk and even an overnight stay in a canopy treehouse with a cruise in the Pacaya-Samiria Reserve in the north. These are two of the most bio-diverse areas on earth, yet in totally different parts of the country. A canopy walk gives you the opportunity to look that bird in the eye as it flies by, while a cruise gives you a sense of true vastness, with all those rivers, lakes and streams going somewhere and yet always taking you back to the comfort of your ship.

If the rainforest is only part of a larger experience, combine it with another country highlight. In Peru that could be the Lost City of the Incas, Machu Picchu, or Lake Titicaca, the highest navigable lake on earth, or even Colca Canyon, the second deepest in the world. In Ecuador it could be the Galápagos Islands, nature's greatest show. In Brazil you could venture to the Pantanal for more wildlife, or to Rio de Janeiro, one of the world's greatest cities.

US-based LADATCO has been introducing travellers to the intriguing places, special lodgings and rewarding experiences of the Amazon for 45 years. All trips are tailored to the customer's interests and needs, with an emphasis on insight into the destination and providing hassle-free arrangements on the ground. We spoke to Michelle Shelburne of the company.

📞 +1 800 327 6162 or 305 854 8422 ✉ tailor@ladatco.com
🖑 www.ladatco.com

Rio Negro Palace in Manaus is evidence of a bygone age during which vast fortunes were made and then lost (KHY/DT)

houses the state art collection, the fourth-largest collection of currency in the world and various exhibits. Also worth a visit is the restored former home of rubber-boom governor Eduardo Ribeiro beside the Palace of Justice, in front of the opera house. It houses a small museum featuring a biography of the state's most important governor, complete with multi-media presentations.

Day trips from Manaus

Within day-trip distance of Manaus are the waterfalls and caves of Presidente Figueiredo, 60 miles (100km) north of Manaus by highway, and the dolphins and snake park at Novo Airão, about 45 miles (75km) west of Manaus, over the new bridge linking Manaus to towns on the southern peninsula. These and other day trips are available from several tour operators.

One of the city's most impressive buildings, dating from the late 19th century, the **Rio Negro Palace** was once the home of Waldemar Scholtz, a wealthy rubber baron and former Austrian consul. It is the place to go if you have trouble believing the stories of Brazil's rubber wealth. Those days are now long gone, but the building lives on as the home for the administrators of Amazonas' state government. The palace is located on the east side of town at the end of Avenida 7 de Setembro, where it meets Rua Major Gabriel. It is not open to the public but is worth a look from the outside.

The **British Customs House** is an example of 19th-century British architecture. It shows the solid, confident style typical of contemporary government buildings. Built on a square plan and made of English sandstone, the Customs House serves much the same function for which it was originally intended: as an office for Manaus's inspector of port taxes. It's not open to casual visitors, although it is used today for port business, as it has been since its construction, which coincided with that of the floating dock whose traffic it was built to administer. The Customs House is unmistakable and easy to find: just inside the entrance to the floating dock, left as you go through the gate. In the **Port of Manaus Museum** on Travessa Vivaldo Lima 61 (☻ 07.00–11.00 and 13.00–17.00 Monday–Saturday, 12.00–17.00 Sunday) you can have all your questions on the minutiae of the construction and running of the port facilities answered. The displays include photographs, maps, instruments and logbooks. The museum will fascinate anyone interested in the story of the Manaus dock construction.

Further afield

If your trip is mostly around or near Manaus, most tour operators will either include or arrange side-trips to various features and facilities. Here are some of the main options.

The Meeting of the Waters

Along the confluence of the Amazon main stream and the Negro is the so-called Meeting of the Waters (Encontro das Águas). The Rio Negro is, as its name suggests, black, or at least very dark brown, the colour of black coffee, and classified as a black water river. The Amazon main stream is classified as white water, somewhat misleadingly, being caramel-coloured. Where the rivers join up, and for some distance downstream, the two waters remain separate, intermingling in circular, spiral and wavy whorls and eddies.

In Conversation with...

I see that Steppes Discovery offers two options for exploring the Brazilian Amazon. Can you help readers choose between them?

We offer two very different trips to Brazil; the first is our **Jaguars and Amazon Wildlife Tour** that contrasts the Pantanal with the southern Amazon. Here you stay in the little-visited Alta Floresta region at a lodge renowned for its birdlife and primates, and its strong links to the

local community. In the Pantanal, our guides are familiar with the movements of the jaguar and know all the favourite hunting grounds of this apex predator. The second option is our **Expeditionary Amazon Cruise**, a boat-based trip sailing deep into the Amazon along the Rio Negro, with opportunities to explore by foot and by canoe. This voyage takes you away from the more crowded Amazon waterways, visiting the Anavilhanas Archipelago.

Out of your trips to the Ecuadorian and the Peruvian Amazon, which offers the best wildlife-spotting opportunities?

Both destinations offer excellent wildlife viewing. The trip we offer in Ecuador focuses on the Huaorani tribe and their ancestral home in the Amazon, learning from their traditions and spiritual relationship with the forest. You will get involved with a jaguar population project in the Yasuní Biosphere Reserve, setting camera traps and collecting data. In Peru we visit the Tamshiyacu-Tahuayo Reserve, which is one of the most biologically diverse regions of the Amazon, with a new species of saki monkey having recently been discovered here. We also visit the Manatee Rescue and Rehabilitation Centre and have an excellent chance of seeing both pink and grey Amazon river dolphins.

What do you believe makes your trips to the Amazon special?

When you feel as passionate about wildlife as we do it is not enough to offer exceptional wildlife holidays without giving something back. By joining forces with local research projects and carefully chosen wildlife charities, Steppes Discovery is able to offer a privileged insight into the natural world

Steppes Discovery

while supporting conservation and local communities. Our Amazon trips are for travellers with a love of wildlife and wild places, who appreciate that viewing wildlife in its natural habitat is a privilege that should never be rushed or compromised.

How does your experience as a company help you in providing travellers with unique experiences?

Not only have we been in business for 22 years, but many of our staff have been with us for over ten years, giving us what is arguably the most knowledgeable travel team in the UK. It has enabled us to build long-standing relationships with our partners in the Amazon, frequently allowing us privileged access to wildlife-rich areas, off the beaten track. Our long-standing reputation also allows us to set benchmarks in responsible travel, meaning that a trip with Steppes Discovery can be inspiring and uplifting without costing the earth.

What would be your top tip for travelling in the Amazon?

Despite being the most bio-diverse region on the planet, encountering wildlife in the Amazon can be surprisingly difficult. You'll get more from your trip if you eschew travelling with a 'Big Five' mentality and open your eyes and ears to the smaller mammals, birds and insects, not forgetting the staggering diversity of plant life. You will need time and patience to gain the most from your trip, but equally important is a tour operator who knows the area well and can provide the best local guides. A rain jacket and industrial quantities of insect repellent are also recommended!

Steppes Travel was founded in 1989 with the aim of taking travellers to see lesser-known intriguing places off the beaten track. They offer tailor-made trips to Ecuador, Brazil and Peru with Steppes Discovery, specialising in wildlife conservation tours. We spoke to Jarrod Kyte of the company.

📞 +44(0)1285 643 333 ✉ enquiry@steppesdiscovery.co.uk
🖱 www.steppesdiscovery.co.uk

All Manaus tour operators sell trips to see the Meeting of the Waters. At about US$75 it's the cheapest tour in town, with lunch, guide and activities included.

Amazon Ecopark
 www.amazonecopark.com.br

This is a private nature reserve and jungle hotel with a visitors' centre and a variety of animals. Guides lead a course on jungle survival offering you the best non-life-threatening way to learn how people 'live off the land' in the jungle. Figure on US$30–35 for a day trip, including the 30-minute launch trip from Manaus.

Separate from, but adjacent to, the Ecopark is the **Monkey Jungle**. This small wildlife centre run by the Living Forest Foundation is dedicated to the care of confiscated and abandoned animals. Most people come here as part of their visit to the Ecopark.

Black and white tassel-ear marmoset, Brazil (CM/MP/FLPA)

Aerial view of a meandering river in the Amazon forest, Brazil (CM/MP/FLPA)

In Conversation with...

Reef and Rainforest offers tours in the Brazilian, Ecuadorian and Peruvian Amazon. Is the rainforest experience very different between these countries, or could I expect the same wherever I stayed?

There is probably as much variation within each country as there is between them. Brazil certainly has the greatest section of the Amazon rainforest (around 60%) plus the majority of the Amazon River. In the north, you can enjoy classic riverboat cruises along the Amazon, but there is surprisingly little wildlife to be seen. In the far west there is the marvellous floating Uakari Lodge where you explore the flooded forests to see the rare uakari monkey, plus river dolphins. Further south, you have some superb rainforest lodges such as the Cristalino Jungle Lodge (see page 225), which offers excellent birdwatching and wildlife, but on a much smaller river.

Ecuador and Peru sit at the edge of the Amazon basin, on the divide between the Andes mountains and the Amazon rainforest. Here you can see the various sources of the Amazon River: bubbling springs in the high Andean plains, descending through the mid-altitude cloud forests and finally becoming the slow, meandering rivers of the lowlands. This variety of landscape plus the high level of nutrients generally mean a greater biodiversity and abundance of wildlife than in Brazil. Southeast Peru is particularly good for wildlife and is home to Manú National Park (see page 186), one of the most bio-diverse areas on earth.

Which of your tours would you recommend for a first-time visitor to the Amazon?

Both Peru and Ecuador have very accessible Amazon rainforest for first-timers, with excellent lodges only a couple of hours' boat ride from major airports. In Ecuador, you have three superb lodges (La Selva, Sacha and the Napo Wildlife Centre) dotted downriver from Coca and all offering good chances of seeing a wide range of birds and primates. In Peru, there are a series of lodges just a short boat trip from Puerto Maldonado: for example, Sandoval Lake Lodge offers good sightings of giant otters, macaws and a large number of monkeys just 90 minutes from town. Choosing between the countries really depends on what else you want to see: Peru has the Inca citadel of Machu Picchu, whereas Ecuador has the Galápagos Islands. It's a pretty tough choice!

Do you have any top tips for travel in the Amazon that you'd like to share?

The first tip that I was ever given was to take a sieve. This was to pee through to avoid the legendary candirú, a species of parasitic catfish that has nothing better to do than swim into your nether regions while you are relieving yourself in Amazon rivers. The eye-watering reputation of the candirú isn't backed up by much medical evidence, so you can probably leave your sieve at home, but it is still advisable to wear tight-fitting underwear when swimming in the rivers.

Another top tip is to take a jumper. This sounds strange given that you are travelling to the steaming jungles of the Amazon, but cold fronts occasionally come up from Patagonia and can give three or four days of very chilly weather, particularly from June to September.

If you had time to spare at the beginning or end of your Amazon trip, would you recommend combining it with another trip elsewhere in South America?

With a good flight network and the cost-savings of the South American Airpass, it is incredibly easy to combine the Amazon with other attractions anywhere in South America. Popular additions include the Pantanal region of Brazil (excellent for jaguar watching), the magnificent waterfalls at Iguaçu, Machu Picchu in Peru and the Galápagos Islands, part of Ecuador.

Reef and Rainforest specialises in tailor-made wildlife tours to tropical destinations. Within the company's ranks are two biologists (one a PhD) and a graduate in geography who also happens to be an ex-Amazon guide and lodge manager, but all of the consultants share a love of wildlife and nature. They travel extensively to all the destinations in order to find the best wildlife viewing. We spoke to Dr Jonathan Morris, general manager of the company.

☎ +44 (0)1803 866965 ✉ mail@reefandrainforest.co.uk
🖰 www.reefandrainforest.co.uk

Choosing a jungle tour in Brazil

Your most hassle-free option is to pre-book your tour from your home country. It's fine to try and arrange a jungle tour once you're in Brazil, but you'll spend at least two or three days just trying to sort out the options – not a good way to spend your valuable holiday time. Bear in mind that all the forest within 60 miles (100km) of Manaus is secondary rainforest; to reach pristine rainforest you need to travel by boat for a day or more beyond the city.

Whether or not you have a pre-arranged tour, avoid the touts at the airport and in town. Select a reputable tour operator and then visit their office or call from your hotel.

The Amazonas State Tourism Bureau (Amazonastur) has a large stand at the airport where you can get a list of tour operators. Look for companies who are registered with the Brazilian Tourist Board (Embratur) and members of reputable travel associations such as ABETA (Brazilian Ecotourism and Adventure Travel Trade Association; ⁊ www.abeta.com.br) and ABAV (Brazilian Association of Travel Agents; ⁊ www.abav.com.br). Amazonastur also provides maps of the city.

Accommodation

Tour operators can provide details of their recommended accommodation. Here follows a few further suggestions from the author.

Amazon Tupana Lodge ⁊ www.amazontupana.com
Anavilhanas Jungle Lodge ⁊ www.anavilhanaslodge.com
Juma Lodge ⁊ www.jumalodge.com.br
Malocas Lodge ⁊ www.malocas.com

Ariau Amazon Towers

✉ info@ariautowers.com ⁊ www.ariautowers.com

About 35 miles (56km) from Manaus on the Rio Negro, eight wooden towers house 268 treetop rooms, eight suites and 11 tree houses built up to 65ft (20m) high in the canopy. The rustic accommodations are connected by wooden catwalks that meander through the Amazon's thick canopy of native trees and forest at 32ft (10m) high. The main attraction within the lodge grounds for nature lovers is the surrounding forest and birding. For the best wildlife viewing you'll need to take day trips to undisturbed areas.

This is the world's largest treetop hotel, and it employs mostly locals. The facility has environmentally-friendly waste disposal.

Ariau Amazon Towers is the largest and best-known lodge within easy reach of Manaus (SS)

Cristalino Jungle Lodge

✉ info@cristalinolodge.com.br 🖰 www.cristalinolodge.com.br

Located in a 30,000-acre (12,000ha) private reserve connected to the Cristalino State Park, you reach this lodge via Alta Floresta, in the state of Mato Grosso. Your tour operator will book one of the daily flights (or coach lines if you are on a budget) from Cuiaba to Alta Floresta.

The lodge is only accessible by boat. From Alta Floresta, you ride an hour a half by car before a 30-minute boat ride that takes you to the lodge. The Cristalino Ecological Foundation educates local children about the Amazon and the sustainable use of the forest. This programme received the Whitley Fund for Nature Award as a model for environmental education. In 2008, the Cristalino Jungle Lodge was awarded the World Savers Award by *Condé Nast Traveller*. It offers private bungalows, or rooms built with with natural materials, solar water heating and biological treatment of waste residue.

Tree climbing

Not for the faint-hearted, tree climbing is an increasingly popular way to explore the canopy. Expert guides use a pulley system to hoist guests into the treetops. It offers the least environmental impact but is not advised for the unfit.

Two companies in Brazil offer tree-climbing experiences, with different itineraries. A day session focuses primarily on the climb, with the aim of spending several hours in the canopy. Other opportunities include the kind of activities you'd have on a more conventional tour, with climbing sessions as part of the package.

Reaching the heights: tree climbing in the 21st century
Tim Kovar, Tropical Tree Climbing

The rooftop of the forest teems with life – life that very few individuals get to experience. This is where my heart is, opening peoples' eyes to the abundance and variety of life in the rainforest canopy. Over the past 20 years, technical tree climbing has opened up a new world to the intrepid primate within, but only recently has tropical rainforest canopy been open to the general public for exploration and education.

Technical tree climbing adapts caving techniques and arborist tools to create a new type of ecotourism. Sometimes called 'recreational' or 'inspirational' tree climbing, this is an activity that most people can attempt.

A typical session begins with a brief introduction, a safety talk and demonstration from a qualified guide. Then you are on your way to seeing life from a new perspective. You enter 'tree time'.

Key points for a successful tree climb
Know your instructor's history Ensure that your guide is an accredited tree climbing instructor. Ask for credentials. The leading authorities on recreational tree climbing are Tree Climbers International (✌ www.treeclimbing.com) and the Global Organization of Tree Climbing (✌ www.gotc.org).

Spend minimum time in the branches and maximum time on the rope The canopy is a fragile place, it is important to limit your contact with the tree. On some itineraries, hammocks will be available for your time aloft. You relax in a hammock 100ft (33m) off the ground while watching the wildlife interact within the canopy around you.

Family tree-climbing in the Amazon (TK)

Proper gear = safety and comfort Tree climbing is an on-rope activity, so you will be suspended in a saddle for the majority of your climb. The aim is to connect with nature comfortably and safely.

Take your time Go at your own pace; don't rush or you will miss the wonder around you. A relaxing climb may take several hours in one tree. The quieter and more still you are, the more you will experience the canopy's wildlife. Imagine you are a sloth rather than a monkey. This is slow travel at its best.

Climbing party Tree-climbing teams are small so as to limit the activity's impact. For safety, each guide is responsible for no more than three climbers.

Fitness Being in good shape will make the climb easier. You don't need to be a professional athlete, but you must be in relatively good shape.

Costs Because of the personal attention you will receive, expect to pay from $50 for a two-hour climb to $500 for an overnight experience, where you get the opportunity to sleep in the arms of the jungle.

Tree-climbing operators

Tropical Tree Climbing ⚲ www.tropicaltreeclimbing.com. Week-long tours or instruction with expert tree-climbing instructor Tim Kovar.

Amazon Tree Climbing ⚲ www.amazontreeclimbing.com. Specialises in tree-climbing tours and offers a wide variety of day climbs and multi-day expeditions, including Rio Negro cruises.

8 The Colombian Amazon

Although the country is named after the 'discoverer' of the Americas, Colombia was never visited by Christopher Columbus. Presumably, he had no idea what he was missing, for even today Colombia compels the attention of the curious traveller. It is the land of emeralds and legends of El Dorado. From snow-capped volcanoes and sunny beaches to the vast tropical woodlands, Colombia – more than most countries – merits the tour brochure's description, 'a land of contrasts'. Because of the Colombian Amazon's underdeveloped infrastructure, travel there can be a challenge. The most popular place to start, and with most options for an organised tour, is Leticia, reached by air from Bogotá, or by ship from Iquitos or Manaus.

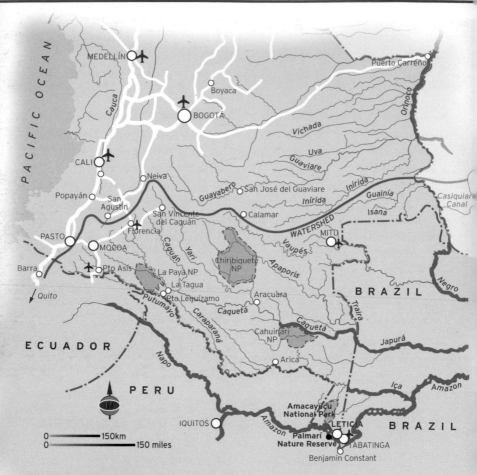

The Colombian Amazon

Leticia

Leticia's beauty is in the eye of the beholder. It's a bustling jungle town in the cool of morning and a lazy backwater during a sultry siesta. It's clean compared with most Amazon towns, and most buildings are cinder block and concrete, or wood, nails and plastic. Leticia is waking up to tourism. People are friendly and welcome *extranjeros* (foreigners).

The town is at the junction of three countries: Leticia proper in Colombia, Tabatinga in Brazil and the mid-river island of Santa Rosa in Peru, hence the area's informal name, Tres Fronteras (Three Frontiers).

Looking across the Amazon River towards Leticia (DD/A)

With around 40,000 inhabitants, Leticia is Colombia's largest settlement east of the Andes and, after Iquitos, the second-largest town on the Amazon River west of Brazil. It is also Colombia's southernmost town, and the region's commercial centre. Compared with that of Brazil or Peru, Colombia's Amazonian territory is small, but it covers a third of the country. Amazonas is Colombia's largest province – four-fifths the size of England. Iquitos in Peru is the nearest big city: it's just over 250 miles (400km) from Leticia as the parrot flies. By river, the distance is about 350 miles (560km).

Originally part of Peru, Leticia was founded as San Antonio in 1867. The town was jump-started into industrialisation by the 19th-century rubber boom. Regional conflicts in the early 20th century prompted the Peruvian and Colombian governments to establish the present-day borders in 1922.

In the 1970s and 1980s, Leticia became a waypoint for cocaine shipments to the US and Europe; it was drug baron territory. You can see this legacy in the form of incongruously luxurious houses dotted around the town. From the late 1980s to the present day, anti-drug enforcement efforts have all but eliminated organised crime operations in Leticia.

Practicalities

Four **currencies** are in everyday use in the Tres Fronteras area: US dollars, Colombian pesos, Peruvian soles and Brazilian reais. Peruvian soles are sometimes refused, but the others are always accepted. To help you budget while planning your trip, we use approximate US dollar prices.

Along the lower part of Calle 8, near the riverfront, small shops house **moneychangers** with desk and calculator. If staying in Leticia or if you don't want to withdraw additional cash from an ATM (see below) you will need them to change small banknotes. Rates are reasonable; the occupants are honest and there's not much difference between them. However, they may refuse to change travellers' cheques or amounts under US$10, and they won't change any dollar bills with the slightest imperfection. If you need a **bank**, hours are from 08.00 to 12.00 (as for the post office and museums), with a long siesta until 14.00, after which places stay open until 18.00. If you're going onwards to Brazil or Peru, get pesos from an **ATM** in Leticia, then go to the moneychangers and exchange into your desired currency. This is the best course of action, because the ATMs in Tabatinga don't seem to work with overseas cards, and the exchange rate for Brazilian reais (pronounced 'hay-ice' in Brazil, but 'ray-al-ess' in Colombia) in Leticia is much better than that in Manaus.

Accommodation

The tour operators featured within this guide will be able to recommend accommodation if you are staying in Leticia. Here follows a few further suggestions from the author.

The Amazon Bed & Breakfast Calle 12 #9-30
Decalodge Ticuna Carrera 11 #6-11 ✆ 098592 6600 🖰 www.decameron.com
Hotel Anaconda Carrera 11 #7-34 ✆ 098592 7119
🖰 www.hotelanaconda.com.co
Hotel Yurupary Calle 8 No 7-26 ✆ 098592 4743 🖰 www.hotelyurupary.com
Maloka Amazonas Avenida Internacional ✆ 098592 6642
🖰 www.hotelmalokamazonas.es.tl
Waira Suites Carrera 10 #7-36 ✆ 098592 4428 🖰 www.wairahotel.com.co

Eating out and nightlife

If you are on your own for meals, several bars and restaurants serve inexpensive dishes or snacks. Restaurants along Avenida Internacional serve mostly

Leticia is connected by road only to a few outlying towns. A new road completed in 2008 provides reliable transport to 11 miles (18km) from the city. **Minibuses** (*combis*) travel along the road at regular intervals throughout the day. If you have a moment on your own, you can choose a **motocar** or a **taxi** to get around town. Motocars are motorbike rickshaws from Peru. They carry three people and are about half the cost of a taxi (up to US$1 per journey). Few drivers speak English, so if your Spanish is sketchy, hire a guide. Agree on the fee and length of the tour before setting out.

For **orientation**, look out for Carrera 11 and Calle 8. These are the two main streets. Explore them and you'll soon be comfortable finding your way around.

For **city tours**, tour operators use minibuses to take up to seven passengers. A standard city tour takes in the museum, fish market and border crossing. If your organised tour does not include a city tour, arrange one at any of the local tour operators, and ask for an English-speaking guide. Do not hire guides you meet in cafés or bars or who approach you in the airport.

To make cheap **international calls**, go to the Telecom office on Carrera 11. Look for the giveaway high mast. Ask for a cabin, dial, talk, and pay afterwards in pesos. Leticia has several **internet** cafes. Look on Carrera 9 near the Leticia-Tabatinga shuttle stop. Facilities open and close frequently so just ask around.

chussos (small kebabs) or fried chicken. Regional dishes include caiman and palm grubs (called *mohohoy*). Check what locals pay before you order. Below are a few suggestions from the author. Not all have phone numbers; you can just drop by or ask your guide or locals about opening times and prices.

Tierras Amazónicas (chicken & steak) Calle 8, #7-50; ☎ 098592 4748
La Varsia (authentic local food) Av Vasquez
Estanco de Fercho (authentic local food) Carrera 11
El Viejo Tolima (bar & restaurant) Calle 8
Pizzeria Preciado Av Internacional 3-45 ☎ 098592 5561
Tio Tom (bar) Corner of Carrera 11 & Calle 7

Leticia's music includes homegrown *cumbia* and *vallenato*, popular genres of local folk music, plus imported styles. The best nights for partying are from Wednesday to Saturday. The hottest part of town is along the Avenida Internacional; here you'll find salsa bars where you can party until the early hours. Some of these establishments are brothels or strip joints (or both). You'll get the general idea from the dress of the patrons and others hanging around.

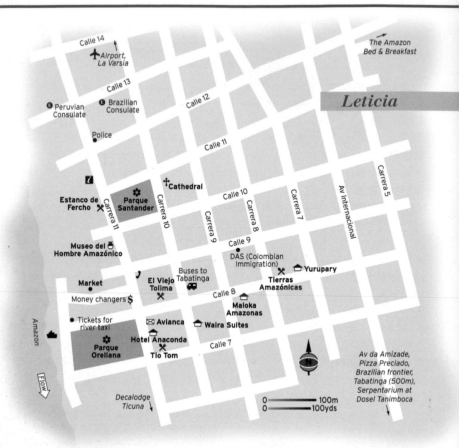

Leticia

Leticia highlights

Leticia Market

Although small, Leticia's main market is worth exploring. You'll see how locals live. It's a bit tricky to find. Look for a narrow opening on Calle 8, just below the moneychangers and opposite a bakery. Ask for '*el mercado*'. Head for the rear of the market to see what fish is on sale – it's an education on the biodiversity of Amazon fishes.

Parque Orellana

Overlooking the riverfront, Parque Orellana has one of the few busts of Francisco Orellana, the first person to sail the whole length of the Amazon (see page 5). A corner of the park has a concrete map of Colombia, where you can stand on Leticia. The park is linked by an indoor arcade of shops to a promenade on the riverside. Here you can see small boats arriving with cargo and passengers. The promenade is currently being extended to the Brazilian frontier.

Shopping in Leticia

Leticia is the place to buy a T-shirt claiming 'I survived the Amazon', a giant carved balsa parrot, precious stones or painted postcards. Near Parque Orellana you'll find several **curio stores**. These are Aladdin's caves for the souvenir hunter – packed from floor to ceiling with masks, carvings, palm-fibre baskets and hammocks, seed necklaces and less desirable items like caiman skulls and mounted piranha. An arcade of shops behind the stage in Parque Orellana through to the Promenade (El Cai) is a treasure trove of souvenirs, snacks, bootleg branded products and odds and ends.

Whether or not souvenirs are on your shopping list, visit **Uirapuru**. It's around the corner (turn right) from the Hotel Anaconda on Calle 8. Shelves are piled high with carved animals, bark cloth paintings, toy blowguns and preserved piranhas. Towards the back of the store is a small 'museum'. One wall is adorned with wasps' nests and on shelves opposite are fossils, birds' nests and animal parts. A glass cabinet holds pieces of native pottery.

Hammocks are cheap (starting at about US$20) but well made. In Leticia you'll find them in shops near the Anaconda. However, you'll find a better selection and lower prices in the Fera Market in Tabatinga (see page 238). Other good buys are woven goods from the Andes area (but cheaper in highland areas) and leather products.

On the lower part of Calle 8, towards the riverfront (turn right as you leave the Hotel Anaconda), are small stalls selling everything from fake designer watches and shoes to haircuts. The best deal here is the famous Colombian **coffee**. You can buy ground or whole beans. The best brand is Sello Rojo ('red seal'), at less than US$2 a pound. Whole bean is scarcer than ground coffee, which is available only in one consistency – very fine – suitable only for espresso or filter machines.

The market in Leticia includes vegetable stalls that give an idea of the diversity of local agricultural produce (ss)

Parque Santander

Parque Santander was completely renovated for the visits of three presidents and Shakira in 2008. It has an ornamental lake, with giant water lilies, fountains and tasteful statues of indigenous scenes. If you're there in the evening you can see thousands of lorikeets arriving to roost. A small amphitheatre hosts the occasional performance.

Serpentarium at Dosel Tanimboca

⌐ www.tanimboca.org

Just off Km11 outside Leticia, this serpentarium gives visitors the chance to see snakes, a large black caiman, frogs, turtles and other exhibits. The animals are kept in large terrariums that simulate their natural environments. You wander around the facility on raised walkways. It's located in the Tanimboca Reserve, and well worth the visit and modest entry fee (US$4).

Museo del Hombre Amazónico (Museum of Man in the Amazon)

Carrera 11 #9-43 🕘 08.00-12.00 & 14.00-18.00 Mon-Fri

This museum consists of one room inside the Banco de Colombia. It houses a small but well-displayed collection of artefacts from the Tikuna and Huitoto tribes. The museum's collection gives a good sense of how indigenous people use rainforest materials to survive day to day.

Tres Fronteras

A floating bar greets arriving travellers from the Peruvian settlement of Santa Rosa across the river (WP)

Leticia marks the boundary of Colombia with Peru and Brazil. Leticia and Tabatinga merge imperceptibly with one another, except that signs in Tabatinga are in Portuguese. The only sign of the frontier is a simple

Practicalities

The Tres Fronteras area uses the currencies of the three countries that meet there (Colombian pesos, Peruvian soles and Brazilian reais), plus US dollars. See page 232 for more information on withdrawing and changing **money** in Leticia.

Santa Rosa is a short ride over the river by **water taxi** from Leticia or Tabatinga. Agree on the price (around US$2–3 is adequate) and pay on arrival. The quickest way to Tabatinga is by **taxi**, which will take you to your exact destination. Taxis are always parked across the road from the Tio Tom bar on the Parque Orellana side. Be sure to agree on a price – US$7 is about right. The cheapest method of getting these is the regular van shuttle every 20 minutes (fare about US$2). The bus stop is in the centre of Leticia on the corner of Carrera 9 with Calle 8, opposite a chemist's shop.

Customs formalities are only necessary if you're staying in a country more than a day. Immigration offices are open during business hours only. Officials may ask to see your yellow fever vaccination card. The customs offices of the three countries are located as follows:

Colombia DAS office in Leticia town centre.
Brazil Policia Federal on Av Amizade in Tabatinga.
Peru Santa Rosa Island just across the Amazon River. Peru's consul in Leticia does not process immigration.

If you are entering or leaving the country for more than a day, you will need to visit the various immigration authorities for exit and entry stamps (or visas if necessary). To enter the national parks in the region, you need an entry permit (US$1) from the Colombian National Parks Authority (✆ www. parquesnacionales.gov.co).

monument on one side of the road. You can breakfast in Colombia, lunch in Peru and have dinner in Brazil. Just in case, carry your passport.

Santa Rosa, Peru

Santa Rosa in Peru has the smallest population of the three towns of Tres Fronteras. It serves primarily as a waypoint for traffic up- and downriver. There are a few shops, bars, police, immigration and customs. Sit at a bar to watch waterfront activity – small boats coming and going, and cargo or passenger vessels heading to or from Iquitos.

Annual festivals in the Tres Fronteras region

The **Confraternidad** celebrates the friendship between the three countries whose frontiers border Leticia. Held in mid-July every year, this week-long music and culture festival features nightly shows in the Parque Orellana. Each country presents dancing, music and food. In early December, the **Pirarucu de Oro** festival features regional musicians.

Young boy from the Tukano tribe dressed up for a festival (ss)

Tabatinga, Brazil

Avenida Internacional is the main road to Tabatinga, where it becomes Avenida da Amizade. Just inside the Brazil–Colombia border, Tabatinga forms a single urban area with Leticia, but is rather more sprawling and down-at-heel. Its main attraction is its lively market, a great place for people-watching and snacking on grilled catfish and other more exotic street food.

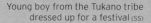

Amacayacu National Park

In the wedge of rainforest reaching down to the Amazon River, Amacayacu ('hammock river') is the only national park in the Amazon Basin to include a portion of the main stream. The Tikuna tribe lives in the park, mostly around San Martín.

Within the park are typical tropical flora and fauna. Plants include teak, mahogany, capirona, acacias and uncounted herbaceous plants and epiphytes. Mammals include jaguar, anteater, armadillo, sloth, tapir and peccary, with pink dolphin and manatee along remote tributaries. Reptiles include anaconda, caiman, river turtles and the green iguana. Some 500 birds are known from the park, a third of Colombia's total.

A few areas can be visited on foot but access is reduced at high water; as with elsewhere in the Amazon, you generally travel around by canoe. To explore the area on foot, the best time to go is at low water from

August to January. At the visitors' centre, you can hire a guide to take you along the well-marked trails into the forest. On an organised tour you'll be accompanied by a guide, essential to point out wildlife you may otherwise miss.

Your tour operator will be able to arrange trips to the park. Tour agencies in Leticia can also arrange excursions, and freelance guides will offer less expensive trips (but see caveats in the box *Choosing a jungle tour*, page 240). Always check what's included. Alternatively, book through the UAESPN offices in either Leticia or Bogotá (www.parquesnacionales.gov.co). The **village of San Martín de Amacayacu** is worth a visit.

The **visitors' centre** has lodgings for 40 people (about US$30pp), a museum and research centre. Unless it is included in a tour, everyone who enters the visitors' centre (even if just for a meal) has to pay the park fee of US$16 (payable in pesos) on top of any other charges.

The brown-throated three-toed sloth is among many arboreal mammals to see in Amacayacu National Park (TM/MP/FLPA)

Choosing a jungle tour in Colombia

Leticia lacks the urban sprawl overtaking Iquitos and Manaus, so you only need to go a short way out of town to get into the jungle proper. The forest starts 1–2 miles (2–3km) from the city, and you only need to go 12 miles (20km) to reach virgin forest. You can enjoy a real jungle experience just with day trips from the town.

The per-day cost of tours from Leticia is comparable to Manaus, Iquitos or Ecuador. However, the cost of a tour to good forest from Manaus or Iquitos involves an overnight stay at a lodge or on board a boat. In Leticia, you can have city amenities while exploring nearby pristine forest.

You can use the internet to arrange a tour from Leticia before you get there. Tour operators in Bogotá can also make arrangements. In Leticia, there are a handful of tour operators and freelance jungle guides. For up-to-date recommendations on freelance guides, ask around at hotels or the recommended local tour operators (see page 137). Do not book a tour from a guide who approaches

Long, narrow boats are ideal for exploring small tributaries that wind through the Amazon (CTB)

you on the street: they may not be reliable. The industry is more or less unregulated, so a guide's licence is no guarantee of honesty.

Accommodation

For tour-operator recommended jungle lodges, contact the listed tour operators offering tours in Colombia (see pages 134–7). Here follows a few further suggestions from the author.

Albergue Tacana ᐤ www.alberguetacana.com
Reserva Natural Heliconia ᐤ www.amazonheliconia.com
Palmari Jungle Lodge ᐤ www.palmari.org
Reserva Natural Amarasha ᐤ www.reservamarasha.com

Palmari Nature Reserve

Located about three hours by motor launch from Leticia, this private nature reserve protects an area of virgin rainforest near the confluence of the Javari and Palmari rivers in Brazilian territory. As the reserve is just over the Brazilian border, you will need your passport. Indigenous groups include Yagua and Mayorana. Accommodation was being built within the reserve at the time of writing. You can also stay at the Jungle Lodge in the village of Palmari, where you can observe rubber-tapping techniques.

Local guides will help identify plants such as this huge liana at Palmari Nature Reserve (PPP/A)

9 The Ecuadorian Amazon

Ecuador's conservation areas protect some of the best scenery and highest biodiversity in Amazonia. The country boasts five national parks in the Amazon watershed, more than any other country. The Ministry of the Environment manages government conservation areas, and private organisations run a number of small biological reserves. The country's Amazon region is called the Oriente, meaning east. The main towns for trips to the Amazon are Lago Agrio, Coca and Tena. Quito is close enough to these that it can be considered the 'gateway' town, but there is no single dominant city like Iquitos in Peru, or Manaus in Brazil.

Ecuador is perhaps South America's most visitor-friendly country. Its official currency is the US dollar, and it's small enough to get around easily, but varied enough to offer endless cultural and wildlife opportunities. Hotels are inexpensive, but of a high standard. The infrastructure is geared to meeting the needs of foreign tourists.

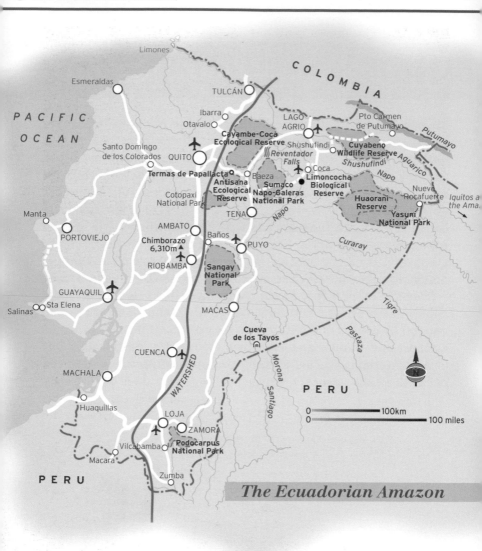

The Ecuadorian Amazon

National parks and wildlife reserves

Ecuador has an extensive system of nature reserves and parks, administered by the Ministry of the Environment. Nine of these are national parks, five of which (Yasuní, Sumaco Napo-Galeras, Sangay and Podocarpus national parks and Cayambe-Coca Ecological Reserve) are in the Amazon watershed. Tour operators will arrange the required permits for entry into national parks and reserves.

Long dugout canoes are the principal form of transport for locals, such as these villagers near Coca, Ecuador (SS)

Cuyabeno Wildlife Reserve

Established in 1979 to preserve one of the world's richest biodiversity hotspots, Cuyabeno holds the world record for plant diversity, with 277 tree species recorded in just one hectare. Its 520 bird species include toucans, hoatzins, antbirds, tanagers, parrots and macaws. The boundaries encompass much of the Aguarico River watershed. The

Cuyabeno Wildlife Reserve is a maze of rivers and lakes such as Laguna Grande (UR/DT)

Ecuadorian Amazon practicalities

No settlement in the Ecuadorian Amazon has a population over 30,000, and most jungle towns only began to grow significantly following the discovery of oil in the 1970s. Most visitors travel from the capital, **Quito**, to one of the three stopping-off points for trips into the Amazon – Coca, Lago Agrio or Tena. Tour operators offer **flight transfers** from Quito's Mariscal Sucre International Airport, plus onward travel to your lodge or reserve of choice. However, a cheaper (and more interesting) option is to travel overland by **bus**. Higher-end

Choosing a jungle tour in Ecuador

For its relatively small size, Ecuador offers perhaps the widest range of options for jungle tours in the smallest area. On the other hand, the possible combinations of lodges, camps, tours, expeditions and guides can be truly baffling. Consider that in Ecuador you can easily experience lowland tropical forest and cloudforest in the same day. Once you have narrowed down the focus on what you want to do, choosing how you will do something becomes a lot easier. If you are doing your research at home and booking in advance, spend time on the internet to get as much information as you can. If you are already in Quito, the best strategy is to visit the tour operators listed on page 137.

Do bear in mind that the best wildlife and culture experiences are in the remotest areas. However, the further you travel from the main towns, the more you will pay for transport and, all else being equal, for accommodation. Most tours include a combination of wildlife-viewing opportunities with visits

reserve is reached from the oil town of Lago Agrio. Excursions include trips to meet the Cofán, Siona and Secoya peoples.

The most comfortable place to stay within the reserve is **Tapir Lodge** (⌘ www.tapirlodge.com), with double rooms, private bathrooms, hot water and electricity generated using solar panels. Other options are the Grand Cuyabeno Lake Lodge (⌘ www.cuyabenolodge.com), on a lake island, and Siona Lodge (⌘ www.sionalodge.com), which offers easy access to primary forest along a trail. Both can be booked through local and international tour operators.

Cayambe-Coca Ecological Reserve
Protecting the country's third-highest mountain peak, this is Ecuador's second-largest conservation area. Protected habitat includes tropical

tours will provide a private vehicle and driver. If you travel by bus, it's a bit more uncomfortable, and you are constrained by the bus schedule, but it will bring down the cost of the tour and you will get to experience more of how the locals live and work.

The US dollar is Ecuador's official **currency**. If your tour is prepaid, you'll need money for tips and minor expenses. Don't count on finding an ATM away from the larger towns, and most vendors don't take credit cards, so you should carry as much cash as you think you will need in small notes. Allow US$200–50 to cover souvenirs, drinks, tips and other miscellaneous expenses.

to indigenous communities, adding a cultural component to the rainforest experience. These may include the possibility for you to witness shamanism, herbalism and the daily life of a rainforest tribe.

Accommodation

The tour operators featured within this guide will be able to recommend accommodation if you are staying in the Ecuadorian Amazon. Here follows a few further suggestions from the author.

Kapawi Lodge (on the Pastaza River) ⁀ð www.kapawi.com
La Selva Lodge (between Cuyabeno and Yasuní)
⁀ð www.laselvajunglelodge.com
Liana Lodge (near Tena) ⁀ð www.lianalodge.ec
Yachana Lodge (Misahuallí, southern Napo) ⁀ð www.yachana.com

rainforest on the easternmost margins of the park up to subtropical forest, cloudforest and paramo. Visits to Cayambe-Coca Reserve can be arranged through Quito-based tour operators.

Oyacachi is a Quechua community in the reserve that some tour operators include on their itineraries or can arrange for you to visit. There is no permanent accommodation within the reserve, but some tour operators can arrange camping trips.

Yasuní National Park

Between the Napo and Curary rivers, and accessed via Coca, Yasuní is Ecuador's largest protected area. The park encompasses tropical lowland rainforest, *várzea* and terra firme forest; over 700 woody species have been identified. Animal life comprises some 200 types

In Conversation with...

Out of Nomadtrek's trips, which Amazon lodges offer the best wildlife opportunities?

Lodges in the Cuyabeno Region, such as Tapir Lodge, and some located in the lower Napo, including Napo Wild Center, La Selva and Sacha Lodge, are very interesting for birdwatchers. We can provide tailored packages from four days and three nights to seven days which should give you a good chance of glimpsing some interesting species.

It is important to remember that there is no guarantee of spotting particular animals – luck and time are important factors.

What do you believe makes the Ecuadorian Amazon special?

The Ecuadorian Amazon is not as vast as the Brazilian Amazon, of course, but the biodiversity of our forests is immense. You can cover Ecuador pretty quickly and smoothly by air or overland. We can travel all over Ecuador at any time in search of the region's rich bird life, which numbers 1,650 species. The cloudforests to the east and west offer 350-450 bird varieties. Ecuador is also a paradise for orchids (4,200 species), and insects such as beautiful morpho butterflies and iridescent beetles can be found everywhere, and at different heights. From the fantastic snow-covered volcanoes of the Andes to the very rich flora and fauna of the Amazon, Ecuador can provide travellers with an amazing experience.

The Ecuadorian Amazon offers some wonderful rainforest experiences, such as cloudforest, or trips into the national parks and reserves. Can you help readers choose?

There are a whole range of outstanding rainforest experiences. The Cuyabeno Reserve, located near the Equator, is home to Tapir Lodge, and is in my opinion a real highlight. There are 12 lagoons where you can paddle or drive a motorised dugout canoe, and enjoy looking for river dolphins, monkeys, parrots, toucans, hoatzins, sloths and much more.

NOMADTREK
Tour Operator

Cloudforests are found on both the eastern and western slopes of the Andes. The environment of some areas of cloudforest lodges means that you will have a good chance of spotting spectacled bears, giant anteaters and other exciting mammals. On the eastern slopes you can go to Baeza or Reventador and stay in places like Cabañas San Isidro in the Sierra Azul. If you head to the western cloudforests of the Andes and driving to Mindo, Nambillo or Tandayapa, you can reach other private reserves, such as Maquipucuna and Bellavista.

For those who are short on time, we have pleasant day trips to Cotopaxi National Park, Antisana Ecological Reserve, or overnight stays in haciendas, with trips to the famous Otavalo Indian market!

If you only had ten days, would you combine other experiences in Ecuador with your Amazon tour?

With ten days at my disposal, I would opt to go on an Amazon tour lasting about five days, combining this with excursions to the Cotopaxi National Park in the Andes, two days in Otavalo, and two days in the western or eastern cloudforests. The packages that we handle include airport pickups, accommodation in hotels all over Ecuador, internal flights, meals, park fees, multilingual naturalist guides and 4x4 vehicles or vans.

Nomadtrek is a family-run tour operator which has been doing business for almost 30 years, with a variety of tours in mainland Ecuador and the Galápagos Islands. Nomadtrek offers trips to a number of ecotourism lodges in the Amazon, and work with expert guides. We spoke to Kurt Beate of the company.

℡ (5932) 290 2670, (5932) 290 6036 ✉ info@nomadtrek.com
🐾 www.nomadtrek.com

Bird life in Yasuní National Park is almost unbelievably rich in species, including the crested owl (PO/MP/FLPA)

of mammals and 500 birds. Huaorani (Waorani) Reserve is part of the park (see below). There are a few lodges on the edge of the park, and basic camping facilities are available. Most local tour operators offer Yasuní itineraries. Nomadtrek offers 8–10-day expeditions based on a minimum of four guests.

Napo Wildlife Center
⏗ www.napowildlifecenter.com
The Napo Wildlife Center is a two-hour motorised canoe ride from Coca. Large rooms in ten luxury cabins sleep up to three people. Rooms have private bathrooms with hot water, porches with lake views, electric light and 120V outlets. Screened rooms have ceiling fans. Viewing towers close-by take you into the canopy. Accommodation here can be booked through major tour operators.

Huaorani Reserve
⏗ www.huaorani.com
The Huaorani Reserve allows the Huaorani people relative independence from industrial and urban development. To get there, travel two and a half hours by road from Coca to the Shiripuno River, and it's then a four-day journey downriver to the community. Some tribal elders dress in the traditional *komi*, a type of loincloth. Men hunt and fish, clear forest for gardens, make weapons and protect the family. Women cultivate crops, cook food, raise children and make items used in daily life.

Accommodation at Huaorani Lodge is in covered tented cabins with private bathrooms, and you can make visits to the community during

A shaman at the Huaorani Reserve (K/FL)

the day. Electricity is supplied by solar panels. Opened in 2008, the lodge has won LATA's award for the 'Best Sustainable Tourism Project in Latin America'. Book directly or through major tour operators.

Manatee Amazon Explorer

🖥 www.manateeamazonexplorer.com

The three-deck *Manatee Amazon Explorer* has 13 double cabins with air conditioning and hot water. Facilities include dining room, bar and lounge area, and laundry service. The crew includes English-speaking naturalist- guides. From Coca, the boat heads down the Napo to Yasuní National Park. Book through tour operators or the company's website.

Limoncocha Biological Reserve

This reserve protects a small area along the middle Napo River, and is reached by a three-hour boat ride down the Napo from Coca; the *Manatee Amazon Explorer* visits here on its regular itineraries. The Reserve protects Limoncocha Lagoon, a lake lined with semi-aquatic and aquatic plants. Microscopic phytoplankton give the lake's water the lemon-green colour after which it is named (*limon* means 'lemon'; and *cocha* 'lake'). Most tour operators can arrange trips to Limoncocha.

Trekecuador
tourism & conservation

What do you at Trek Ecuador consider to be special about the Ecuadorian Amazon?

Because of Ecuador's small size, the Ecuadorian Amazon offers a wide range of options within a short distance from the Andes, the cloudforest and even the Pacific Coast. There are several air and overland access routes and departure points that allow you to make the most of your time.

What things should I bear in mind when booking an Amazon adventure?

A true Amazon adventure includes activities that allow you to experience the rich diversity of fauna and flora and learn about the region's ancient cultural heritage. You should look for ecotourism options that allow you to discover the relationship between local indigenous communities and the incredible biodiversity of the Amazon rainforest.

Can you combine a trip to the Ecuadorian Amazon with other tours?

You can combine a trip to the Amazon with a visit to Ecuador's other geographical regions. If you travel overland, you only need to go a short distance to come into contact with the diversity of Ecuador: active volcanoes, colonial towns, protected areas, indigenous markets, ecolodges and more. You can also add the Galápagos Islands, Ecuador's most renowned destination, to your itinerary.

Trek Ecuador is an Ecuador-based operator specialising in taking small groups on expeditions that support conservation and sustainable development in the Amazon Rainforest and the Galápagos Islands. We spoke to Juan Carlos García of the company.

☎ +593 2 227 7916, +593 9 775 6340 ✉ info@trekecuador.com
🐾 www.trekecuador.com

Sumaco Napo-Galeras National Park

In Napo province to the north of Tena, Ecuador's newest national park protects a unique ecosystem of lowland rainforest in the upper Napo watershed. The region encompasses Volcán Sumaco, which rises like a giant pimple from an ocean of green. Some tour operators offer several days' trekking in the park.

Sangay National Park

This UNESCO World Heritage Site protects the habitat surrounding Volcán Sangay, Ecuador's second-highest active volcano. The volcano's peak is often cloaked in clouds. On the slopes of the volcano are representative habitats of all the major biomes, from tropical rainforest to alpine. A few tour operators offer trekking in the park, using mules to carry expedition equipment.

Podocarpus National Park

Named after a species of indigenous pine, Podocarpus National Park is the southernmost of Ecuador's national parks. Rising to elevations over 9,800ft (3,000m), the park protects extensive cloudforest and diverse wildlife. Permits only allow day trips into the park. Activities include hiking and birding, and marked trails lead to swimming holes and waterfalls. From Loja you can travel to Zamora or Vilcabamba, the nearest large town to the park. Do not accept offers from guides in the village. Several local tour operators will arrange tours to the park or include them in a package tour itinerary.

Podocarpus tree in Podocarpus National Park (PO/MP/FLPA)

In Conversation with...

Adventure Life offers tours in Ecuador and Peru. How does the rainforest experience differ in these countries?

Most Amazon lodges are located in the upper headwaters of the Amazon Basin, with a comparable diversity of the flora and fauna. As a first step we generally find out whether travellers are interested in visiting regions other than the Amazon in one of the countries to help match them with the ideal Amazon lodge. So if someone wants to see Machu Picchu, the Peruvian Amazon is the best match, whereas if a group is interested in the Galápagos, we suggest a trip to the Ecuadorian Amazon.

That said, some lodges in each country are unique. Manú and Tambopata in Peru are more remote and in areas less impacted by humans, so the wildlife is denser. These lodges make good bases for seeing giant river otters and elusive jaguars. However, you won't be missing out on an authentic Amazon experience if you stay in lodges with a shorter transit time by boat, such as Sacha or Sandoval in Ecuador; your days will still be full exploring the forest on foot, in dugout canoes or in the forest canopy.

With all the options out there, we recommend that travellers contact us to help them assess which characteristics are a priority and thus make sure that your experience suits your interests, budget and timeframe.

What's involved in an adventure tour, where you go off the beaten track into remote parts of the jungle?

Just getting to the lodge, whether by motorised canoe or small plane, is an adventure in itself. Gliding upriver to a lodge by boat allows you to see the local communities that rely on this ecosystem and glimpse the wildlife you will be spotting over the next few days. The biggest advantage of lodges is certainly their location in protected areas teeming with wildlife. The rainforest's sights, sounds and smells – and tastes, as the food is often prepared with local ingredients – surround you throughout your visit. During the day you may visit clay licks that attract animals, or climb towers in the forest canopy with a local naturalist guide, who is also likely to be a fantastic wildlife spotter.

Overnight camping and kayaking trips can also be arranged, along with tailored trips for adventurous types who are interested in more activities or looking to visit indigenous communities.

There are many different options for Amazon River cruises. How should I make a choice, aside from the price?

When it comes to Amazon cruises, bigger is definitely NOT better! Travellers after the best opportunities for spotting wildlife should look for small expedition cruises that head off the major rivers and into the less travelled tributaries where wildlife is less likely to be disturbed. A good Amazon cruise will break travellers into very small groups (six or fewer is ideal) for excursions, as large groups are often too noisy to allow much wildlife viewing. Further, it should offer a mix of Zodiac cruising and hikes, particularly at dawn and dusk, to give everyone the best chance of seeing animals during their most active times.

Price differences often reflect the quality of service on board. Look for a good balance between value and the amenities that you consider to be important. Great Amazon cruises can be found for anywhere between around US$700–7,000 per person, so it is important to be clear about your priorities (cost, large cabin, five-star cuisine, etc) so that you are paying only for what you really need.

Can an Amazon trip be combined with a Galápagos tour?

The Ecuadorian Amazon and the Galápagos make a great combination. For wildlife lovers, particularly birdwatchers, Adventure Life highly recommends extending a Galápagos trip with a 4–5 day tour to the Amazon Basin to experience something completely  different. Logistically, combining the two is easier on the wallet than splitting them into two separate trips, especially as the Amazon is so accessible from Quito on a 45-minute flight to Coca, where most itineraries begin.

US-based Adventure Life provides quality small group tours to the Ecuadorian, Peruvian and Bolivian Amazon, and further afield. On tours group size is kept to a minimum and the company aims to have a positive impact on local culture and the environment. We spoke to Beth Conway of the company.

📞 800 344 6118 (US) +1 406 541 2677 (international)
✉ trip.center@adventure-life.com 🌐 www.Adventure-Life.com

Volunteering in the Ecuadorian Amazon

Ecuador is a magnet for volunteers. Inexpensive facilities, plus a wide range of ecologically and socially conscious programmes, attract volunteers from around the world. Global Vision International (🌐 www.gvi.co.uk) offers a volunteer programme based in the village of Mondaña, on the Napo River. The cost is about US$2,200 for five weeks. Volunteer opportunities are posted online for members of the South American Explorers' Club (🌐 www.saexplorers.org) website and at their Quito clubhouse.

Major cloudforest areas

Around Papallacta and Baeza

Papallacta Pass (pronounced pop-eye-auk-tah) is the highest easily accessible point in Ecuador. It links Quito and the lowland rainforest. On the way there you encounter a wide range of montane habitats. Papallacta's main attraction is its hot springs. You can visit on a day trip from Quito or as part of a longer itinerary. Termas de Papallacta resort (see below) is popular with Quiteños looking for escape. It charges US$18 to access the pools.

Baeza is the largest town between Quito and the lowland rainforest. It's a good starting point to explore the surrounding area, but the town is not strongly oriented to tourists. It has no bank or telecommunications and only a handful of basic inns and restaurants.

Termas de Papallacta Lodge
🌐 www.termaspapallacta.com
Termas de Papallacta is located 40 miles (65km) east of Quito. The lodge offers thermal baths on the banks of the Papallacta river in a unique natural environment. It is a full-service resort, ideal for relaxing after a trip to the lowland rainforest. Soak in the thermal baths, get pampered by spa treatments and experience the surrounding nature. Accommodation can be booked directly or included as part of a cloudforest tour.

Cabañas San Isidro
🌐 www.cabanasanisidro.com
San Isidro Lodge is within a few hours' drive of Quito and 20 minutes from Baeza. The chalet-style cabins offer spectacular views from a

vantage point 6,800ft (2,000m) high on the eastern slope of the Andes. The lodge specialises in meeting the needs of devout birders, who will appreciate the diversity of rare species in the vicinity. Accommodation includes 11 comfortable double rooms with hot water and electricity, and San Isidro caters to guests with dietary restrictions. It an ideal base for exploration, particularly when combined with Guango Lodge, only an hour's drive away. It is included in the itinerary of some tour operators, or can be booked directly.

Guango Lodge

Managed by the same company that runs Cabañas San Isidro, Guango Lodge opened in 2000. About one hour away from San Isidro, it lies at a higher elevation (about 8,800ft; 2,700m). It's readily accessible, only 7 miles (11 km) down the main Interoceanica Highway from the town of Papallacta. This area is in humid temperate forest, characterised by more stunted trees with a thicker canopy, and a cool climate. The hummingbird feeders here bring species not often seen elsewhere or in wild settings. Rooms include private bath and hot water. Book through Cabañas San Isidro (see opposite) or other tour operators.

The thermal springs in Papallacta are a great place to unwind after a trip to the lowland rainforest (JM/A)

In Conversation with...

Which experience would Rainbow Tours recommend for a first-time visitor to the Amazon?

I would say that it is essential for any first-time visitor to the Amazon to go on one or more night walks: it is one of those experiences that really takes you out of your comfort zone. The rainforest comes alive after dark, and a night walk will immerse you in a cacophony of noise. The feeling of being completely surrounded by so many creatures you can only hear is truly amazing. The density of the rainforest makes it difficult to spot wildlife during the day, but it's much easier at night, as many of the creatures who live here are nocturnal hunters, and you can catch the reflection of their eyes in the light cast by your torch. A night walk may make you check your bed and mosquito net a few extra times before going to sleep, but it's an experience that no visitor should miss.

What kind of involvement do your tour and lodges have with local Amazon communities?

The lodges that we use in the Ecuadorian Amazon have a very strong relationship with the indigenous communities. In 1998 Ecuador changed its constitution to ensure that the indigenous peoples of the Amazon owned the land rights to their reserves. This was to stop widespread oil speculation, a problem that has dogged the Amazon for decades. From then on, any company wanting to prospect had to get the permission of the indigenous communities to use their land. With the help of private partners, tourism lodges were set up to make sure these people had a sustainable income, halting a lot of the oil prospecting that would have otherwise taken place. This initiative has meant that some lodges now offer an experience of indigenous culture that is seldom found elsewhere in the Americas, or indeed the world.

Rainbow's pick of lodges with strong community connections include the Huaorani Eco Lodge, which offers visitors the chance to sample and learn about the traditional way of life of the Huaorani people; the Napo Wildlife Centre, which is fully owned by the Anagu Kechua people and offers fantastic interaction with the community and the rainforest; and the award-winning Kapawi Lodge, this time owned by the Achuar people, and again offering access to the community and their way of life.

Rainbow Tours

Do you cover any areas that are particularly good for wildlife-viewing? What might you see there?

Although only a small percentage of the total mass of the Amazon Rainforest lies within Ecuador's borders, roughly one third of its diversity can be found there. Wildlife viewing in the Amazon is best attempted at night, but sightings of tropical parrots, macaws and toucans, various types of monkeys, river turtles, caimans and tree frogs are common during the day. Daytime sightings of larger, more reclusive mammals such as tapirs, cougars, sloths, spider and woolly monkeys and capybaras are also possible.

In Yasuní National Park alone there are 610 bird species, and from every lodge you have the chance of seeing a hoatzin, cock of the rock, scarlet macaw or the harpy eagle, as well as many varieties of hummingbirds, parrots and toucans. Sightings of large mammals and manatees, black caimans and bushmasters are also a rare treat in the Ecuadorian Amazon.

Please could you share your top tips for travel within the Amazon with us?

My top tip would be to go with an open mind. You might be set on spotting a specific animal, but the magic of the Amazon will really hit you when you least expect it – when you're sitting on the lodge deck in the evening listening to the incredible sounds of the forest, on a trek with your guide, seemingly lost in a sea of green and brown, or being told you can swim in a lake whilst the guests next to you have been told they can also fish for piranha!

I recommend that visitors take the time to talk to the guides one-on-one whenever they get the chance. You may have questions that were not answered on a trek or that occurred to you afterwards, and if there's time to chat with your guide then you may be rewarded with some incredible insights.

Rainbow Tours Latin America specialists have been providing expert advice and tailormade tours to the region for over a decade. Focusing on comfortable adventure, Rainbow's trips are aimed at allowing travellers to get to the heart of the Amazon through their contact with local communities and accompaniment by specialist naturalist guides. We spoke with Simon Forster of the company.

☎ +44(0)20 7704 3931 ✉ info@rainbowtours.co.uk
🖰 www.rainbowtours.co.uk

Antisana Ecological Reserve

From Baeza you can explore the Antisana Ecological Reserve. Besides spectacular scenery, the reserve offers a mix of elfin forest at lower elevations and grassland páramo higher up. Highlights for birders include the Ecuadorian hillstar, black-faced ibis and silvery grebe. Raptors are common, notably carunculated caracaras and puna hawks. There's also a chance of seeing the Andean condor. The shores of Lake Mica bustle with Andean gulls, Andean coots, Andean and blue-winged teals, ruddy ducks and yellow-billed pintails. Rare mammals often seen at the reserve include the South American fox and white-tailed deer. There is no accommodation here, but tour operators offer day trips into the reserve.

Ecuador's cloudforests harbour a rich array of colourful hummingbirds, such as the hillstar (MC/MP/FLPA)

Rio Reventador and San Rafael Falls

San Rafael is Ecuador's biggest waterfall at 492ft (150m) high. It's about an hour past Baeza by road. A nearby oil pipeline stretches from the Amazon lowlands to highland refineries, but don't let that put you off. Slivers of waterfalls cascade off thousand-foot (300m) cliffs and the forest is otherwise unspoiled. Nearby looms Volcán Reventador, which erupted in late 2002. Along the trail to the falls, you may see cock-of-the-rock. At the foot of the falls are weird sculptures formed by mineralised water coating rocks and branches. The nearest accommodation is at Cascada de San Rafael Lodge; its rooms are in prefabricated buildings built for pipeline workers and there is a simple restaurant. Several tour operators can book trips here.

San Rafael Falls on the road from Quito to Baeza is well worth a stop (PO/MP/FLPA)

When in Ecuador...

While you're in the country, you might also like to visit a few other cloudforests. Not strictly part of Amazonia, the cloudforest region on the western slopes of the Andes offers outstanding biodiversity and some excellent facilities with a high quality of service. You can see birds here that are absent or rare on the Amazon side.

Another major draw is the Mindo cloudforest area, about 90 minutes' drive from Quito, which offers some of the world's top birdwatching. It's also one of the most-visited cloudforests in Ecuador, but it's worth a stop on your way over the Andes to lowland Amazonia. Your tour operator will help you figure out the options.

Cueva de los Tayos

Hike along the Cacapischo River to explore a cave that is home to the endangered oilbird (*tayo*). A few tour operators offer a day trip here that includes a hike to the Rio Malo Waterfall, where you can swim in a pool at the base of the falls, and incorporates the Amazon Orchid Garden at Puyo.

Appendix 1

Language

Useful Spanish words and phrases

Spanish is spoken in Peru, Colombia and Ecuador. Here is a brief list of commonly used words and phrases with Spanish equivalents, including weekdays, months and numbers. Phonetic pronunciation is given for each word. The list gives a visitor with no knowledge of Spanish enough to get around, find luggage, ask the time, look for food and communicate other basic needs. See also *Cultural etiquette*, page 168.

For a more extensive foray into Spanish or Portuguese, we recommend a travellers' dictionary or electronic translation device (see page 167).

Courtesies

English	Español	Pronunciation
		(accent on underlined syllable)
hello	*hola*	<u>oh</u>-la
goodbye	*adiós*	ah-dee-<u>oss</u>
how are you?	*¿como está usted?*	<u>coh</u>-moh eh-<u>stah</u> ew-<u>stayd</u>
see you later	*hasta luego*	astah lew-aygoh
good day	*buenos dias*	boo-<u>eyn</u>ohss <u>dee</u>-ahs
good afternoon	*buenas tardes*	boo-<u>eyn</u>ahss <u>tarr</u>-dayz
good evening	*buenas noches*	boo-<u>eyn</u>ahss <u>noh</u>-chayz
morning	*mañana*	man-<u>nya</u>-na
afternoon	*tarde*	<u>tarr</u>-dayz
evening	*noches*	<u>noh</u>-chayz
very good	*muy bien*	mwee bee-<u>en</u>
thank you	*gracias*	<u>grah</u>-see-ahs
please	*por favor*	pohr fah-<u>vor</u>
excuse me	*perdóneme*	pehr-<u>dohn</u>-ay-may
many thanks	*muchas gracias*	<u>moo</u>-chas <u>grah</u>-cee-yahs

Basic words

yes	*sí*	see
no	*no*	noh
what is your name?	*¿como se llama?*	<u>koh</u>-moh say <u>jah</u>-mah

my name is...	*mi nombre es...*	mee <u>nohm</u>-bray ays
I don't understand	*no comprendo*	noh cohm-<u>prayn</u>-doh
do you speak...	*Habla...*	<u>a</u>-blah...
...English	*...inglés*	...en-<u>glays</u>
I'm hungry	*tengo hambre*	<u>ten</u>-goh <u>am</u>-bray
how much?	*¿quanto es?*	<u>kwahn</u>-to ayss
that's expensive!	*¡está caro!*	eh-<u>stah</u> kar-oh
that's too much!	*¡está demasiado!*	eh-<u>stah</u> day-mah-see-ah-doh
I want	*quiero*	kee-<u>eh</u>-ro
I don't want	*no quiero*	noh kee-<u>eh</u>-ro
I would like	*quisiera*	kee-see-<u>eh</u>-ra
I am lost	*estoy perdido*	eh-<u>stoy</u> pehr-<u>dee</u>-doh
to the right	*a la derecha*	ah lah day-<u>ray</u>-chah
to the left	*a la izquierda*	ah lah eez-kwee-<u>ehr</u>-dah
where is...	*¿donde está...?*	<u>dohn</u>-day eh-<u>stah</u>...
restaurant	*el restaurante*	el reh-staw-<u>rahn</u>-tay
bathroom	*el baño*	el <u>bahn</u>-yo
hotel	*el hotel*	el oh-<u>tehl</u>
bedroom	*la habitación*	la ab-ih-tas-<u>yon</u>
towel	*la ropa*	la <u>roh</u>-pah
soap	*el jabón*	el zhah-<u>bohn</u>
telephone	*el teléfono*	el tay-<u>lay</u>-foh-noh
currency exchange	*la casa de cambio*	la <u>kas</u>ah deh <u>cahm</u>-bee-oh
bank	*el banco*	el <u>bahn</u> coh
river	*el río*	el <u>ree</u>-oh
forest	*la selva*	la <u>sehl</u>-bah
airport	*el aeropuerto*	el ahy-roh-<u>pwahr</u>-toh
Indian village	*el pueblo de los Indios*	el poo-<u>weh</u>-bloh day loss <u>een</u>-dee-oss
boat	*el barco*	el <u>bar</u>-koh
bus station	*estación del autobús*	stah-see-<u>ohn</u> dehl ow-too-<u>boos</u>
street	*la avenida, la calle*	la ah-vehn-<u>ee</u>dah, la <u>cah</u>-yay
house	*la casa*	la <u>cah</u>-sah
guide	*el guía*	el <u>gee</u>-yah
luggage	*equipaje*	eh-kee-<u>pah</u>-hey
what time is it?	*¿que hora es?*	kay <u>or</u>ah ays
what time is...	*¿que hora...*	kay <u>or</u>ah...
the meal	*la comida*	la koh-<u>midh</u>-ah
breakfast	*desayuno*	day-say-<u>ooh</u>-noh
lunch	*almuerzo*	ahl-moo-<u>ehrt</u>-soh

dinner	*cena*	<u>say</u>-nah
what is your...	*que es su...*	kay ays soo...
phone number?	*número de teléfono?*	nume-eh-row day tay-<u>lay</u>-foh-noh
address	*dirección*	dee-rek-shee-<u>yon</u>

Weekdays — Días laborables

Sunday	*domingo*	doh-<u>min</u>-goh
Monday	*lunes*	<u>loo</u>-ness
Tuesday	*martes*	<u>mahr</u>-tess
Wednesday	*miércoles*	mee-<u>ehr</u>-coh-less
Thursday	*jueves*	hoo-<u>ay</u>-bess
Friday	*viernes*	bee-<u>err</u>-ness
Saturday	*sábado*	<u>sah</u>-bah-doh

Months — Meses

January	*Enero*	ay-<u>nay</u>-rho
February	*Febrero*	fay-<u>bray</u>-roh
March	*Marzo*	<u>mahr</u>so
April	*Abril*	ab-<u>reel</u>
May	*Mayo*	<u>my</u>-oh
June	*Junio*	<u>hoo</u>-nee-oh
July	*Julio*	<u>hoo</u>-lee-oh
August	*Agosto*	ow-<u>go</u>-stoh
September	*Septiembre*	sayp-tee-<u>aym</u>-bray
October	*Octubre*	ock-<u>too</u>-bray
November	*Noviembre*	noh-bee-<u>aym</u>-bray
December	*Diciembre*	day-see-<u>aym</u>-bray

Numbers — Números

zero	*cero*	zay-roh
one	*uno*	<u>oo</u>-noh
two	*dos*	dohs
three	*tres*	trayss
four	*cuatro*	<u>kwat</u>-roh
five	*cinco*	<u>seen</u>-koh
six	*seis*	says
seven	*siete*	see-<u>ay</u>tay
eight	*ocho*	<u>oh</u>-cho
nine	*nueve*	noo-<u>ay</u>-bay
ten	*diez*	<u>dee</u>-ayz

eleven	*once*	<u>ohn</u>-say
twelve	*doce*	<u>doh</u>-say
thirteen	*trece*	<u>tray</u>-say
fourteen	*catorce*	kaht-<u>ohr</u>-zay
fifteen	*quince*	<u>keen</u>-zay
sixteen	*diez-y-seis*	<u>dee</u>-ayz ee <u>says</u>
seventeen	*diez-y-siete*	<u>dee</u>-ayz ee see-<u>ay</u>tay
eighteen	*diez-y-ocho*	<u>dee</u>-ayz ee <u>oh</u>-cho
nineteen	*diez-y-nueve*	<u>dee</u>-ayz ee noo-<u>ay</u>-bay
twenty	*veinte*	bay-<u>ihn</u>-tay
twenty-one	*veinte-y-uno*	bay-<u>ihn</u>-tay ee <u>oon</u>-o
thirty	*treinta*	<u>trayn</u>-ta
forty	*cuarenta*	kwahr-<u>ehn</u>-ta
fifty	*cincuenta*	seen-<u>kwen</u>-tay
sixty	*sesenta*	says-<u>ehn</u>-ta
seventy	*setenta*	say-<u>tehn</u>-ta
eighty	*ochenta*	oh-<u>chen</u>-ta
ninety	*noventa*	noh-<u>ben</u>-ta
one hundred	*cien*	<u>see</u>-ehn
two hundred	*doscientos*	dhos see-<u>ehn</u>-toss
one thousand	*mil*	meehl
one million	*millón*	meeh-jee-<u>ohn</u>

Useful Portuguese words and phrases

Portuguese is the official language in Brazil. Although Brazilians will often be able to understand what you are saying if you speak some Spanish, the chances are that without any knowledge of Portuguese you may not be able to understand their reply. The following is a list of commonly used words and phrases with Brazilian Portuguese equivalents, including weekdays, months and numbers. Phonetic pronunciation is given for each word. The list gives a visitor with no knowledge of Portuguese enough to get around, find luggage, ask the time, look for food and communicate other basic needs.

Stress

If a word ends in a vowel with a tilde (~), stress the last syllable, unless another vowel in the word is accented. If a vowel has an acute (´) or circumflex (^) accent, stress that vowel no matter where in the word it comes. If a word ends in r, stress the last syllable, unless there's an accented vowel somewhere else. Otherwise, in words of two or more syllables, stress the penultimate vowel.

Courtesies

English	Português	Pronunciation
hello	*olá!*	ol-lah
goodbye	*adeus!*	er-deoosh
cheerio	*tchau!*	chow
how are you?	*como vai?*	comb-oh v-eye
see you later	*até breve!*	er-teh-brev
good day	*bom dia!*	bom dee-er
good afternoon	*boa tarde!*	bow-ah tardee
good evening	*boa noite!*	bow-ah noy-chee
morning	*manhã*	mer-nyah
afternoon	*tarde*	targee
evening	*noite*	noy-chee
very good	*muito bem*	mween-too bem
thank you	*obrigado/a*	oh-bree-gah-do/dah
please	*por favor*	poor fah-vor
excuse me	*desculpe*	dish-koolp
many thanks	*muito obrigado/a*	mween-too oh-bree-gah-do/dah

Basic words

yes	*sim*	seem
no	*não*	nawm
what is your name?	*como se chama?*	koo-moo set sha-mmer
my name is...	*chamo-me...*	sha-moo mer
I don't understand	*não entendo*	nawm ayn-tay-doa
do you speak...	*fala...*	fa-ler
...English	*...inglês*	een-glaysh
I'm hungry	*estou com fome*	e-stoo com fom
how much?	*quanto custa?*	kwan-too cush-ter
that's expensive!	*é caro*	eh ka-roo
that's too much!	*é muito caro*	mween-too karoo
I want...	*queria...*	ker-ree-er
I don't want...	*não queria...*	No ker-ree-er
I am lost	*estou perdido/a*	ish-toh per-dee-doo/er
to the right	*à direita*	a dee-ray-ter
to the left	*à esquerda*	a ishkairder
where is the...	*onde é...*	ond eh.....
restaurant	*o restaurante*	o rish-tow-rawnt
bathroom	*a casa de banho*	a kasah deh ba-nyoo
toilet	*o banheiro*	a bah-nyay-ro

the hotel	o hotel	o ot-tehl
bedroom	o quarto de dormir	o kwar-too deh door-meer
towel	a toalha	a too-al-yer
soap	o sabonete	o ser-boo-nayt
the telephone	o telefone	o ter-ler-fon
currency exchange	o câmbio	o kawm-byoo
bank	o banco	o bawn-koo
river	o rio	o ree-oo
forest	a mata/a floresta	a floo-resh-ter
village	a aldeia	a al-dag-ea
airport	o aeroporto	o eh-ro-poartoo
boat	o barco	o bar-koo
bus station	a rodoviária	a hodo-vyar-rhea
street	a rua	a rhu-a
house	a casa	a ka-saa
guide	a guia	a gee-er
luggage	a bagagem	a ber-gaz-haym
can you tell me the time?	diga-me as horas	dee-gah-er mer er zor-ush
a meal	comida	co-mee-dah
breakfast	café da manhã	ka-feh dah man-yah
lunch	almoço	al-moa-soo
dinner	jantar	djan-tar
can I have your...	pode dar-me o seu...	pod dar-mer oo se-oo
phone number?	número de telefone?	noo-me-roo der ter-ler-fon
address?	endereço?	arn-der ray-soo

Weekdays — Dias

Sunday	domingo	doo-meen-goo
Monday	segunda-feira	ser-goon-der fay-rer
Tuesday	terça-feira	tart-ser fay-rer
Wednesday	quarta-feira	kwar-ter fay-rer
Thursday	quinta-feira	keen-ter fay-rer
Friday	sexta-feira	says-ter fay-rer
Saturday	sábado	sa-ber doo

Months — Meses

January	janeiro	zher nayroo
February	fevereiro	fer ver ray-roo
March	março	mar-soo
April	abril	er-brill
May	maio	migh-hoo

267

June	*junho*	zhoo-nyoo
July	*julho*	zhoo-lyoo
August	*agosto*	er-goash-too
September	*setembro*	staym-dro
October	*outubro*	oh-too-broo
November	*novembro*	noo-vaymbroo
December	*dezembro*	der-zaym-broo

Numbers · Números

zero	*zero*	ze-hroo
one	*um/uma*	oom/er
two	*dois/duas*	doysh
three	*três*	traysh
four	*quatro*	ka-troo
five	*cinco*	seen-koh
six	*seis*	saysh
seven	*sete*	set
eight	*oito*	oy-too
nine	*nove*	nov
ten	*dez*	desh
eleven	*onze*	onz
twelve	*doze*	doaz
thirteen	*treze*	trays
fourteen	*catorze*	ker-toarz
fifteen	*quinze*	keenz
sixteen	*dezesseis*	dzer-saysh
seventeen	*dezessete*	dzer-set
eighteen	*dezoito*	dzoy-too
nineteen	*dezenove*	dzer-nov
twenty	*vinte*	veent
twenty-one	*vinte e um/uma*	veen-tee oom/er
thirty	*trinta*	treen-ter
forty	*quarenta*	kwer-rayn-ter
fifty	*cinqüenta*	seenkwayn-ter
sixty	*sessenta*	ser sayn-ter
seventy	*setenta*	ser tayn-ter
eighty	*oitenta*	oy tayn-ter
ninety	*noventa*	noo vayn-ter
one hundred	*cem*	saym
two hundred	*duzentos/as*	doo-zayn toosh/ush
one thousand	*mil*	meel
one million	*um milhão*	oom mee-lyawn

Appendix 2

Selected reading

Travelogues

Angus, C *Amazon Extreme: Three Ordinary Guys, One Rubber Raft, and the Most Dangerous River on Earth* (Broadway Books, New York, 2002). Five-month endurance test by three inexperienced rafters shouldn't put you off rafting with established tour operators.

Cousteau, J Y and Richards, M *Jaques Cousteau's Amazon Journey* (Harry N Abrams, New York, 1984). A coffee-table book replete with colour photos telling the story of Cousteau's 1981 Amazon expedition.

Ghinsberg, Y *Lost in the Jungle* (Skyhorse Publishing, 2009) True story account of a dream adventure in the Bolivian Amazon turning into a nightmare.

Gordon, N *Tarantulas, Marmosets and Other Stories: An Amazon Diary* (Metro, London, 1997). A highly readable account of travelling in the rainforests of Venezuela and Brazil based on the author's wildlife filming.

Harrison, J *Up the Creek* (Bradt Publications, London, 1986). To be reissued in February 2012. Essential reading for anyone planning an independent canoe trip who needs a little preparation.

Kane, Joe *Running the Amazon* (Knopf, New York; Pan, London, 1997). Account of a full-length voyage by kayak. Good background for anyone doing a whitewater trip in the upper Amazon.

Kelly, B and London, M *Amazon* (Harcourt, Brace Jovanovich, New York, 1983). Travelling the main stream by plane and boat during the pre-tourist boom era in the 1970s, with chapters on Iquitos and Leticia at the time.

MacCreagh, G *White Waters and Black* (University of Chicago Press, 2001). Humorous account of a 1923 scientific expedition to the upper Amazon where everything seems to go wrong.

Mohlke, M and Strel, M *The Man Who Swam the Amazon: 3,274 Miles on the World's Deadliest River* (The Lyons Press, 2007) Inspiring but somewhat coloured account of what was certainly an amazing accomplishment.

Shoumatoff, A *The Rivers Amazon* (Sierra Club Books, San Francisco, 1986). The author's tale covers his voyage up the full length of the Amazon from its mouth to Pucallpa, Peru.

History

Gheerbrant, A *The Amazon: Past, Present and Future* (Harry N Abrams, New York, 1992). Well-written and beautifully illustrated book that tells the story of the Amazon from its early discovery to the present day. Has a full chronology of events in Amazonia, mostly in Brazil.

Grann, D *The Lost City of Z: A Tale of Deadly Obsession in the Amazon* (Doubleday, New York, 2009). Spell-binding story of British explorer Percy Fawcett's doomed attempt to find a lost city in the heart of the Amazon.

Hemming, J *Red Gold: The Conquest of the Brazilian Indians* (Macmillan, London, 1978). A detailed and highly readable historical analysis of the exploitation of the Indians of Brazil and the Amazon.

Hemming, J *Amazon Frontier: The Defeat of the Brazilian Indians* (Macmillan, London, 1987). Continuing the story set in *Red Gold* explaining the continued decimation of the Indians of the Amazon from 1755 up to 1910.

Hemming, J *Tree of Rivers: The Story of the Amazon* (Thames & Hudson, London, 2009) A history of the Amazon from the perspective of today's threats to the rainforest.

Millard, C *The River of Doubt: Theodore Roosevelt's Darkest Journey* (Anchor Books, New York, 2006) The story of how the former US president almost met his end due to bad planning and disease.

Muscutt, K *Warriors of the Clouds: A Lost Civilization in the Upper Amazon of Peru* (University of New Mexico Press, 1998). Illustrated well-written text places the Chachapoya, or Cloudforest people, in the larger context of Andean prehistory.

Smith, A *Explorers of the Amazon* (Viking/Penguin, New York, 1990). The most comprehensive history of the Amazon from early discoverers to the rubber boom.

The Latin American Bureau has an *In Focus* series providing a guide to the people, politics and culture of each country bordering the Amazon Basin. International mail order available. Contact **Latin America Bureau (LAB)**, 1 Amwell St, London EC1R 1UL ✆ 0171 278 2829 🖱 www.lab.org.uk/.

Ethnology

Campbell, D *A Land of Ghosts: The Braided Lives of People and the Forest in Far Western Amazonia* (Houghton Mifflin, Boston, 2005). Personalised travelogue by professional botanist describing travels and long-term study of rainforest trees.

Davis, W *Lost Amazon: The Photographic Journey of Richard Evans*

Schultes (Chronicle Books, San Francisco, 2004). Moving, evocative pictorial essay based on 1940s photos of Schultes, considered the father of ethnobotany. Davis was a student of Schultes.

Davis, W *One River* (Simon & Schuster, New York, 1997). Nicely written scientific adventure. Two tales entwined tell of the author's explorations during the 1970s and those of his mentor, Richard Evans Schultes.

Descola, P *The Spears of Twilight: Life and Death in the Amazon Jungle* (Flamingo, London, 1997). A detailed insight into the life of the Achuar Indians of Ecuador based on the anthropologist author's two years spent living close to the banks of the Pastaza.

Graud, C *Jungle Medicine* (Center for Spirited Medicine, Minneapolis, 2004) A memoir of a decade spent as a shaman's apprentice in Peru's Amazon.

Kane, J *Savages* (Vintage Books, New York, 1996) The impact of the modern world on the Huaorani of Ecuador.

Plotkin, M J *Tales of a Shaman's Apprentice: An Ethnobotanist Searches for New Medicines in the Amazon Rainforest* (Penguin Books, New York, 1994). Account of medicinal plants used by various tribes and prospects for curing major diseases.

Rabben, L *Brazil's Indians and the Onslaught of Civilization: The Yanomami and the Kayapo* (University of Washington Press, Seattle, Washington, 2004) Documents the impact of modern life on Brazilian tribes.

Reel, M *The Last of the Tribe: The Epic Quest to Save a Lone Man in the Amazon* (Scribner, New York, 2010) Insight into the politics and economics of conflicts over exploiting resources and preserving heritage.

Schultes, R E and Raffauf, R F *Vine of the Soul: Medicine Men, Their Plants and Rituals in the Colombian Amazonia* (Synergetic Press, Santa Fe, New Mexico 2004) Essential reading on the role of ethneogens in native cultures of the Colombian Amazon.

Tidwell, M *Amazon Stranger* (Lyons Press, New York, 1997). A reporter's touching account, told with wit and sensitivity, of the Cofan, a small Ecuadorian Indian tribe, and their American chief's battle to save the Cuyabeno Reserve from the big oil companies.

Up de Graff, F W *Headhunters of the Amazon: Seven Years of Exploration and Adventure* (reprinted: Kessinger Publishing, Montana, 2004). A fascinating account of the upper Amazon at the beginning of the 20th century, including descriptions of Iquitos at the time, as well as graphic descriptions of the now-outlawed practice of headhunting.

Wheeler, J *The Adventurer's Guide* (David MacKay Inc, New York, 1976). Describes, among other things, the author's year-long experience living with Shuar Indians of the Ecuadorian Amazon. Lots of detailed information on how he prepared for his adventure.

Conservation

Caufield, C *In the Rainforest: Report from a Strange, Beautiful, Imperiled World* (University of Chicago Press, Chicago, 1984). This book highlights the causes and consequences of rainforest destruction, with emphasis on the fate of the Amazon.

Cousteau, J Y *The Cousteau Almanac: An Inventory of Life on Our Water Planet* (Doubleday, New York, 1981). An encyclopaedic source of information on all aspects of the aquatic realm, with comparative data on the world's rivers and a useful section on Amazon conservation.

Hecht, S and Cockburn, A *The Fate of the Forest: Developers, Destroyers and Defenders of the Amazon* (HarperCollins, New York, updated 2011). Rainforest conservation is the major theme of this outstanding book in which the authors do a fine job of untangling the knotty issues and personalities.

Lewis, S *The Rainforest Book* (Living Planet Press, Berkeley Books, New York, 1990). Accessible to school-age children, this is a useful source book on rainforest conservation issues.

London, M and Kelly, B *The Last Forest: The Amazon in the Age of Globalization* (Random House, New York, 2007) Balanced firsthand perspective comparing changes in Brazil's Amazon over 25 years of development.

O'Connor, G *Amazon Journal: Dispatches from a Vanishing Frontier* (Plume Books, 1998). Unbiased documentary of consequences of modern encroachment on the Brazilian Amazon.

Slater, C *Entangled Edens: Visions of the Amazon* (University of California Press, 2001). Impassioned and well-reasoned plea to emphasise conservation of Amazon cultures as well as natural resources.

Natural history

Barthem, R and Goulding, M *An Unexpected Ecosystem: The Amazon as Revealed by Fisheries* (Missouri Botanical Garden Press, Saint Louis, 2007) A broad perspective of the diversity and productivity of the Amazon's fisheries.

Bates, H W *The Naturalist on the River Amazons* (University of California Press, Riverside, 1962). A classic Victorian travelogue and natural history of the author's years spent in Brazil during the middle of the 19th century.

Campbell, J A and Lamar, W *The Venomous Reptiles of the Western*

Hemisphere (Cornell University Press, Ithaca, New York, 2004) Authoritative and comprehensive guide for reptile enthusiasts and professionals.

Castner, J L *Amazon Insects: A Photo Guide* (Feline Press, 2000). Pocket guide to common insects, but not comprehensive.

Emmons, L H *Neotropical Rainforest Mammals: a Field Guide* (Chicago University Press, Chicago, 1990). A must for scientists and naturalist-guides interested in Amazon mammals. Every known mammal species is fully described and illustrated in colour or black-and-white, with scientific name.

Forsyth, A and Miyata, K *Tropical Nature: Life and Death in the Rainforests of Central and South America* (Scribner, New York, 1984). Just about the most readable text on tropical rainforest ecology and evolution. The authors draw on extensive experience in Ecuadorian and Costa Rican rainforests to paint a dramatic and sometimes amusing picture of the inner workings of tropical plants and animals.

Goulding, M *Amazon: The Flooded Forest* (Sterling Publishing Co, New York, 1990). Based on a BBC documentary series, this book is written for the layman (ie: no scientific names) interested in the flooded forest habitats of the Amazon.

Goulding, M, Barthem, R and Ferreira, F *Smithsonian Atlas of the Amazon* (Smithsonian Books, Washington DC, 2003) A wide-ranging review of statistics and geographical data, with many informative charts and diagrams.

Goulding, M *Palms: Sentinels for Amazon Conservation* (Missouri Botanical Garden Press, Saint Louis, 2007) A guide to the hundreds of commercially and ecologically important palms of the Amazon.

Gordon, N *Wild Amazon* (Evans Mitchell Books, London, 2007) A coffee-table book that gives photographers a standard to aspire to.

Hilty, S L and Brown, W L *A Guide to the Birds of Colombia* (Princeton University Press, Princeton, NJ, 1986). Although it technically covers only Colombia, this is the most comprehensive field guide (some 1,500 species described with hundreds of colour drawings) of the upper Amazon avifauna and will be useful for birdwatchers visiting Ecuador and Peru.

Kricher, J C *A Neotropical Companion,* (2nd edition) (Princeton University Press, Princeton, NJ, 1997). Written for the informed layman, it offers useful insights into rainforest ecology and evolution.

Lowman, M *Life in the Treetops: Adventures of a Woman in Field Biology* (Yale University Press, New Haven, Connecticut, 2000) Autobiographical account of the challenges of working as a woman in the world of field biology.

Mee, M *Margaret Mee's Amazon: The Diaries of an Artist Explorer* (Antique Collectors Club, 2004) Beautiful illustrations combine science and art to reveal more than any photograph of Amazon flowers and plants.

Montgomery, S *Journey of the Pink Dolphins: An Amazon Quest* (Simon & Schuster, New York, 2000). Naturalist and columnist's lyrical and rather uninformed account of the myths and biology of the cetaceans.

Pearson, D L et al. *Brazil – Amazon and Pantanal* (a volume in the *Ecotravellers' Wildlife Guides Series*) (Academic Press, 2001). Information on the most frequently seen animals, including identification, ecology, behaviour, and conservation.

Pimm, S L *A Scientist Audits The Earth* (Rutgers University Press, New Brunswick, New Jersey, 2004) Puts Amazon deforestation into a global context and details the costs to the global economy and biodiversity.

Prance, G T and Lovejoy, T E *Amazonia* (Pergamon Press, New York & London, 1985). An excellent photo-essay of the Amazon's floral and fauna wealth, written by two of the world's foremost tropical biologists.

Smith, N *The Amazon River Forest: A Natural History of Plants, Animals, & People* (Oxford University Press, 1999). Authoritative exploration of ecological, historical, cultural, and socioeconomic issues, with practical suggestions for developing the Amazon floodplain to enhance biodiversity.

Smith, N *Amazon River Fruits: Flavors for Conservation* (Missouri Botanical Garden Press, Saint Louis, 2007) An excellent review of edible fruits from the Peruvian Amazon. Ideal for identifying all the fruits in your photos after your trip.

Wheatley, N *Where to watch birds in South America* (Princeton University Press, 1995). A comprehensive guide to birds and the best birding sites throughout the Amazon and South America.

Websites

Sites are in English unless otherwise stated. There are literally thousands of relevant websites on Amazon travel, natural history and various speciality topics. We've curated some of the best, which we think will be most useful.

General

www.amazontravelbook.com Companion website to this book. Includes travel deals, example itineraries, wildlife checklists, extended bibliography and even Amazon recipes.

tripadvisor.com Possibly the single most useful site for travellers. Offers user reviews and ratings. Best for checking any accommodation your tour operator recommends.

earth.google.com Fly anywhere on Earth to view satellite imagery, maps and terrain.

www.worldairportguide.com Information on airport facilities worldwide.

www.mapquest.com Printable maps of locations around the world.

www.wunderground.com Weather forecasts for virtually any city in the world.

www.latinamericapress.org Award-winning journalism on Latin America.

forests.org Worldwide forest biodiversity campaign news.

www.nativeweb.org International, non-profit, educational organisation with information about indigenous nations, peoples, and organisations.

www.ayahuasca.com A reference site reflecting the growing global interest in ayahuasca and traditional South American shamanism.

www.junglephotos.com/amazon Amazon plants, animals, people and conservation photos and information from Roger Harris, author of this book.

www.embassyworld.com Up-to-date contact info for all the world's embassies.

www.cia.gov/library/publications/the-world-factbook Detailed, well-organised summary information on the world's countries.

www.wikipedia.org/wiki/Amazon_Rainforest Good overview of the Amazon rainforest with some useful links.

www.geographia.com Comprehensive but succinct general information on the world's countries.

translate.google.com Use this site to translate emails, websites and brochure text into English.

travel.state.gov Latest US government travel updates and information on countries worldwide.

Countries

Peru

www.iquitosnews.com Good source of unbiased information for Peru's Amazon gateway city.

www.cusco.info Comprehensive site for travel to Peru and Cuzco. Package tours, hotel booking, Inca trail hikes, travel information.

www.peru.travel Official government site: useful data for travellers, travel FAQ, weather, accommodation, travel agents, restaurants and other tourist services, tourism for people with disabilities.

www.perulinks.com Peru links directory – most complete index of Peru web links. Lists around 800 Peru-related sites, including over 200 travel sites.

www.peru.com Comprehensive information about Peru including history, geography, statistics and useful sections on each department. (Spanish)

www.andeantravelweb.com The most comprehensive site on travel in Peru.

www.projectamazonas.com Non-profit research, conservation, education and humanitarian-oriented organisation with operations in the upper Amazon.
www.cuscoperu.com Travel-related information on Peru.

Brazil

www.braziltour.com Official website of Embratur, the Ministry of Tourism.
www.brazilink.org Educational portal on Brazilian development issues, edited by experts.
www.braziltravelinformation.com A plethora of useful travel information about Brazil.
www.v-brazil.com Comprehensive information on all aspects of Brazil.
www.braziltravelnews.com Extensive resource about travel in Brazil.
www.braziltravelvacation.com Covers scenic tours, attractions, hotels, motels, resorts, spas, maps and much more.
www.amazonia.org.br Packed with general Amazon information, travel, conservation updates, news, economics, science, photos and videos.

Colombia

www.colombia.travel General information on travel in Colombia, including Amazonas.
www.colombiaemb.org Colombian Embassy in the US; covers economy and culture, US-Colombia relations, and travel and visa information.
www.presidencia.gov.co Official government presidency site covers government, history, geography, human rights issues, and drug policy.
www.birding-colombia.com Information guide to birding in Colombia.

Ecuador

www.ecuadordaily.com Latest news on happenings in Ecuador and Latin America.
ecuador.travel Official Ministry of Tourism site. Easy to navigate. Overview and details of destinations, trails, travel updates, and directories of hotels, restaurants, tour operators, etc.
www.igm.gob.ec Official site of *Instituto Geográfico Militar* – source of official maps and geographical information. (Spanish)
www.ecuador.com Informational resource for travel, e-commerce and business.
www.ecuaworld.com All you need to know about Ecuador. Navigation is a bit clunky but the content is there.

Index

Index

First edition published November 2011
Bradt Travel Guides Ltd
IDC House, The Vale, Chalfont St Peter, Bucks SL9 9RZ, England
www.bradtguides.com
Published in the USA by The Globe Pequot Press Inc,
PO Box 480, Guilford, Connecticut 06437-0480

ISBN: 978 1 84162 374 0

British Library Cataloguing in Publication Data
A catalogue record for this book is available from the British Library

Photographs
Alamy: Danita Delimont (DD/A), Octavio Campos Salles (OCS/A), John Mitchell (JM/A), Porky Pies Photography (PPP/A); Amazon Tree Climbing (ATC); Colombian Tourist Board (CTB); Bill Cooper (BC); Dreamstime: Daniel Budiman (DB/DT), Deb22 (D/DT), Dirk Ercken (DE/DT), King Ho Yim (KHY/DT), Uros Ravbar (UR/DT), Xura (X/DT); David Fernandes (DF); Flickr: Keith Morris (KM/F)FLPA: Theo Allofs/Minden Pictures (TA/MP/FLPA), Ingo Arndt/Minden Pictures (IA/MP/FLPA), Luciano Candisani/Minden Pictures (LC/MP/FLPA), Murray Cooper/Minden Pictures (MC/MP/FLPA), Reinhard Dirscherl (RD/FLPA), Suzi Eszterhas/Minden Pictures (SE/MP/FLPA), Guenter Fischer/Imagebroker (GF/IB/FLPA), Tim Fitzharris/Minden Pictures (TF/MP/FLPA), Michael and Patricia Fogden/Minden Pictures (MPF/MP/FLPA), Foto Natura Stock (FNS/FLPA), GTW/Imagebroker (GTW/IB/FLPA), ImageBroker (IB/FLPA), Gerard Lacz (GL/FLPA), Frans Lanting (FL/FLPA), Oliver Lucanus/Minden Pictures (OL/MP/FLPA), Thomas Marent/Minden Pictures (TM/MP/FLPA), Claus Meyer/Minden Pictures (CM/MP/FLPA), Mark Moffett/Minden Pictures (MM/MP/FLPA), Flip de Nooyer/FN/Minden (FDN/FN/M/FLPA), Rolf Nussbaumer/ImageBroker/FLPA (RN/IB/FLPA), Pete Oxford/Minden Pictures (PO/MP/FLPA), Photo Researchers (PR/FLPA), Tui de Roy/Minden Pictures (TR/MP), Kevin Schafer/Minden Pictures (KS/MP/FLPA), Ingo Schulz (IS/IB/FLPA), Jurgen and Christine Sohns (JCS/FLPA), Roger Tidman (RT/FLPA), Terry Whittaker (TW/FLPA), Konrad Wothe/Minden Pictures (KW/MP/FLPA); Roger Harris (RH); W W Lamar/GreenTracks (WWL/GT); Tim Kovar (TK); Stuart Pimm (SP); SuperStock (SS); Wikimedia Commons (WP)

Front cover (Top, left to right) Blue-headed parrot (IA/MP/FLPA), Phyllomedusa tomopterna (MPF/MP/FLPA), Member of the Jivaro tribe (SS)
Back cover Toco toucan (SS), Brown-throated three-toed sloth (SS)
Title page Cattelaya orchid (WWL/GT), San Rafael Falls, Ecuador (PO/MP/FLPA), Red-tailed Amazon parrots (CM/MP/FLPA)
Part & chapter openers
Page 1: Indigenous man fishing with a bow and arrow (SS); Page 2: An indigenous settlement on the Rio Negro, Brazil (SS); Page 3: Member of the Kaiapo tribe (SS); Page 16: Terrestrial bromeliad (WWL/GT), *Heliconia psittacorum* (WWL/GT); Page 17: Amazon tree boa (SS); Page 49: White-fronted capuchin monkey (PO/MP/FLPA); Page 123: Tourist on canopy walkway in Yasuní National Park, Ecuador (PO/MP/FLPA); Page 149: Tourist lodge on the Brazilian Amazon (FDN/FN/M/FLPA); Page 169: Flooding in banana grove (SS); Page 170: Curl-crested araçari (RT/FLPA); Page 171: Kinkajou (SS); Page 200: Red-tailed Amazon parrots (CM/MP/FLPA); Page 201: Brazil rainforest (FL/FLPA); Page 228: Squirrel monkeys (TM/MP/FLPA); Page 229: Keel-billed toucan (MC/MP/FLPA); Page 242: Black-mantled tamarin (PO/MP/FLPA); Page 243: Rainforest, Ecuador (X/DT)

Maps Artinfusion

Typeset and designed from the author's disk by Artinfusion (www.artinfusion.co.uk)
Production managed by Jellyfish Print Solutions; printed in India